Vocabulary Plus High School and Up

A Source-Based Approach

ALLEEN PACE NILSEN

DON L. F. NILSEN

Arizona State University

PEARSON

Boston   New York   San Francisco

Mexico City   Montreal   Toronto   London   Madrid   Munich   Paris

Hong Kong   Singapore   Tokyo   Cape Town   Sydney

To our grandchildren
who helped us in more ways than they know

Taryn, Britton, Kami, and Erich
David, Lauren, Michael, and Jenna
Jim and Luke

Series Editor: *Aurora Martínez Ramos*
Series Editorial Assistant: *Katie Freddoso*
Senior Marketing Manager: *Elizabeth Fogarty*
Composition Buyer: *Linda Cox*
Manufacturing Buyer: *Andrew Turso*
Editorial-Production Administrator: *Karen Mason*
Editorial-Production Services: *Walsh & Associates, Inc.*
Design and Electronic Composition: *Ellen Pettengell*
Cover Administrator: *Joel Gendron*
Cover Designer: *Jenny Hart*

For related titles and support materials, visit our online catalog at www.ablongman.com

Library of Congress Cataloging-in-Publication Data

Nilsen, Alleen Pace.
    Vocabulary plus high school and up : a source-based approach / Alleen Pace Nilsen,
Don L. F. Nilsen.
        p. cm.
    Includes bibliographical references and index.
    ISBN 0-205-36014-9
    1. Vocabulary–Study and teaching (Secondary)–United States. 2. English teachers—In-service training.
I. Nilsen, Don Lee Fred. II. Title.

LB1574.5.N53 2004
428.1'071'2—dc21   2003050296

Photo credits: All photographs by A. P. Nilsen.

Printed in the United States of America

10 9 8 7 6 5 4 3 2 1   09 08 07 06 05 04 03

Contents

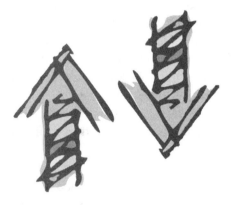

Preface

Several events convinced us that this was a good time to turn our attention to the teaching of vocabulary. An early clue came from our college students, who in the semesters prior to student teaching are required to observe and, where possible, participate in classroom instruction. A disproportionate number of them were asked on Mondays to give out the weekly list of words and then on Fridays to administer and grade the test. Obviously, this is the kind of discrete task that an outsider can do; however, our students suspected that teachers were passing this job along to them mostly because they did not like to do it themselves.

Except for saying, "You might be tested on this word," the regular teachers were as unable as were our college students to answer complaints and questions about why students should be memorizing the meanings of words they had never heard spoken, never seen in writing, and never anticipated using. As we pondered this situation, we concluded that the main problem is that until the last few years the teaching of vocabulary was not a high priority in teacher education programs, thus until recently teachers gave little thought to the matter. The result has been that, when faced with an unexpected emphasis on vocabulary, teachers naturally turned to the source with which they were the most familiar—they modeled their classroom instruction on the techniques used by testmakers.

As we will show throughout this book, the goals of teachers and testmakers appear at opposite ends of a spectrum, and the techniques of teachers should be quite different from the goals and techniques of those who devise the high-stakes tests.

We owe a special thanks to Arizona State University for supporting Alleen in a sabbatical leave during which we began this research. We also wish to thank the English Department at McClintock High School in Tempe, where during the spring semester of 2001 we were guest teachers in a sophomore English class taught by Diana Dwyer, an advanced ESL class taught by Janis Huerbsch, and a class of seniors taught by Nicole Ainsworth. We also wish to thank our graduate students at ASU: Carol Smith, Andrea Low, and Gail Spiegel, who let us come and work in their classrooms. Colleague Micaela Muñoz let us work with her students and take photographs of them at Fees Middle School in Tempe, and James Blasingame used a prepublication version in his Methods of Teaching English class at ASU. We also tried out several ideas and lessons with future teachers in our ASU classes and with ASU undergraduate English majors who enrolled in a special seminar on metaphor that Don taught in the fall semester of 2002. Many of the photographs in this text are of work done by these students.

While the source-based approach that we are advocating is an outgrowth of all that we have learned in two lifetimes of working with English, the specific comments about, and ideas for, classroom practices come from our guest teaching over the past several years. We also thank our Allyn and Bacon Longman editor, Aurora Martínez, and the reviewers that she arranged for: Eileen E. Moore, Birmingham-Southern College; Leif Fearn, San Diego State University; and Mary-Catherine Sableski, University of Dayton/Kettering City Schools.

We are grateful for their many helpful suggestions and for their catching some of our errors. We humbly take the blame for any that remain.

CHAPTER ONE

The Theory behind a Source-Based Approach

Initially, we described what we were working on as "a metaphorical approach to the teaching of vocabulary," but when we approached schools with the idea of coming to classrooms to try out our lessons, they misunderstood our goals and thought we wanted to be "poets-in-residence." It is true that poets use metaphors, especially when searching for concrete ways to talk about abstractions, but, in reality, all speakers use metaphors as part of their everyday speech as well as when they are stretching their imaginations to say something new.

Nevertheless, we decided that the term *source-based* would be more accurate because we are working, not with poetic "frills," but with basic, everyday language. And, contrary to popular thinking, it is not easy to determine the exact point at which a particular usage leaves the literal and becomes metaphorical. This is especially true when changes are brought through the adding or subtracting of morphemes. *Morphemes* are the smallest units of language that carry meaning, and the mixing and matching of morphemes (what we call *lexical extension*) is a key component of our approach.

Teaching vocabulary through a source-based approach means starting with basic concepts that have been in human language for as long as people can remember and then working with lexical and metaphorical extensions of these basic words. The concepts we work with are such things as animals, weather, plants, the human body, families, food, containers, clothing, work, play, and life and death. The reason for working with words that have been used to refer to these concepts for centuries is not so much to teach history, but to take advantage of the way that over time these basic words have given birth to whole *families* of related words. When we teach these families of words, we naturally end up teaching through *webs* or *gestalts*, which allows learners to make connections and to gain confidence in language as a system.

A source-based approach might also be called a process or a generative approach because it follows the ways that both individuals and cultures develop language in moving from the known to the unknown, from the simple to the complex, and from the literal to the metaphorical. The approach taps into the collective unconscious because it starts with the concepts that have been in languages the longest and have therefore served as the foundations on which many other words have been built. As students and teachers work with variations of words, they will become adept at figuring out the meanings of words they have not seen before, a skill that in today's fast moving, high-tech "global village," is increasingly important. We hope that users of this book will inductively learn:

- How English is enriched by words from other languages.
- How basic words carry dozens of meanings.
- How the meanings of words move from literal to figurative.
- How words follow regular patterns as they acquire new meanings.

An Explanation of Morphology

Thanks to computer graphics, students already know that to *morph* is to change. By bringing the language-related concept of *morphemes* and *morphology* to students, we will encourage them to look at words as a detective might. Even one or two familiar morphemes in a word can serve as the key that will unlock the meaning of an unfamiliar word. In English, *bound morphemes* include such prefixes as *anti-, ambi-, co-, dis-, mal-, non-, pre-,* and *un-,* and such suffixes as *-ed, -er, -ess, -ful, -ing, -s,* and *-y. Free morphemes* are those that can either stand alone or be used in combinations—for example, *any, berry, child, man, room,* and *way.* They are what are commonly called *root words.*

J. K. Rowling's *Harry Potter* books are a wonderful place to gain an appreciation of the power of mixing and matching morphemes. (See our article "Lessons in the Teaching of Vocabulary from September 11th and Harry Potter," in the November 2002 *Journal of Adolescent and Adult Literacy*). One reason she does not have to include a glossary of the many new words that she uses is that she creates them from morphemes that are familiar to readers. In *quidditch,* the small black balls that fly fast and hit players are named *bludgers* (c.f. *bludgeon*) while *sneakoscopes* (c.f. *sneak* and *telescopes*) emit a piercing whistle when they come close to anyone doing something untrustworthy or dishonest. The *floo powder* that enables the Weasleys to travel through their chimney has a wonderful name because it is a play on several words including the verb *flew,* the noun *flue* (part of a chimney), and *flea* (interpret *flee*) *powder.*

Because of the way related words are grouped in a source-based approach, students will get extended practice in working with morphemes in a systematic way. Between the workshops in each chapter and the less structured end-of-chapter activities, students should spend enough time with productive morphemes that their minds will be able to absorb (as opposed to just memorize) the meanings. The main problem with teaching randomly organized lists of words or alphabetized lists of prefixes and suffixes is that students' minds do not have time to absorb the meanings, nor do they have mental hooks on which to hang the ideas.

An Explanation of Metaphorical Connections between Language and Life

Words communicate to people only if they are based on things that most speakers know about. Between 1910 and 1920, one-third of all Americans lived on farms; today, that number is less than 2 percent. But because it takes longer for terms to disappear from a language than to be introduced into it, modern English is filled with metaphorical idioms based on what, for farm people, was common knowledge. City folk have had to learn the meanings of such idioms, not from first-hand observations, but from the situations where they see the idioms used. In this context, Editor Jack Rosenthal, writing in the *New York Times Magazine* cited such language "fossils" as *making hay while the sun shines, being taken to the woodshed, living in a pig pen, separating the sheep from the goats, making a silk purse out of a sow's ear, waiting until the cows come home,* and *holding your horses.*

Paul Fussell, in his prize-winning *The Great War and Modern Memory,* also wrote about how the metaphors that Americans relied on in the early part of the twentieth century were based in nature. Fussell explained that when bad things happened, people felt *thrown,* as if from a horse. They would respond to feeling *swamped* or being led into a *wasteland of uncertainty* with *showers* of complaints and *storms* of protest.

But once the majority of young men were drafted and attention turned to the Great War, a new set of metaphors entered U.S. English. Instead of feeling *swamped,* people *in the trenches* felt *shell-shocked* as they were *barraged, bombarded,* and *torpedoed* by *lousy* (from the lice in battlefield trenches) events. Even civilian life was divided into the *rank and file, platoons,* and *sectors.* World War II added such metaphors as *to blitz* (from Hitler's *blitzkrieg,* i.e., lightning wars) and *Pearl Harbor* as the name for any disastrous surprise attack.

Ken Ringle writing in the *Washington Post* said that from the Korean War came such metaphors as *brainwash* and *flameout,* while from the Cold War (itself a metaphor) came such metaphors as *fallout* for unexpected results and *Siberia* for any perdition. In relation to the Vietnam War, he asked, "Will *domino theory* ever again refer to dominoes, or *quagmire* to swampy land, or *light at the end of the tunnel* to an actual tunnel?"

Even eponyms (words created from someone's name) are subject to metaphorical changes, as shown by the word *sandwich.* In the late 1700s, John Montagu, the Earl of Sandwich, was an enthusiastic gambler who did not want to stop long enough to eat and so asked that someone bring meat between slices of bread to his gaming table. His invention of *sandwich*es proved to be so practical that both the food and the eponym were soon known around the world.

Once a word is in common use, it is subject then to the kinds of metaphorical extensions that will be talked about throughout this book in which words acquire both more general and more specific meanings. Through lexical extensions, we have *club* or *triple-decker sandwiches, ice cream sandwiches, Oreo® cookie sandwiches,* and *submarine, hero,* and *hoagie* sandwiches. Moving closer to metaphor, a person who walks around advertising something by wearing a *sandwich board* is the "meat filling" for what looks like a giant-sized living sandwich. More metaphorically, adults might recall bad memories of childhood vacation trips when they were *sandwiched* between older siblings who always claimed the windows in the back seat of the family sedan. And even more metaphorically, the generation who used to be known as the *Baby Boomers* are now talked about as the *sandwich generation* because they are caught between taking care of their elderly parents and their own teenaged and adult children.

While we realize that even 3- and 4-year-olds know what a sandwich is, we still view talking with students about the kinds of information we have just presented to be a valuable kind of vocabulary study because it teaches students about language processes and gives them the kinds of information they need for developing their reading skills.

Language Is Spoken before It Is Written

Just as with poetry, the teaching of vocabulary is best done orally. The power of listening and talking is demonstrated by how many words your students miraculously learned during their first few years of life. And while the process may have seemed effortless both to the children and their caregivers, there was plenty of direct teaching. When, in William Gibson's *The Miracle Worker*, Helen Keller's mother grows discouraged at how slow Helen is to make the connection between a fingerspelled word and a concept, she asks teacher Annie Sullivan how many times the mothers of sighted and hearing children have to repeat a word before a child learns it. Miss Sullivan replies, "No mother ever minded enough to count."

Because teachers are overburdened with multiple responsibilities, they are more likely to count and, like Helen's mother, grow impatient. But once in the habit, teachers will find it easy to involve students in conversations about words and to provide them with opportunities to use new words in different contexts and with different meanings. Only then will the words roll off their tongues in ways that feel and sound natural. Here are some ways to increase the amount of meaningful talk that goes on in a class.

- Plan lessons so that students frequently work as partners or in small groups. This gives more students a chance to talk, and the more often learners hear and say the words being studied, the more natural they will seem.
- To keep students from getting bored, use a variety of activities. One of our most successful lessons was when we provided small groups with sacks of material from which they were to prepare a learning center. They used half of the class period in preparation and the other half in traveling around the room to view and participate in the different learning centers. We did not have many props for the group working on clothing and so we gave them colored chalk. They filled the whole front chalkboard with wonderful cartoon-style drawings, which they were happy to explain.
- Provide opportunities for students to make mini-speeches to their classmates. Encourage them to bring in visual aids or to explain a poster they have made or a news clipping or cartoon that illustrates something you are studying.
- Let the students do some of the teaching, but keep it special by spreading their experience over the course of a semester making sure that everyone gets a turn.
- In the beginning you will need to supply most of the ideas and materials, but as the semester goes along, students may surprise you with their creativity in devising games and activities.

Our students respected such tasks more when they were given unique information to present. They appeared to feel manipulated if we asked them to teach information that fellow students had already been given in print form, and they were out-and-out resentful if they had prepared something to give and we accidentally jumped in and shared the information before they had their chance.

An Overview of the Kinds of Language Change That Will Be Illustrated in the Following Chapters

INHERITING WORDS

No one knows for sure how long people have been speaking because histories were not written until long after language was developed. However, from the oldest written records and from reconstructing similarities in the languages of peoples now far removed from each other, linguists have compiled histories of language that go back approximately eight thousand years. The core vocabulary of English consists of two kinds of words: One is limited and "closed," while the other is ever-expanding. The closed set includes function words that serve as glue to hold everything else together. Included in these function words are the conjunctions *and, but,* and *or*, as well as such common prepositions as *among, by, for, in, of, on, to,* and *with*. Auxiliary and linking verbs are also in this category—for example, *am* and *are, be* and *is, can* and *could, may* and *might, will* and *would, shall* and *should,* and *must, ought to,* and *have*. These words are among the 1,000 most commonly used words in English and are in the vocabularies of most 5-year-olds. We know so little about how these words were developed that most linguists describe them simply as *inherited words*. Such pronouns as *I, we, they, he, she,* and *it* are also in this closed category, although they share some of the characteristics of the ever-expanding category because of the way they act as replacements for nouns.

The second type of words is comprised of the lexical categories of nouns, verbs, adjectives, and adverbs. These are nonfinite categories. Unlike the function words, which have stayed basically the same for thousands of years, these words have undergone tremendous growth and change, a phenomenon that will be emphasized throughout this book. Language has been compared to a large and fertile field, which is always growing, albeit in irregular fits and starts. Allan Metcalf, executive secretary of the American Dialect Society and author of *Predicting New Words: The Secrets of Their Success*, has explained that whenever the majority of people in a society focus their attention on a particular section of the field, it is as if that section is receiving a huge dose of fertilizer, rain, and sunshine. Words change and grow and mix with other words to sprout all kinds of new meanings.

Although Metcalf was talking specifically about the large number of computer-related usages that English speakers developed during the 1990s, he could have also cited the Industrial Revolution, the invention of the automobile, either World War I or World War II, and any time when speakers of different languages were somehow pushed into close contact with each other.

BORROWING WORDS

English is filled with words borrowed long ago from Latin, Greek, and French, and more recently from Spanish and dozens of other languages. Knowing a little about the historical connections among speakers of different languages will help students understand some of the things about English, which on the surface appears chaotic. For example, English has several words for basic numbers because traders who went to different countries had to learn "foreign" number words to keep from being cheated. This left English with *uni, primus, mono, solo, once, only, first,* and *single* all with the basic meaning of *one*, and *bi, duo, duet, second, twice,* and *twin* all with the basic meaning of *two*. Because these terms are not interchangeable but are still related, students need to know what the words have in common as well as how they differ.

A more recent example of borrowing relates to the September 11, 2001 terrorist attacks. Suddenly, Americans began hearing *jihad, fatwa,* and *madrasah*. Since these words name things that were not part of U.S. culture, they were borrowed directly into English. However, some of the complications of word borrowing are illustrated by such arguments as whether *jihad* is supposed to refer to an actual war or to an overall goal for one's life, whether Osama bin Laden was an authorized Muslim cleric with the authority to issue a *fatwa* against Westerners, and whether the Koranic schools called *madrasahs* should be called "schools" or "indoctrination centers."

Even in the same culture, words have many different meanings. When they are transferred to a different culture, it is impossible for them to carry the same sets of meanings. Also, the longer they are in the new language, the more likely they are to acquire still further meanings as they are influenced by new speakers.

Speakers' minds are so eager to connect new words to ones they already know that when they borrow words from other languages, they adapt their sounds and their spelling so that they "make sense." For example, Albert H. Marckwardt in his *American English* shows how English speakers created the word *woodchuck* from an Ojibwa word that appeared variously as *wuchak, otchak,* and *odjig.* Since the word named an animal that lived in the *woods,* English speakers could learn it and remember it by adapting the Native American name to *woodchuck.* Speakers did something similar to the Algonquin word *muscassus,* which they interpreted as *muskrat,* because they were thinking of "a rodent with a musky odor."

A more recent example is the way U.S. speakers changed the name of *gyro sandwiches* to *hero sandwiches.* The original name of these sandwiches comes from Greek *gyros,* referring to something that is circular or that winds around, as seen in the words *gyroscope* and *gyrate.* In Greek restaurants a big piece of meat is speared onto a revolving wheel that the cook spins around as he cuts off fresh, thin slices to go on the sandwich. But as processed meats have become more popular, people seldom see spinning wheels of meat, so the connection to *gyro* is lost. And since English does not have the kind of guttural *gh* sound that Greek has, it was easy for the word to slip over and become *hero.* Semantically, it makes sense because these sandwiches are so big it is easy to think of them as food fit for a hero.

When people hear terms they are unfamiliar with, they often interpret the terms as metaphors based on animals because such terms can include emotions and humanlike behaviors. With *guerilla warfare,* the image that pops into many speakers' heads is of gorillas climbing in trees and dropping or throwing projectiles at intruders. Actually, *guerilla* is Spanish for *little war.* With *pidgin* English, people get an image of pigeons cooing and nodding their heads at each other. *Pidgin* is actually an altered form of *business,* relating to the fact that *pidgins* are the simplified languages that traders used (and still use) in the various ports they visit.

COINING NEW WORDS (NEOLOGISMS)

It is relatively rare for brand new words to be coined, and even more rare for new sound combinations to be invented. Many people, including babies, create new sound combinations, but such sounds do not really become part of a language until many other speakers recognize the sounds and begin to use them to represent the same concept.

It is much more common for speakers to come up with using old words in a new way as with the phrase *24/7* used first by advertisers, and then by the general public, to describe something available 24 hours a day, seven days a week. New words that are created as analogies to older words have a head start in acquiring this kind of recognition. For example, the meaning of *oldster* is recognizable because of its similarity to *youngster,* while *headnote* is understandable because of its similarity to *footnote.*

Advertisers create product names that are different enough to be registered as unique trademarks, while still fitting into the sound patterns of a language so they will be easy to say and easy to remember. They also want names to remind speakers of the product in a positive way without making claims that a company has to legally defend. For example, the makers of *Viagra* probably hope that it will remind people of such concepts as *vigorous* and *viable,* just as the name of the Honda *Acura* was designed to make people think of such concepts as *accurate* and *acumen.*

CREATING EPONYMS

Another way that new words come into languages is from the names of people and places, both real and literary as with the *Franklin stove* (from inventor Benjamin Franklin), the *sousaphone* (from musician John Philip Sousa), and *cesarean section* (from the manner of Julius Caesar's birth). With literature, the more people who have read a book, the greater the chance of characters' names becoming eponyms. This is why so many names from the Bible have become common parts of the language. The projection of cartilage in a man's larynx is called an *Adam's apple*. The name actually came about from a mistaken interpretation of Hebrew, but people believe the playful explanation that when Adam and Eve were eating the forbidden fruit a piece of the apple stuck in Adam's throat. *Maudlin,* meaning an exaggerated or overly sentimental sorrow, comes from the name of Mary Magdalen, the reformed prostitute of the New Testament, who in paintings always looks sad.

From places, we get such food names as *Boston baked beans, Buffalo wings, Cheddar cheese, Chicago beefsteak sandwiches, Tex-Mex food,* and *Manhattan clam chowder* versus *New England clam chowder*. The words *denims, dungarees, jeans,* and *levis* are used almost interchangeably. The first three terms are place name eponyms, while the last one comes from the name of Levi Strauss, a man who went to California during the Gold Rush and found his gold by turning tent cloth into sturdy pants that he riveted together at points of stress. *Dungarees* are named for a Hindi town where the heavyweight cloth was woven, while *Denim* is named for Nimes, France, a city famous for making *serge de Nim,* a durable, twill cloth that was good for the sails of ships as well as for heavyweight pants. *Jeans* are named for *Genoa,* Italy, another source of heavyweight cloth.

USING METONYMY AND SYNECDOCHE

Metonymy is a process of language invention in which speakers give something the name of something else with which it has been associated. For example, male athletes are sometimes referred to as *jocks*, women as *skirts*, and business executives as *suits*. *Synecdoche* is closely related to metonymy because a part of something is used to stand for the whole thing. For example, when someone buys *three hundred head of cattle*, or orders *all hands on deck*, it is not just the heads or the hands that are being referenced. In some clear examples of synecdoche, popular culture figures have been associated with parts of their anatomy. Football kicker Lou Groza was called *The Toe*, while comedian Jimmy Durante was called *The Schnoz* (Yiddish for *nose*). Softbound books are called *paperbacks*; a television set may be referred to as *the box* or *the tube*, a car as *wheels*, a football as a *pigskin*, and a movie theater as *the big screen*. We put metonymy and synecdoche together because of the difficulty of deciding whether a feature is a quality or an integral part of something.

COMPOUNDING

When two or more words are said together so often that they develop a meaning that is more than or different from the sum of their parts, they become a compound. A *redcap* does not have to wear a red cap, some *blackbirds* and *black bears* are actually brown in color, and some *blackboards* are green. The process of compounding is surprisingly open to different rules. One of the most puzzling is that some compounds have hyphens, some stay as separate words, and some are pushed together as single words. The best advice that we can give is, "When in doubt, look up the compound in a good dictionary," but sometimes even dictionaries disagree. In most compounds, the latter part names the item while the first part modifies it. A *guest house* is a kind of house, but a *house guest* is a kind of guest, while a *tire iron* is a kind of iron, but an *iron tire* is a kind of tire.

CLIPPING AND BLENDING

People often clip words to save time in speaking and space in printing. Of course, most of us would rather write and say *meds* rather than *medications, bus* than *omnibus, deli* than *delicatessen, gym* than *gymnasium, exam* than *examination*, and *zoo* than *zoological garden*. Occasionally, the clipping will come from the middle of a word if that makes pronunciation easier as when we clip *bicycle* to *bike* and *tricycle* to *trike*. Also, speakers may clip both the beginnings and the endings of words as when *influenza* gets changed to *flu* and *refrigerator* to *fridge*.

With well-known words we can leave off the beginnings, as when we refer to *Las Vegas* as *Vegas*, to a *helicopter* as a *copter*, and when we say *bye* instead of *goodbye*. The latter example is especially interesting because *goodbye* is itself clipped from "God be with ye." The tendency to clip words is even stronger when two or more words are going to be blended as with the recently developed *abs* from *abdominal muscles, humint* from *human intelligence* and *hazmats* from *hazardous materials*. Other examples of clipped and blended words that proved to be so efficient that they have become part of everyday language include *motel* from *motor* and *hotel, smog* from *smoke* and *fog, brunch* from *breakfast* and *lunch*, and *flurry* from *flutter* and *hurry*.

Tarmac, a term that today's speakers nearly always reserve for the asphalt area of airports, is an eponym that has undergone specialization. It came from the name of John L. McAdam, a Scottish engineer who in the 1800s devised the system of layering different sizes of gravel to make roads. Such roads were called *Macadamized*. Then, when someone devised a method of adding tar to the top level, the roads were called *Tarmacadam*, eventually clipped to *tarmac*. At least in U.S. English, speakers have come to use *tarmac* mostly for airports, while they refer to roads, parking lots, and playgrounds as *pavement* or *asphalt*.

RELYING ON INITIALS AND ACRONYMS

In an extreme kind of clipping, speakers rely just on initials as when we say *TV* instead of *television, CD* instead of *compact disk*, and *COD* instead of *Collect On Delivery*. The custom of using initials gained wide acceptance during World War II when there were suddenly more governmental bureaus and agencies and more new technologies than people had time to write out. For example, it was much more efficient to talk about the *AK-47* or the *Ak-Ak gun* than to refer to the Russian *Avtomat Kalashnikov*. Today, playful writers of e-mail use such initialisms (text messaging) as *ROTFL* (Roll on the Floor Laughing), *GIGO* (Garbage In, Garbage Out), *ASAP* (As Soon As Possible), and *BCNU* (Be Seeing You).

When initials happen to make a word, speakers find it more efficient to say the word than to pronounce each of the initials with a separate syllable. These are called acronyms. Well-established examples include *radar* from *RAdio Detecting And Ranging, sonar* from *SOund Navigation And Ranging*, and *laser* from *Light Amplification by Stimulated Emission of Radiation*. A fairly recent example is referring to the *President of the United States* as *POTUS* and to the *First Lady of the United States* as *FLOTUS*.

CHANGING PARTS OF SPEECH

One of the hallmarks of English is its flexibility. As speakers we easily shift words from one grammatical function to another. For example, native speakers would have little trouble in understanding these sentences in which *dress* is used as different parts of speech and as parts of compounds, both joined together and free-standing, and as the basis for metaphors.

- My niece always resisted wearing **dresses**.
- My **dress** coat is at the cleaners.
- Do we have to **dress** for dinner?
- People come to the Academy Awards all **dressed up**.
- Men are more restricted than are women when it comes to formal **dress**.
- When I was a child, most neighborhoods had at least one **dressmaker**.
- She is so successful she gets her own backstage **dressing room**.
- Turkey **dressing** is my favorite part of Thanksgiving dinner.
- **Dressers** are so useful that you seldom see them at garage sales.
- The new receptionist cannot even type; I think she was hired mostly as window **dressing**.
- The boss gave him such a **dressing down** that he went home early.

These kinds of lexical extensions make up a huge percentage of the changes in word meaning and word forms that will be studied throughout this textbook.

CHANGING MEANINGS THROUGH GENERALIZATION AND SPECIALIZATION

Words sometimes undergo changes in meanings without any purposeful action on the part of speakers or any change in the appearance or sounds of the word. *Generalization* or *broadening* is the process by which a term acquires a larger meaning. For example, the *Motel Six* chain began by charging $6 per person per night. Inflation soon made that impractical, but the company did not want to waste the money it had spent acquiring name recognition, so it kept the name. Now the more generalized name simply communicates that this is an economy hotel. Similar commercial examples include the *7-Eleven* convenience stores, which no longer restrict themselves to staying open just from 7:00 A.M. to 11:00 P.M. as indicated by their original name, and *Arby's* (*R.B.'s*) restaurants, which no longer restrict themselves to selling only roast beef as indicated by their original name.

Other examples of generalization include today's *linens* (tablecloths, napkins, sheets, and towels), which are usually not made from linen but from cotton blended with synthetic fibers. Most of us *butter* our bread with margarine, while we wear *glasses* made of plastic and eat with *silverware* made from stainless steel. *Dilapidated* from the Latin word *lapis* (stone) used to refer to worn-down stones as in a building or a road, but today we can have *dilapidated* bicycles, furniture, and wooden buildings.

Specialization or *narrowing* occurs when words become more restricted in their meaning. In Shakespeare's time, *meat* was a general term for food. When people asked for *meat* and *drink*, they were asking for food and drink. Today we reserve the term *meat*, at least in its literal sense, for the flesh of such animals as chickens, turkeys, sheep, pigs, and cattle. *Disease* used to be a simple compound whose meaning could be figured out from its parts: *dis* (out of) and *ease* (comfort). When people were embarrassed or were cold, they could be described as diseased, but today a diseased person has an illness usually caused by some kind of an organism as with AIDS, chickenpox, measles, or mumps.

Long before we had the oil-based substance that today is known as *plastic*, the meaning of *plastic* was "moldable." It was with this meaning that the medical world developed the term *plastic surgery* for reshaping someone's body. Then in the 1930s and 1940s, when technologists developed the oil-based substance that today is molded into hundreds of different items, they gave it the name *plastic*. Because plastic items are so ubiquitous, today's speakers associate *plastic* with the substance rather than with the idea of something being moldable. They are surprised to learn that *plastic surgery* has nothing to do with the substance called plastic.

CHANGING MEANINGS THROUGH IRONY, PEJORATION, AND AMELIORATION

The most obvious instances of irony are seen in slang where playful speakers begin using a word with an "opposite" meaning, as when teenagers call something they like *fat* or *phat*, or when they say a good movie is *bad*. Ironic meanings can also result from the slower processes of pejoration and amelioration, in which the prestige associated with particular words changes. Words lose status through pejoration or gain status through amelioration.

Just as when people suffer some kind of public embarrassment and are disappointed to find that it was much easier for their reputation to be lowered than for it to be raised, words are more likely to go down in status than to rise. In ancient Greece, a *demagogue* was simply a public leader, but once the word was connected to Hitler and Mussolini, no one wanted to be known as a *demagogue*. The word *depression* used to be a less ominous term than *recession*, but in the 1930s government officials tried to ward off people's fears by referring to the country's economic problems as a *depression*. As the problems increased and the 1930s became known as the era of *The Great Depression*, people's experiences made them view a *depression* as something worse than a *recession*.

It is a little harder to find examples of amelioration, but there are some. In 1750, Louix XV appointed Etienne de Silhouette as the Court's Controller General. Extravagant members of the court ridiculed his cost-cutting measures by labeling anything cheaply made as à *la silhouette*. This included coats without pleats, trousers without pockets, and cheap portraits. Today the word refers mainly to pictures made in outline form, or in seeing someone's outline against a light background, as in "She was *silhouetted* against the sunset." The idea of cheapness has disappeared.

Derricks, such as those used for oil wells and for lifting heavy objects, started out with a gruesome connection, which has now been lost. Godfrey Derrick was an infamous public executioner in England supposedly responsible for killing 3,000 individuals in the late 1500s. His method of execution was by hanging, for which he built elaborate wooden towers—hence the transfer of his name to structures similar in shape.

Both amelioration and pejoration usually occur over long periods of time without people giving much thought to the matter. For example, the word *pastor* for a religious leader used to mean something like *shepherd*, a *knight* was a stable boy, and *dextrous* and *dexterity,* which refer to skill, started out referring to right-handedness. A word that has fairly recently changed from a negative connotation to a positive one is *default*. It used to mean failure as when someone "defaulted on a loan," but now for anyone who uses computers, the *default* value is the standard, the one you prefer for most situations.

When words lose their power in this way, they are said to have undergone *bleaching* or *weakening*. Examples include the way that speakers describe events as *awful* when they do not really inspire *awe* and as *terrible* when they do not really inspire *terror*. *Awful* was bleached in the direction of pejoration, while *terrible* was bleached in the direction of amelioration. Swear words and insults undergo similar bleaching, which is one of the reasons that grandchildren sometimes shock their grandparents by what they say, and vice versa.

The Problem of Testing versus Teaching

"What gets tested, gets taught" is an adage that many political leaders believe in, and well they might, judging by the proliferation of vocabulary lessons that students are currently being subjected to. An incident in one of our local high schools is just one example of how things go wrong when faculty members are "forced" to teach subjects or processes they do not believe in and do not understand the value of. A teacher who used the common method of passing out alphabetized lists of words, which students were to "look up" and memorize for a weekly quiz, learned that her bright students were dividing up the research part of the assignment and posting their findings on a website for everyone's use. She accused the students of cheating and asked the principal to devise "appropriate punishment." Parents, the local school board, and the press got involved. Once it was understood that the students had cooperated only on finding the definitions and that the quizzes had been given in class with students being individually responsible for their own answers, the idea of punishing the students received little support because people realized that sitting alone and copying a definition from a dictionary was not a worthwhile activity. It would have been better for the students to work in groups and to come up with several meanings instead of one. Language is a social phenomenon, which means that students need to interact with other speakers and hear pronunciations and intonations, as well as words used in more variety than brief dictionary entries can capture.

We empathize with teachers' concerns about the high-stakes tests. It is likely that relatively large numbers of vocabulary items will continue to appear on such tests because:

- Testmakers find it easy to devise questions about particular words.
- The answers can be machine-scored at little cost compared to the expensive individualized scoring demanded for writing samples.
- Unlike questions on literature, vocabulary items do not force testmakers to choose between being inclusive and focusing on the "literary canon."
- While there is little agreement on the value of teaching isolated examples of grammatical niceties to students, virtually everyone agrees that understanding the meanings of words is crucial to reading, listening, writing, and speaking.
- Questions based on analogies are especially discriminating in that they test students' abilities to see patterns and to make connections.

Many teachers, when faced with an unexpected emphasis on vocabulary, turned to the source of the problem—the tests themselves—and used the tests as a model for their teaching. This has caused undue frustration because, as shown in Table 1.1, the goals and the methods of testmakers differ considerably from those of teachers.

Table 1.1 Goals and Methods of Testmakers and Teachers

Characteristics of Standardized, Machine-Scored Testing	Characteristics of Good Classroom Teaching and Learning
Students work silently.	Students and teachers engage in lots of talk.
Students work individually.	Students work in small and large groups, as well as individually, so that they have more opportunities for hearing and speaking the words.
Words are tested for single meanings.	Students learn multiple meanings along with linguistic principles about the way words acquire extended and metaphorical meanings. This gives students predictive abilities to figure out new usages and new meanings.
Students spend only a few seconds focusing on any particular word.	Students engage in various activities including puzzles, discussions, artwork, creative writing, drama, extensive reading, and the making of individual notebooks because their minds need time to absorb new meanings while their tongues learn new pronunciations.
The focus is on obscure words.	The focus is on words students are likely to meet in everyday life. While using the old to teach the new, teachers start with basic words and move into increasingly complex terms.
Clear-cut answers and an easy-to-grade format are important.	Teachers encourage conjecturing and intelligent guessing because with the meanings and the histories of many words there are no "right" or "wrong" answers.
Words are tested in random or alphabetical order.	Words are taught in gestalts so that related meanings reinforce each other. Students work with both similarities and differences among lexical extesions and metaphors.
The premium is on getting a wide range of scores.	The premium is on success for all students.

When teachers have students memorize the meanings of long and obscure words that they think might be on the standardized tests, they are trying to outguess the test-makers, an activity doomed to failure because there is no end to the obscure words that can be chosen for tests. What makes more sense is to equip students with the skills they need to be more effective communicators in all aspects of their lives, which includes test taking. Here are ways that a source-based approach will help students score better on standardized tests:

- Because students have extensive practice in mixing and matching morphemes, they will have the confidence and the skills they need to search for familiar morphemes and to use these to unlock the meanings of new words.
- Because of "overlearning" basic words and of having meaning-related hooks on which to hang morphemes (including prefixes and suffixes), students' minds will not go blank as often happens when people try to remember the meaning of a word they memorized, but did not connect to their own life.

- Through working with the multiple meanings of words, students will be aware of the fact that single words have many meanings. This will make them better prepared for the challenge of using context clues to figure out which of many meanings is the one intended by the writer.

English and reading teachers frequently tell students to "use the context" to figure out a word's meaning. However, this is easier said than done, because rather than telling readers what a word means, context clues serve primarily to screen out meanings that will not fit. The reader is then left to come up with a meaning that makes sense in a particular context. Students are at a disadvantage if they do not know several meanings of a word or if they mistakenly think words have only one meaning.

Understanding what we are reading or hearing is truly a challenge because our minds are forced to play two games at the same time, and these games have contradictory rules. Game One is played in the social arena. It consists of mapping whatever we are hearing or reading onto whatever we know or can imagine about an expanding and ever-changing world. This free-flowing and flexible game is part of what in literature is called *reader response*. Because the world, as well as what speakers know about it, is constantly changing, this part of the game expands choices.

However, Game Two, which is played in the linguistic arena, does just the opposite. Linguistic clues (determiners, verb markings, plural markings, co-occurrence restrictions, etc.) narrow the possible interpretations, and so do all the ways the word has been used by previous speakers. In spite of Lewis Carroll's claim, through Humpty Dumpty, that words "mean" whatever a speaker wants them to mean, words have socially agreed-upon meanings. There are many more of these meanings than most speakers realize, and they are exceedingly flexible. Nevertheless, the meanings are there, and a listener or reader who does not know the options is handicapped in playing both Game One and Game Two. It is because the balance between these two games is so intellectually demanding that testmakers rely heavily on questions relating to vocabulary and reading comprehension to predict student aptitude. If we have successfully equipped students with the skills they need to play Games One and Two simultaneously, then they will be more effective communicators in all aspects of their lives, including testing.

Right Answers Are Better Than Wrong Answers

A common testing technique, which unfortunately has been transferred into many classrooms as a teaching technique, is the creation of four reasonable-sounding sentences all using the word that is being taught. Students are asked to select the one sentence out of the four that is correct. Since all the sentences are made to sound acceptable, this is a "good" testing technique in that it truly discriminates. However, it is counterproductive to learning because three-fourths of the students' time is spent looking at wrong or inappropriate usages, which, as students read and reread them, begin to sound more and more acceptable.

A better kind of exercise is to present sentences requiring students to think—not about faulty usages—but about correct ones. One of the reasons to work with gestalts is that sets of words can provide material for exercises without asking students to focus their attention on wrong answers. When working with words in a set, you can also provide multiple clues about the meanings of words as in these sentences in which students are to fill in the appropriate words, all built on *amble*.

1. By remembering that *insomnia* relates to sleeping, I can figure out that someone who walks while sleeping is a _____.

2. What U.S. mothers call *strollers*, British mothers call_____, or *prams*, for short.

3. The first _____ were stretchers and medical kits carried onto battlefields where their name meant something like *walking treatment*.

4. In nursing homes, the cost of care is less for _____ patients, that is, for patients who walk.

Answers: 1. somnambulant, 2. perambulators, 3. ambulances, 4. ambulatory.

These sentences are forthright in sharing basic information about the words while at the same time providing raw material for a teacher to use in a mini-lesson. In such a lesson, teachers can go on to lead students to think about how the *preamble to the Constitution* walks in front, and how efficient it is to refer to overly enthusiastic lawyers as *ambulance chasers*. *Ambulatory* also has a meaning in formal, legal language, where it is used to describe the fact that wills can be "moved" or changed up until the time the writer dies or is declared incompetent.

Intelligent Guessing Should Be Encouraged

Teachers have told us that guessing should have no place in a vocabulary lesson. We argue that children would never have learned how to speak if they had not made thousands of guesses. Besides, we quickly add, we are encouraging *intelligent*—not *wild*—guessing. What we mean by intelligent guessing is the taking of all the clues a person can find—grammatical, metaphorical, morphemic, and whatever else is available—and then trying out tentative ideas to see if they make sense in the given context.

If students become intellectually involved and do some heavy thinking before they go to the dictionary, they will get more from the experience. One reason we say this is that social and technological developments are bringing changes to English faster than dictionaries can be compiled. The person not able to make an intelligent guess about a new term will be left out. For example, in the 2000 Presidential election, as the officials in the state of Florida began recounting the votes, the public was introduced to the *butterfly ballot*, one in which candidates' names are printed on both sides (the wings) with the holes to be punched running down the middle (the body). Such a concept was not in any dictionary that we could find. The public was also introduced to *chad*, a word that has been in standard dictionaries since the 1950s but is still so uncommon that many newspapers put it in quotation marks and gave such definitions as "a small piece of paper or cardboard produced in punching paper tape or data cards." The bigger problem was to figure out such metaphorical usages as *hanging door chads* (one corner of the box is still attached), *swinging door chads* (two corners are attached), and *tri-chads* (three corners are attached). These were counted as votes. Those that did not count were the *dimples* (the box was indented) and the *pregnants* (the box bulged but all corners were intact).

The fact that readers could not find these terms in a dictionary does not mean that dictionaries are unimportant. We love dictionaries so much that whenever we are asked what book we would most like to have with us on a desert island, we always answer "a good dictionary." Nevertheless, we have two main concerns about the way dictionaries are used in many schools. First, they are stacked in the corners of classrooms available only for special assignments rather than being stored in the bottoms of students' desks to be used as a constant resource. And second, they are often used to keep students busy looking up the meanings of words.

Students need lots of experience with dictionaries, but not the kind of artificial experience that they view as painful busywork. The work is painful because in dictionaries the print is small, the definitions are too succinct for many students to understand, and the entries are filled with unfamiliar abbreviations and symbols. To help students get the most from the time they spend with dictionaries, make arrangements to take students for a visit to the school library where the librarian can introduce them to many different kinds of dictionaries, including bilingual dictionaries, slang dictionaries, specialized subject dictionaries, general-purpose dictionaries, and the so-called unabridged dictionaries. Help students explore the dictionaries that are available on the school computers as well as through the Internet so that students can use them at home. Compare Internet to handheld dictionaries by watching for new words and new usages and checking to see what you can learn from various dictionaries. Work with students to help them understand some of the decisions that dictionary editors must make and what decisions the editors of your classroom dictionaries have made. For example:

1. Is the first meaning that is listed in an entry the oldest usage or the most common usage?

2. Are there separate entries for the same words when they are used in different lexical categories?

3. Do different dictionaries agree on how many "senses" a word has?

4. Are the histories of words given in each entry or, as with the *American Heritage Dictionary*, put in a separate section of Indo-European roots?

Once students begin relating words to each other and looking in dictionaries for more than how to spell a word, they will begin to see relationships among words that go beyond the ones the teacher brings to class. For example, in one of our class discussions, a student added the word *ramble* to our list of *amble* words. When we embarked on a dictionary search, we found *amble* defined as "a leisurely walk," while *ramble* was defined as "an aimless walk." *Ramble* has been in the language since 1620, while *amble* dates back to the 1300s. Webster's Tenth New Collegiate Dictionary dictionary said that *ramble* was "perhaps" related to the Middle English *romblen* meaning "to roam."

Students were surprised that even by looking in other dictionaries they could not find a definitive answer as to whether *ramble* descended from *amble*. Before going on with the discussion, we listed four criteria on the board. These are the ones we have used throughout this book to decide whether words are related to each other:

- Phonological (sound) similarities
- Orthographical (spelling) similarities
- Semantic (meaning) similarities
- Pragmatics (common sense and knowledge about historical connections between the users of both words)

We explained that by examining the two words on each of these points, we would be preparing ourselves to make an *intelligent guess*. After looking at each of these points, most of us agreed that at the least, the pronunciation of *ramble* was probably influenced by its similar meaning to *amble*, a word that Webster's Tenth cited from the fourteenth century as compared to 1620 for *ramble*. We also agreed that even though *ramble* might not be etymologically related to *amble*, their meanings, their sounds, and their spellings reinforce each other in people's mind. Such connections are important in languages and should not be ignored.

We laminated clippings from newspapers and magazines to illustrate the difference between puns and metaphors. The clippings are distributed to students, who figure out where they go and then come up and explain their decision as they tape the clipping to the appropriate poster. Among the puns are *Pets-mart, Caricature Builder, Cloning Around, Kidnip TV,* and *Lives at Steak.* Among the metaphors are *Hot Deals, Driving Down the Cost, Warring Couples,* and *Residents Drawn to Valley's Fringe Locations.*

These kinds of research problems make dictionary work interesting, but we are quick to caution students that tracing the histories of words and their connections will not "prove" the meaning of any particular word as it is used today. However, knowing earlier meanings of words can provide valuable insights. For example, when a student told us that *managers* are supposed to be men because "it says *man* right in the word," we were happy to lead the class on a search for words that have come into English from the Latin *manus*, meaning hand. We were probably more surprised than were the students at how many direct connections we found. Our biggest surprise was discovering that the word *emancipate* means something like "being freed from the hands of someone else." Clearer examples include the way that *manuals* are also called *handbooks;* a *manuscript* is prepared *by hand* as opposed to being published or printed on a press; to *manacle* a prisoner is to *handcuff* the person; a *manicurist* takes care of people's *hands*, while the *manual alphabet* allows deaf people to communicate through fingerspelling. After hearing these examples, the class was more willing to believe that *manual training*, the *manual arts*, and *manual labor* all relate to people – either male or female — developing skills with their hands and that a *manager* is someone who *handles* the affairs of a business.

The students were also interested to learn how words change meanings based on different conditions. In the 1500s when the term *manufacture* came into the language, it meant *made by hand* as opposed to something grown or made by nature. But then the industrial revolution brought about the building of factories, and the term *manufacture* developed the new meaning of something made in a factory most likely by a machine rather than by hand.

Knowing the Difference between Metaphors and Puns

Although puns are occasionally based on metaphors, more commonly they are based on homonyms—words that accidentally or coincidentally sound alike. *Puns* are bits of language creativity based on words that happen to sound like each other while not being semantically related—for example, the old joke about the Texas ranch where the *sons raise meat* versus the Texas ranch where the *sun's rays meet*. In contrast, when we refer to *metaphors* and *metaphorical extensions*, we are talking about language creativity based on semantic relationships—for example, allusions to such things as *a favorite son candidate, the raising of taxes, the meat of an argument, a sunny disposition, a ray of hope*, and *a meeting of the minds*.

Puns are created for purposes of amusement: They are conundrums that cannot be figured out logically. Metaphors are created for purposes of communication (and sometimes amusement). They are riddles that can be solved through applying what one already knows about the world and the language to the subject of the metaphor. In Chomsky terminology, puns are based on surface structure (phonology, morphology, and syntax), while metaphors are based not only on surface structure, but also on deep structure (semantics and pragmatics).

While homonyms are accidents, metaphors have an inherent system that speakers can apply across categories and rely on to figure out new meanings. Homonyms make us laugh because they do not fit into our expected system. The fact that they surprise us illustrates the old saying that "the exception proves the rule." It is fine to enjoy accidental puns and homonyms, just as we might amuse students with George Bernard Shaw's spelling of *fish* as *ghoti* (the *gh* of *enough*, the *o* of *women*, and the *ti* of *nation*), but we are doing a disservice if we fail to explain that in the great majority of situations, it is worth our time and effort to search for the meaning relationships that underlie similar-sounding words.

Understanding the difference between puns and metaphors is not an easy concept. When a group of preservice teachers in one of our classes was making a poster of animal metaphors related to bears, they included *bare feet* and *bare naked* along with *bear hug, teddy bear,* the *Chicago Bears*, and a *bear market.* Another student giving a speech on clothing metaphors confidently stated that *afraid* was related to the metaphor of having *frayed* nerves, while one working with food metaphors brought in a basket of plastic potatoes (*taters*) as a prop to use with teaching children about such words as *commentators* and *agitators*.

Failing to distinguish between puns and metaphors undermines the idea that language is systematic. With a "woe-is-me" expression on his face, one of our students brought in a newspaper clipping that ran under the headline, "No wonder the English language is so difficult to learn." There was no documentation of where this one came from or who compiled it, but other students said they had also seen it on the Internet. It consisted of twenty-one sentences, designed to "prove" that English is hard to learn. However, a careful look at these "demon" sentences showed that about half were coincidental puns, while the others were metaphorical extensions. The puns were admittedly hard to recognize because they were based on words that are spelled the same but pronounced differently—for example, "We *polish* the *Polish* furniture," "He could *lead* if he would get the *lead* out," and "The bandage was *wound* around the *wound*." Only those who have had previous experience with both the words and the situations can possibly understand them.

However, the other sentences that were intermixed in the article were based on metaphorical extensions, a fact that whoever collected them seemed not to realize. Rather than being viewed as puzzling anomalies, these sentences should be viewed as illustrating the flexibility of English by showing how the same basic word, with slight changes in pronunciation, can serve as different parts of speech. Table 1.2 shows some of the sentences and comments that our students made as we talked about relationships between the two italicized words in each of these sentences.

Table 1.2 Metaphors in Which Pronunciation Changes

Examples of Metaphorical Word Play	Classroom Observations by Students and Teachers
The dump was so full it had to *refuse refuse*.	*Refuse* is garbage. It is the exact thing that people would want to *refuse*.
The insurance for the *invalid* was *invalid*.	To call a person an *invalid* seems mean—or at least not politically correct. It implies that a person who is really sick is not *valid*— not a real person.
They were too *close* to the door to *close* it.	When you *close* a door, you put it *close* to the frame that goes around a door. Someone must have been standing between the door and the frame.
How can I *intimate* this to my most *intimate* friend?	*Intimate* friends are close friends. They know you well enough that they can guess what you mean when you *intimate* (hint at) something.
The soldier decided to *desert* in the *desert*.	I think *deserts* got their name because they look so *deserted*.
I'm going to *present* her a *present*.	Of course, if you *present* someone with something, it should be called a *present*.
Farms *produce produce*.	This also makes sense if you need a word to refer to lots of different vegetables and grains.

This is a continuation of the kind of intelligent guessing that we talked about in relation to dictionary work. It is a good classroom activity even if you cannot find definitive answers. Just talking about possibilities keeps students' minds involved long enough to help them remember particular words. For example, we could not decide if *minute steaks* are so named because they cook in a minute or because they are *minute* (small). Neither could we decide if the noun *wind* is related to the verb *wind*, but after we talked about how on *windy* days, flags get *wound* around their poles, everybody in the class knew the meanings of both kinds of *wind*. And while we were trying to figure out whether *memento* was related to something *of the moment* or to something *of one's memory*, class members learned the meaning and also the spelling when we finally decided that it was a metaphorical extension of *memory*. Bilingual students have an advantage over native speakers because when they translate a questionable item into their native language, the metaphors will make sense while the coincidental puns will not.

People who prepare word-study materials know that the human mind has to make connections in order to remember things, so they exert themselves to devise "memory hooks." Unfortunately, these mnemonic devices are often based on accidental puns rather than on genuine semantic connections. For example, one popular book ties *palpable* in with the *pulp* of an orange, *tangible* with a *tangerine*, and *tentative* with a *tent to live*. On the page devoted to *quarantine*, the "memory device" is the phrase *GUARANTEED Time Alone*. In the small print explanation, the authors do say that *quarantine* comes from the Latin word *quarant* meaning "forty," but the big print "memory device" leaves the impression that *quarantine* somehow relates to *guarantee*, which it does not. A major advantage of a source-based approach is that it does not have to rely on these kinds of artificial connections.

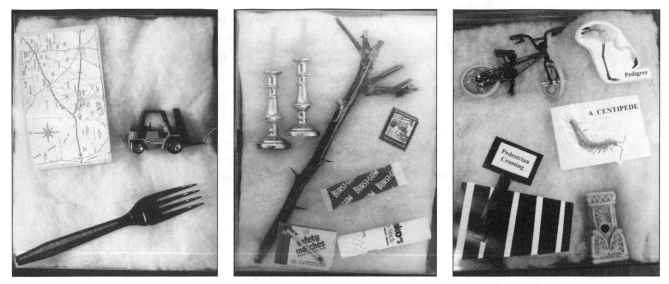

These acrylic boxes (recycled from holders of old computer manuals) are good for getting students to start thinking metaphorically. The items are held in place with thick quilt batting.

One way to get students talking at the same time you introduce them to a metaphorical approach to word study is to distribute preselected tangible objects or pictures to small groups. We were fortunate to inherit several heavy-duty acrylic covers from out-of-date computer manuals, which we filled with little items that are semantically related and share a name in some way. When we distribute the boxes, we ask the groups to figure out the following:

- Is one of the items most likely the source of the name? If so, which one?
- If the source is not represented, what do you think it was?
- Estimate which item has had the name the longest and which is the most recent.
- What feature(s) do the source word and the various target words have in common?
- Which items are most closely connected with the source word? Which names are most metaphorical and which are more literal?
- Think of other terms and metaphors related to the same source word.

For purposes of illustration, we are including photos on our website of some of the boxes along with a list of the contents and sample comments made by students. (See www.ablongman.com/nilsen for photos and information on the other boxes.) As you will see in Table 1.3, the contents come mostly from what we happened to have around the house or could easily acquire. The lesson could be just as effective with other items and with other source words.

Table 1.3 Looking for Similarities

Contents	Sample Student Comments
plastic fork map cut-out of a junction toy forklift	*Forks* in nature had to come first, as when rivers or canyons split into two parts. Forks to eat with probably got their name from these natural forks, but their shape is more likely to have been based on human fingers. The newest word is *forklift*, based on the two prongs that stick out to pick things up sort of like a *pitchfork*. The towns of *Spanish Fork* and *American Fork* in Utah got their names because they are located where different explorers forked off from the main trail to find a way through the Wasatch mountains.

stick with stickers matchstick gluestick stick of chewing gum paper sticker candlestick lipstick	The **stick** from nature probably is the source. The stickers on it look like they could stick into something, almost like thumbtacks. Maybe this is how the verb meaning of *stick* developed. A candlestick is shaped like a stick and so are a matchstick and a lipstick. The paper sticker is the only thing not shaped like a stick. Its common feature is that it sticks to things. The newest term here is *gluestick*. Probably the reason people learned its name so easily is that it is doubly appropriate. It sticks things together, plus it is shaped like a stick.
pedestal pedestrian crosswalk crane (labeled *pedigree*) centipede bicycle with pedals	Once we realized the common word was **ped,** Latin for *foot*, we know that a *pedestrian* is "on foot," a *pedal* is pushed by feet, a *pedestal* is the foot or base of something like a statue. We had to ask for help in figuring out the picture of the crane. It made sense once we learned that *pedigree* comes from French *pied de gris* (foot of crane). The lines on a pedigree chart look like the legs of a crane with the names sticking out. *Centipedes* have lots of feet but not really 100.

Working with the examples of word play in Table 1.4 may help students begin to understand the differences. A good clue, at least with these examples, is that when the word that is given is spelled differently from the word it makes people think of, chances are that the humor is based on a pun. When the spelling is the same or similar (e.g., having the same unusual consonant clusters, etc.), then it is likely that there is a semantic or metaphorical relationship.

Table 1.4 Puns versus Metaphors

Examples of Word Play	Classroom Observations by Students and Teachers
Ad for needlecraft: It's a *crewel, crewel* world.	*Crewel* is a term related to needlework. It is a pun because it accidentally sounds like the cliché about a *cruel, cruel* world.
Ad for a lampstore: Just a *shade* better.	*Shade* is metaphorical because lamp stores sell *shades* and when something is a *shade* better it is the difference between being in a *shadow* and in the light.
Name of restaurant: Paul Perry's *Stake-Out.*	This is a pun because in a *stake-out* police are assigned to watch an area. The restaurant owner wants to make his place seem special while reminding people that he sells *steaks* (meat).
Ad for a drapery shop: After 35 years, we've *got the hang of it.*	*Getting the hang* of something means understanding it or developing skill. The idea is metaphorical because the people in the shop are saying they have the skill to *hang* drapes in the right way.
Christmas ad for a thrift shop. *You'll spend vs. Yule spend!*	This is a pun because *you'll* and *Yule* just happen to sound the same.
Ad for spark plugs: We're *plugging* for better mileage.	This is a metaphor because *plugging* means to be working or filling in where there is a need. The manufacturer is claiming to be doing this on a large scale just as spark plugs do it for individual cars.
One liner: The weather bureau is a *nonprophet* organization.	This is a pun because *nonprophet* sounds like the common phrase *nonprofit*. The joke is that the weather bureau is not good at prophesying or foretelling the weather.
One-liner: Alimony is a *splitting headache.*	The description of a *splitting headache* is an exaggerated metaphor based on how bad the pain would be if your head were split open. The description of a married couple *splitting up* is an allusion to emotional pain.

Teaching students to understand the various senses of words is a practical application of L.S. Vygotsky's sociocultural theory on children's cognitive development. In discussing the *senses* of words (what we talk about as *metaphors* and *metaphorical extensions*), Vygotsky explains that there is no one-to-one correspondence between the literal or basic meanings of words and their extended or metaphorical meanings. He writes that "A word aquires its sense from the context in which it appears; in different contexts, it changes its sense" (p. 245). He believes that children's ability to understand the *sense* of a word is prerequisite for their gradual transition from a social plane to a cognitive plane. It is the understanding of *senses* of words that mediates children's abilities to develop the higher mental functions that can only be developed in educational settings where learning in the zone of proximal development is created and encouraged.

Things We Learned from Our Guest Teaching

The first thing we learned from our guest teaching is that it is much harder—it takes lots more energy—to teach elementary and high school students than college students. If we had been regular classroom teachers over the past two years, even working weekends and summers, we would not have had the time and the energy to do the research and the writing needed for this book. So we take our hats off to classroom teachers as we offer this material in the hopes that it will make their jobs easier, not more difficult. We do not want any teachers losing sleep over the fact that they cannot find the energy and the time to gather up visual aids and art supplies for their students. Instead, we will simply commend teachers for whatever "extras" they can manage.

It is because we appreciate how hard classroom teachers work that we have tried to make our book "teacher-friendly." Workshop answers are printed at the end of each chapter, and the workshop pages are ready to be photocopied for direct use by students. On our Website we have also printed several aids that we hope you can download and use with your own students. In the meantime, here are the activities that worked for us, in descending order of effectiveness and efficiency.

1. Providing students with looseleaf notebooks. In the classes where we taught for a whole semester, we provided looseleaf notebooks that remained in the classroom until students took them home at the end of the semester. In our best classes, students had a substantial book to take home. The books were the kind with clear acetate covers so that we slipped in a preprinted page titled *Changing Words in a Changing World* and then invited students to add what they wanted to the covers. One of our college students confessed that at first she thought decorating her book was silly, but after several weeks of picking her book from the class pile, she came to identify with it and decided the covers were a good thing after all. The books served as a collection point for:

- Completed workshop pages and whatever reading materials we had photocopied for students.
- Notes and writing related to the words being studied.
- Mini-posters and notes used for oral presentations.
- Cartoons, jokes, or newspaper and magazine clippings students had brought to share with the class.

One advantage for us was that rather than giving grades every day, we could concentrate on teaching, then collect and evaluate the books at regular intervals. As an alternative to the notebooks, in one college class we had students keep a word journal that

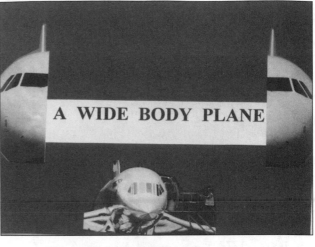

Wordstrips, printed on a computer and then enlarged and photo-copied on card stock, are good for helping teachers remember what they plan to teach. A bonus is that they can also inspire students to search through the classroom picture tub, or through magazines at home, for appropriate illustrations.

encouraged them to make choices about which information of the evening was worth writing down. The journals also provided them with source material for bigger writing and research projects.

2. Making word strips of key words and phrases. We were pleasantly surprised at how useful were the word strips that we typed in all caps on a computer (36 pt. Times Roman type in boldface). We cut our pages in two and photocopied them lengthwise on card stock at 200 percent so the print would be big enough to be read from any place in the room. For your convenience, we have typed key words from each chapter on our Website, which you are welcome to download and print for such uses as these:

- Reminding yourself of the words you are working with and wanting to elicit from students.
- Distributing responsibilities among students for "teaching" particular words or concepts to classmates.

- Inspiring students to do high quality work by providing them with neat beginnings for posters and/or pages in their *Changing Words* books.
- Using them as labels for bulletin boards and other display items.
- Posting words for reference to help students do exercises, complete crossword puzzles, and/or play vocabulary games.

One of our colleagues at ASU West, David W. Moore, takes a playful approach to the posting of word strips FOR THE LONG HAUL. During a unit, he shuttles his word strips from a board identified as THE PARKING LOT (all the words in the unit), to the WORD BENCH (the words the class is working on during a particular lesson), to the PARTS WAREHOUSE (prefixes, suffixes, and roots that relate to the unit).

3. Bringing in a picture tub. Having a box, basket, or plastic tub filled with pictures that students can use for their projects is a time saver. We started our picture collection when we noticed how easily students were distracted if we took in whole magazines. At first, we just tore out interesting looking pages from magazines, but then we found that heavier weight paper worked better and so we began tearing off the covers of performance programs, catalogues, alumni magazines, advertising brochures, and whatever else arrived free in the mail. We also started cutting off peripheral information so that many of the pictures could be transferred directly to posters. A librarian friend donated the book jackets that she didn't need; another teacher brought in old greeting cards and postcards; and we went through our photographs and put in extras from our travels. While always having the main tub handy, we found it worked even better if before class we could pull out pictures in some way connected to the general subject of the day such as food, plants, geology, etc. We spread these out on our teachers' table at the front of the room so they were easily visible, and several students at a time could look at the pictures and pick up what they wanted to take back to their desks. Directions taped onto the tub's lid read:

- Take pictures from here for illustrating posters or writeups.
- Take only what you need.
- Put all cutting scraps in the wastebasket.
- Be considerate of others who may also want to use these pictures.

4. Providing hands-on opportunities. The biggest challenge in teaching vocabulary is to keep students on task and involved in relating to the words. This means constantly coming up with some new kind of activity—for example, bringing in white boards to use in place of paper; letting students use a video or a digital camera to illustrate meanings of words; encouraging students to illustrate their writing about words with computer drawings; making collections of metaphorical headlines, jokes, or advertisements; or drawing the illustrations for such riddles as "What has eighteen legs and catches flies?" "A baseball team." Here the idea is that fly balls are called *flies* because they fly through the air.

If you can afford fancy printed paper (watch the bargain tables), it gives a lift to students to have something different on which to make lists or write explanations of words relating to the design of the paper. In a high school class when we were comparing Latin and English names for body parts, we brought in a big roll of paper and asked two students to trace and cut out a life-sized body that we used for displaying English and Latin word strips. As a concluding activity to the chapter on numbers, we hung cut-out numbers across the front of the room and gave students 3-inch sticky notes on which to write interesting tidbits about various numbers. They shared their observations with the class as they put them on the appropriate numbers. In the last class of the day, we let groups draw and write directly on the numbers. Students liked this better because they had more room.

As we brought in miscellaneous visual aids, we worried about taking a "cutesy" or dollhouse approach because we had read Christina Hoff Sommers's *The War against Boys: How Misguided Feminism Is Harming Our Young Men* and a statement quoted in a BBC report from Britain's Schools Minister Estelle Morris in which she lamented the crisis of "underachievement by boys at school." She gave as a contributing factor "teaching styles that suit girls rather than boys." We made a point to bring in miniature cars, trucks, and forklifts, alongside the dolls and stuffed animals that were easier to find. We also tried to balance out the metaphors connected to sewing and cooking with metaphors connected to tools and weapons. When we brought in a bouquet of sunflowers as a centerpiece for our weather unit, we put the flowers in a cowboy boot instead of a vase, and for whatever art projects we were sponsoring we tried to provide enough basic help that even students without a lot of patience could feel successful. We learned that the older students were, the more they enjoyed the change of pace that came with doing something with their hands. And in relation to gender, we were happily surprised to find that boys enjoyed making things just as much as girls did, and in fact, they often worked more quickly and with fewer inhibitions.

We were surprised at the sophisticated drawings that some students could make for posters and cartoons. If we brought in new, colorful cardstock and pens with plenty of ink, students exerted themselves more than when we came in and said something like, "Take a piece of paper out of your notebooks and . . ." When students make drawings, they want them to be seen, so it's a good idea to post them at least for a few days. We found that it worked well to have students work on 8 1/2 by 11" card stock. We would distribute only compatible colors and let students choose what they wanted to illustrate around a particular theme. The result was unified and attractive bulletin boards, which when dismantled made attractive pages in students' *Changing Words in a Changing World* books.

5. Sharing anecdotes. As long as you remember that your goal is to help students remember the meanings of words, go ahead and tell those true stories that amuse your friends. Alleen tells students about the day she learned what *translucent* meant. It was during summer school when she was teaching two sections of children's literature. She wore a lightweight summer dress and was using a black light to tell the flannel board story of *Why Mosquitoes Buzz in People's Ears*. Not until the second class did a student raise her hand and say, "Dr. Nilsen, do you know that the black light shines through your dress and makes your underwear glow?"

We have an almost equally amusing (or tragic) story about how we learned that *nepotism* originally meant giving special favors to your nephew. We hired our teenaged nephew, who had just graduated from high school and was looking for summer work, to reroof our house. In dry Arizona, it was months before rain came and we discovered that our nephew did not know how to fit shingles into the corners of a sectioned roof.

Don makes the connection between *river banks* and the *banks* that keep people's money by telling how as a child he would hide his treasures in the bank of the irrigation ditch on his parents' Utah farm. When the water would come through every ten days or so, his treasures either got wet or floated away. Finally, he came up with the idea of burying a bottle with a lid in the side of the ditch, thus becoming one of the youngest children in the country to have his own *safe* in a *bank*.

While we are not afraid to encourage students to laugh at our stories, we are more careful about laughing at students. We try to praise their efforts to analyze words and make connections even as we guide them to go a little further and reconsider some of their assumptions. If a classroom has been filled with cheerful acceptance, then even on those rare occasions when someone makes such an outlandish guess that class-mates laugh, the student is not likely to feel embarrassed.

How the Remaining Chapters in This Book Are Organized

Chapters 2 through 9 are not as smooth as we would like because we are writing for two audiences at the same time. Our first audience is adult teachers or preteachers at the secondary and higher levels of classes in English, reading, or ESL. Our second audience is the students in these teachers' classes. We begin each chapter with a "Teacher's Preface" that we hope will make you feel comfortable in teaching the rest of the chapter. We include "Conversation Starters" in several of the chapters because language is primarily an oral phenomenon, and we believe that students will learn more successfully if they are talking with you and with each other.

When we have tried to make this point with our student teachers, they always agree about the benefits of informal discussion and of teaching related words through gestalts or webs, but then they explain in an apologetic fashion that when they are standing in front of a classroom juggling three or four different responsibilities, their minds are too preoccupied to think of the related words that would help them initiate these kinds of discussions with students. It is to help you "talk" the material that we have put the answers at the end of each chapter. From long experience, we know how frustrating it is to have to search out a separate teacher's guide.

We hope you will consider our answers suggestions rather than the final say. On some of the questions designed more for discussion and thinking, we did not take the space to provide answers. Also, depending on your students, you may not want to pho-tocopy all of the workshops. Sometimes you might just communicate the material orally, sometimes pass out one copy to two students, and other times do the work on an overhead. However, when you do the exercises as a group, students will get extra reinforcement if at the same time they fill in the answers on their individual sheets. Also, you need to explain to students that by writing in the words, they are giving their minds extra help in remembering what they are learning. We always had some students who wanted to just fill in numbers or draw lines to the appropriate answers. They seemed more willing to use the words both in writing and speaking after we explained that part of our purpose is to trick our minds into making room for storing this new information.

The end-of-chapter activities are the *Plus* part of this book. They provide opportunities for students to practice their art and writing skills, as well as public speaking. They are more free form and creative than the workshops. We do not expect every student to do every activity. Instead, the purpose is to encourage a sense of ownership by letting students choose one or more of the activities they would like to do.

CHAPTER TWO

Animals

Teachers' Preface

Linguistic principles being illustrated in this chapter include:

1. Animal-based metaphors in English reflect humans' fascination with animals and our instinct for making comparisons.

2. The more closely we associate with a particular species, the more likely we are to create a variety of metaphors based on different features of the same animal.

3. With exotic animals we will have fewer metaphors, and those we have are likely to be based on only one or two dramatic features.

4. Allusions to different animals can be used to express similar ideas, while allusions to the same species of animal can be used to express different ideas.

5. The feature(s) stressed in animal-based metaphors are good illustrations of the concept of metaphorical *grounding*—that is, the *common ground* between the *source* and the *target* or *receiver* of the metaphor.

This souvenir *jackalope* (from *antelope* and *jackrabbit* made in Douglas, Wyoming) inspired thinking about other imaginative animals.

This *In the doghouse* poster came back from a homework assignment.

6. While those who believe in language manipulation might manage to change a basic word, as when purists in the early 1800s changed *roostcock* to *rooster*, it is much harder to change metaphorical allusions as shown by how *cock* has remained a basic word in English to describe a *cocky* person or the action of *cocking a gun*.

You might introduce this chapter by posting on the overhead an enlarged cartoon that uses animals as stand-ins for people. Students could either talk about or write in their journals what they need to know to catch onto the joke. Gary Larson's cartoons often circle around both literal and metaphorical meanings of words. In one he shows a sheep standing on its hind legs and exhorting the rest of the flock, "Wait! Wait! Listen to me! We don't *have* to be sheep." In another one, horses are sitting in school making fun of a fellow student's answer by saying, "Sheila's *cow sense* was always a target of ridicule," while in another one two grizzly bears stare at a fellow bear standing on a pedestal and wearing a sign, "Goodbye World." One of the bears says to the other, "Oh my God! It's Leonard!… He stuffed himself."

Another idea is to encourage students to reminisce about some of their favorite animal characters in children's literature including those drawn by Dr. Seuss, Richard Scarry, Maurice Sendak, or William Steig. They probably have fond memories of Clifford the Big Red Dog, Frances the Badger, and Little Bear and his mother, as well as of old folktales. Students might be interested to learn that one of the reasons so many easy-to-read books are about animal characters—sometimes referred to as "people in fur"—is that publishers think young children can relate to animal characters regardless of their ethnicity or whether they are boys or girls.

A Fish Story was written on bargain-table stationery that we brought in. The student included such phrases as *Something smells fishy, Loan shark, A whale of a tale, A fish out of water, Hook, line, and sinker, Big fish in a little pond,* and *Circling like sharks*.

Around the world, people recognize the symbolism of Hans Christian Andersen's *Ugly Duckling*, and we all know what dragons and unicorns are, even though we've never seen even the bones of such animals. And while we may have seen real storks, not one of us has seen a stork deliver a baby. Talk with students about the messages being communicated in such proverbs as:

- A leopard can't change its spots.
- Let sleeping dogs lie.
- What's sauce for the goose is sauce for the gander.
- There are other fish in the sea.
- His bark is worse than his bite.
- You can't make a silk purse out of a sow's ear.

You might also share the following pieces of information, so that before students launch into the actual lessons, they can see how speakers use animal metaphors to:

1. Illustrate human characteristics.

2. Provide strong visual imagery.

3. Enlarge the lexicon of English.

CONVERSATION STARTERS

- On rare occasions, an individual animal has gotten its name into dictionaries. One such animal was *Jumbo*, an unusually large and smart elephant, which was given the Swahili name for *chief*. In the 1860s and 1870s, he was a prize attraction at the

London Zoo. In 1882, U.S. circus owner P. T. Barnum made the zoo "an offer it could not refuse," and Jumbo came to the United States as the star attraction for Barnum's circus. He was so famous on both sides of the Atlantic that his name became a synonym for *huge* as seen today in such phrases as *jumbo olives, jumbo hamburgers, jumbo shrimp,* and *jumbo jets.* Walt Disney's *Dumbo* character was created as a play on the name of *Jumbo.*

- Walt Disney is also responsible for the most famous cartoon character of all time: *Mickey Mouse.* In his own right, Disney's Mickey Mouse still has plenty of prestige, but dictionaries define his name to mean that something is childish or silly as when students complain about taking *a Mickey Mouse class* or having to abide by *Mickey Mouse rules.* During World War II, Mickey Mouse's name was used as the code name for the invasion of Normandy, but already it was developing the other meaning. A probable contributing factor was that the Navy used *M.I.C.*s (Military Indoctrination Centers) to teach petty rules to sailors.

- The *Trojan horse* from Greek mythology is a well-known symbol for trickery. In the story, the Greeks, who were being kept outside the city of Troy, built a large wooden horse. Several soldiers hid inside before the Greek military commanders delivered the horse to the city supposedly as an offering to the Goddess Athena. When the horse was rolled inside the walls, the soldiers waited until nighttime and then under the cover of darkness climbed out and opened the city gates, thereby allowing the Greek army to enter and conquer Troy. People are alluding to this story when they say things like, "Beware of Greeks bearing gifts." When computer users talk about a *Trojan horse,* they are referring to a file sent by someone who has made it look like a game, a joke, or some useful information. When the file is opened, it releases a virus into the user's computer system.

- Snipes are real game birds resembling woodcocks and living in marshy areas where the vegetation keeps them fairly well hidden. However, they are best known in U.S. folklore because Westerners trick newcomers by taking them on night-time *snipe hunts* (where no snipes really live) and leaving the newcomers out in the wilderness to find their way home. This playful kind of trickery is related to the more serious verb, *sniping,* which is the shooting of enemies from concealed locations. A milder meaning of *sniping* refers to verbal *snipes,* as when a sarcastic family ruins their vacation by *sniping* at each other. The noun *sniper* is used for shooters as in this headline, "Sniper's bullet kills two at mall," but not for the person who *snipes* verbally at others.

- Dictionaries define the word *scapegoat* as someone bearing the blame for others or being the object of irrational hostility. The source of this metaphor is the ancient Jewish celebration of Yom Kippur. As part of the ceremony, the sins of the people were placed on the head of a goat, which was sent into the wilderness. By carrying away the sins of the people, it allowed them to have a fresh start. The first part of *scapegoat* is thought to be a translation of the name of an ancient demon, but most English speakers interpret it to be a shortened form of *escape,* which fits with their mental picture of a goat running off into the wilderness. In the actual ceremony, however, the goat does not escape but is chased away.

- The *magpie* is a colorful and noisy bird that since the 1200s has been called a *pie.* A distinguishing characteristic is its habit of collecting all kinds of odds and ends and using these to make its nests. During the 1300s, when cooks started putting pastry on top of pans full of miscellaneous leftovers—meat, potatoes, carrots, or even various kinds of fruit—the name *pie* was given to the newly invented food because its insides looked like the nest of a magpie.

From the Horse's Mouth

Name: _____ **Period:** _____ **Date:** _____

After you read this essay, do the exercise in which you match up the idiomatic phrases about horses with what they communicate. Not all of the usages are in the essay, so you will have to use what you know about the real world and also pay special attention to the clues that are in the sentences. Perhaps your teacher will let you work in small groups to figure out the answers. That English has so many idiomatic phrases about horses reflects their importance in daily life before the development of bicycles, cars, trucks, tractors, and other conveyances.

HORSE-RELATED WORDS

While some people are cat lovers and others say that dogs are human's best friend, in the history of the world it is the horse that has worked almost as an equal to people. Its importance is reflected in dozens of words and phrases. It even gave its name to other species as with the *sea horse*, whose shape reminded speakers of the elegance of a prancing horse, and the *walrus* (literally, *whale horse*), whose weight reminded speakers of the size and strength of work horses.

When the Spaniards arrived on horseback in the New World, some of the people who first saw them thought that horse and man were one magical creature, sort of like the centaurs in Greek mythology. Further evidence of the importance of horses in world history is the fact that mythical stories gave them additional powers, as with Mercury's winged horse, Pegasus, and Apollo's horses that every day drew the sun's chariot across the sky.

When the French conquered England in 1066 and stayed for the next few hundred years, horses played a big part, as shown by the French words for horse (*cheval, chevalier*) that became part of English. The *cavalry* is the part of an army that is mounted on horseback. Someone who is *cavalier* is aristocratic and disdainful of the common people (he's on *a high horse*), while someone who is *chivalrous* exemplifies the best qualities of a noble soldier.

Words associated with caring for horses also reflect their importance. For example, the rounded shape of horseshoes provides us with a way to describe arches, tables, bars, and even waterfalls and the *horseshoe crab*. Horseshoes are also used as symbols of good luck and as such are nailed over gateways and on fence posts. The idea probably relates to how out of luck someone was when horses provided the only means of transportation and a horse that had lost its shoe was as useless to a rider as a broken-down car would be today.

From *saddle*, comes the idea of a *saddle* as a rounded low place in a mountain chain as well as the more metaphorical idea of someone being *saddled* with responsibility. From *bridle* comes the idea of *bridling one's passions*, which means to get them under control. If someone is *bridling with resentment*, the person acts as offended as does a horse, which rears its head and sticks out its chin to protest the indignity of having the *bit*, which connects the two sides of a bridle, inserted in its mouth. A person who is *chomping at the bit* wants to get started as does a horse that has been saddled up and prepared to go. When solar experts try to *harness* the energy of the sun, they are trying to make it work for the good of people as do horses when they are *harnessed* to wagons, coaches, carts, or plows.

It used to be just horses that were groomed, but today *good grooming* is considered essential for people. Historically, the men on large estates who took care of the horses, the *groomsmen*, were among the most important servants, and so their name became a general term for *man*. It's now archaic, except in the term *bridegroom*, which means something like "the bride's man."

Curry is an Old French word describing the brushing and combing of a horse's coat, as with a *currycomb*. From this came the expression *to curry favor*, which means to try gaining attention or special privileges through insincere flattery. One story says that Napoleon's favorite horse was named *Favel*; another says *favel* was the word for any chestnut-colored horse. Either way, people would try to gain Napoleon's approval by taking extra good care of *Favel*. When English speakers heard about *currying Favel*, they misunderstood and repeated the phrase as *currying favor*.

An equally interesting usage is *curry powder*, which, contrary to general assumptions, is not a spice from India. Instead, it means that the food has been tended and taken care of, which includes applying such spices as cayenne pepper, fenugreek, and turmeric. Not all curried foods taste the same because each cook decides what spices to use in the process of the *currying*.

The horse-related terms we have in U.S. English mostly reflect our rural roots and the years when horses did the work on farms and provided basic transportation even for people who lived in cities. Until the last century, people were so accustomed to riding in horse-drawn vehicles that the first cars were called *horseless carriages*. The word *car* is, in fact, a clipping of *carriage*, which is a noun based on the verb *to carry*.

Horses belong to the category of animals known as *equines*. The horse family includes such animals as zebras, donkeys, and mules, but if a sculptor were hired to make an *equestrian* statue of a town hero, the people would be very surprised if their hero were shown sitting on anything but a horse.

Listed below are several common words and phrases followed by descriptions of the characteristics of horses. Try matching the words or phrases to the descriptions. Write them on the lines, which show how many answers there should be.

horsing around	from the horse's mouth	horsy	hold your horses
long in the tooth	horse-faced	one-horse town	horse feathers
pommel horse	horse laugh	rocking horse	horseplay
sawhorse	to beat a dead horse	horse mackerel	a dark horse
horseradish	vaulting horse	horse sense	
horse of a different color		to look a gift horse in the mouth	

I. As horses grow older, their gums recede from their teeth. This makes it possible for knowledgeable people to tell the age and condition of a horse by examining how long its teeth are.

a. _____   b. _____

c. _____

2. Horses are unusually smart as shown by how cleverly they can help cowboys in tending cattle and how they sense danger and can pick out the best places to walk.

_____

3. Horses sometimes tease as they nicker and reach out to bite each other in a kind of rough play.

a. _____   b. _____

4. Horses occasionally pull their lips back from their teeth so they look as if they are engaged in an exaggerated kind of laughter.

_____

5. When an overworked or frightened horse would lie down, frustrated owners would sometimes try to arouse it through a beating even after the horse had collapsed and died. _____

6. Horses have a lot of qualities, but one thing they don't have is feathers, so this means "nonsense."

_____

7. Because horses are big, their names are used to indicate that something or someone is unusually big or strong.

a. _____   b. _____

c. _____   d. _____

8. When transportation was mainly through horses, people had to keep a tight rein on their horses to keep them from causing traffic accidents.

_____

9. Today, people's wealth is reflected in how many and what kind of cars they own, but the wealth of people, and even towns, used to be judged by how many horses they had.

_____

10. Horses are a perfect shape for holding people as well as other things; hence, we have created several different kinds of artificial horses.

a. _____   b. _____

c. _____   d. _____

11. At horse races, unscrupulous owners would sometimes bring in a winning horse dyed a different color so as to fool the people placing bets.

a. _____   b. _____

From the Horse's Mouth

Other Farm Animals

Name: _____ **Period:** _____ **Date:** _____

Read these paragraphs about common farm animals and then choose which of the given words or phrases best fits in the spaces of the sentences that follow. Talk about the aspect of the animal that is being alluded to in each of the metaphors.

A. *Pigs* (*porcines*) were unusually important to early farmers as shown by the fact that metaphors have been created from five different terms for the animal. *Pig, swine,* and *hog* refer to the living animals, while *pork* and *bacon* refer to the meat. Footballs are called *pigskins*, even though they might be made from synthetic materials. Children save their money in *piggy banks* and ask their parents to carry them *piggyback*. The Bible refers to *swineherds* and metaphorically cautions people against *casting pearls before swine*. *Porpoises* were named by French speakers (*porc poisson=pigfish*) because of their shape, while *porcupines* were named by English speakers (*pork+spines*). Cautions against buying a *pig in a poke* (a sack) are meant to teach buyers to investigate before they agree to something. Because pigs smell bad and cool off by rolling in the mud, and will gobble up almost anything, they are generally associated with negative connotations as when someone is called a *pig* or described as *pigheaded*. In the 1960s, when young people were protesting the Vietnam War, they expressed resentment against police officers by calling them *pigs* and warning against their arrival by saying they *smelled the bacon*.

| gas hogs | guinea pigs | hogwash | hog wild | pork barrel legislation |

1. If your Congressman manages to get the federal government to approve a big project for your state, his work might be described as _____ .

2. Someone who goes _____ will probably regret it the next day.

3. It is against the law for people to be used as _____ without their knowledge.

4. When farmers hose off their pigs or clean out their pens, the runoff smells bad, so you should not be flattered if someone describes an argument you are making as _____ .

5. Many of the same people who preach against environmental abuse drive cars that are _____ _____ .

B. *Cows* (*bovines*) are another important farm animal as seen through such terms as *cow pasture* and *cowboys* and *cowgirls*. Calling someplace a *cow town* is saying that it is small and quaint, while calling a state university a *cow college* is teasing it for receiving land grant money set aside to encourage agricultural education. People whose hair grows in a particular direction are said to have *cowlicks* based on how calves look after their mothers have been licking them. Something that is a *sacred cow* is something that is above criticism. This is based on a custom in India where cows are revered. The males of the species are called *bulls*, a term often associated with macho strength as with the *bullpen*, where baseball pitchers practice throwing, and with *bull sessions* where men come together to talk. *A bull in a china shop* alludes to something big and strong being placed where it is apt to do unwanted damage. Because *beef* is fairly lean and filled with protein and other nutrients, it is used as a metaphor for strength, as when an airport *beefs up* security. When profits are being made on the stock market, it is called a *bull market*, as compared to a *bear market* when people are losing money. The metaphor of a *bear market* is thought to come from an old proverb advising people not to sell the bearskin until they have caught the bear. *To take the bull by the horns* means to face a problem and to attack it directly. Targets are called *bull's eyes* because when people shoot a bull they aim for this vulnerable body part in hopes of killing the bull before it can attack the shooter.

beef	bull market	bulldozers	bullies	cash cow

1. People feel more optimistic about the country's economy when there is a ———————————— with stock trading charging ahead.

2. To ———————————— about something is to complain strongly about it.

3. A ———————————— is a money-maker that keeps producing like a cow keeps making milk.

4. Bulls are so strong and so pushy that they gave their name to mechanical ———————————— as well as to human ————————————.

C. *Chickens* and *Roosters* are important to farms both for the meat and for the eggs. *Roosters* used to be called *roostcocks*, but in the 1800s Americans decided to change the name to *rooster* because of the sexual connotations of *cock*. Although language purists were somewhat successful in changing the name to *rooster*, the word *cock* is still a part of English. A *cocked hat* is bent sideways as is a *cockscomb*. The original *cockpits* were holes in the ground where two roosters were put to fight; hence, the meaning of a small place with lots of action. *Cockpits* on ships came before the *cockpits* on airplanes. The *birdie* in badminton is called the *shuttlecock*, and both *cockamamie* and *cockeyed* are used as terms of disparagement. To *cock a gun* is to get it ready, based on the fact that roosters look ready for anything. Someone who is *cocky* or *cock sure* struts around full of the kind of confidence that roosters show. Some speakers consider it a compliment to call a girl *a chick*, but feminists resent this usage. They say its implications for the future are that they will go to *hen parties*, *cackle* with their friends, *henpeck* their husbands, and turn into *old biddies*. On farms, most chickens were killed by having their heads chopped off. Even after a chicken's head has been severed, it can move for a few seconds, which is the source of the expression *running around like a chicken with its head cut off*, meaning that someone is extremely disorganized and moving to no purpose.

| chicken feed | chickens out | cockeyed | Dixie Chicks | spring chicken |

1. The _____ are an all-girl musical group from the South.

2. If you describe someone as _____, you are insulting the person.

3. Someone who _____ is being a coward.

4. In relation to money, _____ is small change.

5. Someone who is described as no _____ is older and more experienced than someone who would be described as a chick.

D. *Ducks* and *Geese* were almost as important on farms as were chickens. Hans Christian Andersen's story is so famous that anyone called *an ugly duckling* feels confident that better times are coming. To *duck out* on a responsibility alludes to the way ducks dip their head under water. Fairly recently, people have created a saying to help them cut through euphemistic jargon. They say, "If it looks like a duck, walks like a duck, and quacks like a duck, it's a duck." In the days of Elvis Presley, a popular hairstyle for boys was called a *ducktail*. For variety, baseball announcers sometimes refer to the players on base as *ducks on the pond*. If you are cold or scared, you are likely to get *goose bumps* or *goose pimples*. Geese do not have knees and so soldiers who march without bending their knees (as did the Nazis during World War II) are said to be *goose stepping*. Male geese are called *ganders*. Someone taking a *gander* is walking about looking at things as do ganders, who in their own way, are *cocks of the walk*. The saying "What's sauce for the goose is sauce for the gander" is asking for equal treatment for males and females.

If *your goose is cooked*, you are disempowered or disadvantaged because there is no way to bring a *cooked goose* back to life. If you *goose* an engine, you give it a quick infusion of gas so that it jerks forward, much like people do if they are surprised by a goose coming up and snapping at their behind.

| goose egg | gooseneck | lame duck | silly goose | sitting duck |

1. A _____ politician is one whose term in office is almost up, thus the person has limited prestige and power.

2. A _____ is in a bad position, like a target, but not as badly off as a *dead duck*.

3. A _____ lamp is convenient for pointing a light where it is needed.

4. If you say that someone's score is a _____, you are emphasizing that it is a big zero.

5. Calling someone a _____ is a playful kind of teasing.

E. *Donkeys, Mules, Burros,* and *Jackasses* are animals of burden used on farms. Because they do menial work, when their names are applied to people it is in a derogatory sense. You are being insulted if someone accuses you of being *stubborn as a mule* or, even worse, calls you a *donkey*, a *jackass,* or an *ass.* An Old Norse word for buttocks is *ars*, which over the centuries blended with the animal name of *ass*. This allusion to an animal and to a human's backside makes calling a person an *ass* doubly

negative, which is why it is generally considered a vulgar usage. William Shakespeare was making a pun on this usage when he chose the name of *Bottom* for a character in *Midsummer Night's Dream*.

burrito	burro	donkey	easel	mules

1. The Dutch word for *ass* is *ezel*, from which English speakers took the word _____, for a four-footed contrivance that stands patiently holding what an artist needs to paint.

2. Small switch engines for trains are called _____ engines after the smallest of these animals.

3. Drug runners are sometimes referred to as _____.

4. A popular Mexican food is called a _____, or in a smaller version, a _____, because its shape resembles the body of a burro.

F. *Mice* and *Rats* are *rodents,* which are all too familiar to people living in rural areas. These people can easily relate to such terms as *mousy* to describe a small, timid person or someone with grayish-brown hair. Once people have seen a cat catch a mouse, they can understand why the phrase *playing cat and mouse* describes a situation in which a powerful person trifles with the emotions and perhaps the well-being of a less powerful person. They can also understand what is being communicated when business people refer to a venture that has reached the point of diminishing returns as *mouse-milking*. *Rats* are bigger and more vicious than mice, plus they carry more diseases, so their name is more negative. Competitive social behavior is described as a *rat race*, while *to rat* on people is to report their illegal or immoral activities. A *ratfink* (literally, a *rat finch)* is a despicable person.

mice	Mickey Mouse	mouse	muscles	rat

1. If you smell a _____, you sense that something is wrong.

2. People are puzzled about what to say when they want to talk about more than one computer _____.

3. An old proverb is, "When the cat's away, the _____ will play."

4. _____ are named from the word *mouse* because they look like little mice moving under a person's skin.

5. A _____ course in college is one that is too easy.

G. *Dogs (canines)* are one of the few farm animals that earn their keep by working rather than by producing eggs, meat, or wool. Besides being family companions, dogs work as guards and as shepherds. When soldiers talk about their *dog tags* and when pilots recount their *dogfights* in the air, they are subtly complaining that the military treats them like animals. This is similar to a civilian complaining about having to work the *dog shift* (the night shift) or about being *in the doghouse. Hush Puppies* are a popular brand of comfortable shoes. The name is a good pun because people sometimes refer to their feet as *tired dogs*. The shoes were named after the *hush puppies* that you might order at a restaurant. These are little balls of corn meal fried in tasty oil. Fishermen invented this treat to fool their dogs by throwing them pieces of fried cornmeal, while the men ate the fried fish. *Bitch* is the term for a female dog, but the word is so often used as a strong and vulgar insult to women that many people now avoid using it to talk about their dogs. In a joke about a man wanting to call his boss a *son of a bitch*, the man is afraid he will get in trouble for being so insulting, so he settles on saying, "When you get home tonight, I hope your mother comes out from under the porch and bites you."

Canine	dogstooth	dog trot	hangdog	houndstooth	underdog

1. Joggers can get better exercise if they switch off between a _____ and full-out running.

2. The _____ Corps in World War II was sometimes called *The K-9 Corps*.

3. _____ molding is expensive because of the intricate work involved in carving the little niches.

4. Someone with a _____ look can usually get sympathy.

5. It is appropriate that the famous *sleuthhound*, Sherlock Holmes, should have his cape and cap made from wool woven in a _____ check.

6. Because the dog on the bottom is getting the worst of a fight, the _____ in any competition is the one least likely to win.

H. **Cats** belong to the category of *felines*, which is why *Felix* is a good name for a cartoon cat. Cats are able to slink around and get into places people would not expect. From this comes the name for *cat burglars*, those who manage to rob someone's home while the family is there. Another feature of cats, at least on farms where they are more or less wild, is their sexuality, which gives rise to such metaphors as *catting around*. When speakers talk about the *kitty* in a card game, they may be thinking that the extra cards are sitting in the middle of the table like kittens sometimes sit, but the idea originally came from that of a collection of things as in a *shoe polishing kit* or a *sewing kit*. Speakers often make slight changes in words to refer to things that sound more familiar. This happened with the term *catty-* or *kitty-cornered* to describe cutting across a piece of land. The term was originally *cater cornered*, which referred to an eastern diagonal, but speakers probably thought it was an allusion to the way cats take the most efficient route when they are traveling.

cat out of the bag	catbird	catfish	cattail	catty	kittenish

1. _____ reeds grow in marshy places.

2. A _____ has whiskers like a cat.

3. James Thurber wrote a funny story about someone sitting in the _____ seat.

4. To let the _____ is to give away a secret.

5. If a woman is described as _____, she is thought to be cute and flirtatious, while if she is described as_____ she is thought to be mean and gossipy.

I. *Sheep* and *Goats* are common farm animals as reflected in the phrase *to separate the sheep from the goats*, which usually refers to deciding what is good and what is bad. Goats, in general, have a bad reputation because they eat almost anything and are hard to control. Referring to a man as *an old goat* is similar to calling him a dirty old man or to saying that he is grumpy and unappealing. Long before children were called *kids*, young goats had the name because of their rambunctious nature. Sheep and *lambs* are gentle animals that tend to stay close together and close to the *shepherd*. They are famous for following their leader as in the clichéd image of one sheep jumping over a fence with all the others following at the same spot and in the same manner. This boring procession is what people who can't get to sleep are supposed to imagine when they are told to *count sheep*. Female sheep are called *ewes*, while the males are called *rams*. Their strength and pushiness stands out in contrast to that of the more gentle females as reflected in the sentence, "I don't want that *rammed* down my throat." You may have heard something referred to as a *bellwether*, meaning a sign of what is to come. This does not have anything to do with forecasting the weather. Instead, it refers to a castrated ram (a *wether*) that is given the job of leading the flock. A bell is tied to this leader so that the shepherd has only to listen for this bell to know the direction in which the whole flock is likely to be moving.

black sheep	Dodge Ram	goat	goatees	kidding
lambs wool	Rambo	sheepish	sheepskins	shepherd

1. The _____ movies starring Sylvester Stallone were named to make people think of strength.

2. If you are advised, "Don't let them get your _____!" you are being told to ignore someone or something.

3. A slogan for _____ trucks is "Take life by the horns!"

4. When someone says, "I was _____," they are confessing to playing around in a childish and frivolous way.

5. Small, trimmed beards are called _____ because they resemble the natural beards of goats.

6. The Biblical allusion to Jesus as a _____ is similar to calling local religious leaders *pastors*, which in one sense means a herdsman and in another sense a spiritual caregiver.

7. Because most sheep are white, the _____ of a family is a member who stands out, usually for negative reasons.

8. Diplomas are sometimes called _____ because of being printed on parchment, which is fine leather.

9. A _____ person is shy and humble.

10. A _____ sweater is almost as soft as a cashmere sweater.

Animal Homes

Name: _____ **Period:** _____ **Date:** _____

A. *Cages, Coops,* and *Pens* are made by humans for keeping animals. *Cages* can be as small as the little baskets that children in some countries hang around their necks so that they can carry pet crickets to school. Or with an extended meaning, cages can be as big as the steel *cages* that are used as structural frames for modern skyscrapers. *Cage* is related to *cave, cove,* and *cavity,* showing that a *cage* is basically an empty place. Metaphorically, a speaker might talk about someone being as *nervous as a caged tiger* or about a friend being too claustrophobic to work in a *ticket cage* at a movie theater.

The word *coop* is related to an old English word for *basket*, which is probably what people first used to carry their poultry to market. Today, *coops* are mostly thought of as the small buildings on farms where chickens are kept. Because they are so small, people metaphorically compare themselves to chickens when they complain about being *cooped up* or being *in the coop* (in jail).

Pens are less confining because they are open at the top, as when a farmer has a *sheep pen* or when dogs at a kennel are kept in *pens*. The dock or slip that is used to hold submarines while they are reconditioned is known as a *pen*, and so are *penitentiaries*. This latter use makes sense because criminals are kept in penitentiaries much like animals at a zoo are kept in *pens*. However, the word *penitentiary* is not semantically related to these kinds of pens. Instead, a penitentiary is a place to be *penitent* and to *repent* and be sorry for one's crimes. Regardless of this historical mismatch in meanings, *pen* as a shortened form of *penitentiary* is probably here to stay because speakers have made their own semantic connections.

| batter's cage | Caged Bird | cooped up | playpens | tellers' cages |

1. The purpose of a _____ in baseball is to keep practice balls from hurting spectators or players.

2. Banks used to have_____ for those clerks who handled money.

3. Perhaps one of the reasons babies are so eager to get out of their _____ is that they don't want to be treated as if they are animals.

4. Maya Angelou's autobiography *I Know Why the* _____ *Sings* is the first book in a trilogy.

5. Someone who is in jail understandably feels _____.

B. *Fences* and *Corrals* are built to keep animals either inside or outside. The word *corral* is related to *courier* and *current*, meaning *to run*. The first *corrals* were enclosures for carts, but today speakers think of *corrals* as being enclosures that keep horses and cattle from running away. In the 1800s, pioneers moving west would circle their wagons at night to make temporary corrals.

Fence is a shortened form of *defense,* a fact that is more clearly demonstrated by the British spelling of *defence.* "Don't fence me in," are words in a famous cowboy song, which reflects a slightly later period in the history of the U.S. plains. Farmers wanted fences around their fields to protect their crops from being eaten by wandering cattle and horses as well as by wild animals. Cowboys, on the other hand, wanted open-range land so their cattle could forage on whatever land was available. Robert Frost's "Mending Walls" poem closes with the line "Good fences make good neighbors."

corral	fence	fend	fenders

1. To *fend off danger* or to _____ for oneself is to protect oneself, but in a more metaphorical sense than building a fence.

2. Highly emotional people will be counseled to _____, or contain, their feelings.

3. A _____ for stolen goods is a middle man who protects or insulates the thief.

4. The _____ on cars and trucks are there to protect or *defend* the wheels.

C. Sheds, Stables, and **Barns** are built by farmers to protect both their animals and their equipment. *Sheds* are the easiest to build because they have only a roof and perhaps one or more walls. The word relates to *shard* and *shears* in the sense of cutting or dividing something. A *shed* cuts off the light of the sun and sends the moisture from snow or rain in a direction away from whatever is being protected by the roof. In the days when rain was considered pure, women would catch the water that was shed from such roofs to use when washing their hair.

The word *stable* relates to *standing* and *stability.* Once primitive people began building *stables* for their animals, they showed that they were settling in a place and becoming farmers rather than migrant hunters and gatherers. *Stable* families and *stable* societies are peopled by *upstanding* citizens, by people who are likely to *stay* in the same place. In Kentucky, and other places interested in race horses, it is common to talk about someone's *stable of horses.* This means all the horses that belong to one owner regardless of whether they are kept in different stables or barns.

Barns are the largest and most complex of the outbuildings on a farm. They are used to protect both animals and equipment and to store large quantities of hay, grain, and other forms of feed. The largeness of barns is what is communicated when people talk about *a big barn of a restaurant* or a city's *bus* or *trolley barns.* In frontier America, barns were often the biggest buildings in small towns, so they were used as gathering places for traveling performances. Visiting ministers, politicians, actors, and musicians became known as *barnstormers.* The usage spread to other traveling entertainers regardless of whether their performances were conducted in barns.

barn door	barnstormer's	shed	stable	stables

1. The investigation _____ little light on the subject.

2. An old maxim teaches, "There's no use shutting the _____ after the horse is out."

3. Both movie and sports agents work with _____ of athletes or performers.

4. In Richard Peck's *A Long Way from Chicago*, the unconventional grandmother figures out a way to get her granddaughter a ride in a _____ airplane.

5. Most parents want their children's friends to come from _____ families.

D. *Caves, Dens, Lairs, Burrows,* and *Nests* are shelters that animals create for themselves. Wilderness explorers know better than to go blithely into a cave because it may be the home for a family of bears or mountain lions. Because prehistoric people also lived in caves, if we call someone a *caveman*, we are saying that the person is primitive and unsophisticated. *Dens* are also the homes or *lairs* of predatory animals. Some of these may be in caves, but others are in dugouts and in tree trunks. *Lair* comes from an Old English word alluding to a *bed* or to *lie* down. Metaphorically, both *dens* and *lairs* are often associated with hidden criminal activity, as when people talk about an *opium den, a criminal lair,* or a *den of thieves. Dens* with more positive connotations are the *den* (a cozy room) in a house and a group of boys who make up a *Cub Scout den.*

Burrows are underground homes made by such animals as prairie dogs, rabbits, and moles. Metaphorically, in cold climates people *burrow* or *nestle* into warm robes and blankets. *To nestle in* alludes to the *nests* that birds make for the laying and hatching of eggs. Most nests are only a few inches across, but some large birds, such as eagles and falcons, make nests that are two or three feet across. These big nests are made from twigs and grasses, sometimes covered with a layer of mud or with feathers to make them softer.

burrow	Den of Antiquity	den of thieves	feather	nest egg

1. As a play on a *den of iniquity*, an antique shop is named the _____.

2. Ski lodges usually have big fireplaces that encourage people to _____ into their ski sweaters and warm pants while they sip hot cocoa and look through picture windows at the snow.

3. Someone who steals your _____ steals your savings and your hopes for the future.

4. People hoping to get good deals by buying stolen property often find themselves in a _____.

5. When people _____ their nests, they are saving money to make their homes more comfortable.

Figuring out the Grounding of Metaphors

Name: _____ **Period:** _____ **Date:** _____

As the examples in Workshops 2.2 and 2.3 illustrate, each metaphor is based on a feature that the source of the metaphor has in common with the receiver or target of the metaphor. This in-common feature is considered the *grounding*. For the grounding of metaphors, speakers naturally choose those features that are particularly interesting about an animal. For example, while most speakers encounter clams only in *clam chowder,* they have probably seen clam shells or at least pictures of them. The ability that clams have to enclose themselves in the privacy of their own homes is fascinating and from this image comes the phrase *to clam up,* meaning that people abruptly shut themselves off and won't talk as in, "Every time I ask about Uncle Jim, my parents clam up." The other common cliché of being *happy as a clam* does not seem to fit with *clamming up*, but it really does because it is a shortened version of *happy as a clam at high tide*. Clams are assumed to be happy when the tide comes in so that the sand they live in is protected by a covering of water.

In another example, speakers who have never seen a chameleon change colors will nevertheless know that someone who is called a *chameleon* is fickle and will likely agree with whoever happens to be nearby. When someone is described as *floundering*, most speakers picture a fish out of water struggling and thrashing about, even though the usage is thought to come from the word *founder,* as when a ship *founders* and sinks. Saying that someone is a *shrew* or has made a *shrewd* decision is an allusion to a particularly vicious woodland animal. The most interesting thing about crabs is the way they walk sideways. *Crab grass* sends out side runners so that it grows sideways, crowding out flowers and covering walkways. Almost everyone knows that *crocodile tears* are not real tears, but they may not know that the metaphor is based on the fact that when crocodiles open their jaws to eat, their eyes water.

PART I The italicized phrases in the sentences below illustrate other common metaphors related to animals or to items associated with animals. On the space before each sentence, write the name of the animal or the item that the sentence indirectly alludes to. Talk about the connections. If you do not know what they are, someone in your class probably will or you may be able to find them in dictionaries.

_____ **1.** Aunt Suzie has always wanted *to be a den mother*.

_____ **2.** The two of them are working hard to *feather their nest.*

_____ **3.** It has been snowing for four days and she is tired of *being cooped up.*

_____ **4.** In chemistry class, a *beaker* fell on the floor and broke.

_____ **5.** Don't let him drive; he's loaded *to the gills.*

_____ **6.** Con artists are good at figuring out how *to fleece* elderly people.

_____ **7.** It is not fun to be around people who are always trying *to ram something down your throat*.

_____ **8.** Little kids like *to play possum* when their parents open the bedroom door to check on the noise.

_____ **9.** It is embarrassing when your stomach *growls* during a quiet time in class.

_____ **10.** MaryLou has such a *chirpy* personality that it is fun to be around her.

_____ **11.** *Claw hammers* are convenient for both pounding in and pulling out nails

_____ **12.** There was a real *uproar* when they learned that some kids counterfeited prom tickets.

PART II Read the following pairs of sentences and figure out which italicized phrase is based on an accidental similarity and which one is based on a metaphor. With the metaphors, there will be a meaning connection. The accidental relationships are called puns because they sound enough alike to trigger listeners' minds into thinking of a relationship even though they do not actually have a meaning connection. Sometimes, but not always, a different spelling will serve as a clue that the words are not semantically related. You can also find the key words in a dictionary that includes word histories (e.g., *Webster's Tenth New Collegiate Dictionary*) and see if they have the same history. Write ACCID on the space following the sentences where the italicized word is only accidentally related to the specified animal-related term. Write META on the space following the sentences in which a comparison is being made to the animal-related term.

1. The sergeant was always *barking* orders. _____

A DOG'S BARK:

2. You can tell from the *bark* that it is a dogwood tree. _____

1. *Bridal* Veil Falls is a good name for tall waterfalls. _____

A HORSE'S BRIDLE:

2. If you are insulted, it isn't easy to *bridle* your anger. _____

1. Little kids and older people have a hard time *swallowing*. _____

A SWALLOW:

2. A *swallowtail* coat is a tuxedo with tails. _____

1. You are not supposed to enter a restaurant *bare*-footed. _____

A BEAR:

2. I love *bear claw* pastries. _____

1. He is depressed since he got a "*Dear* John" letter. _____

A DEER:

2. Rudolph the Red-Nosed *Reindeer* is a Christmas icon. _____

1. *Guerilla* warfare is a different kind of fighting from that of traditional armies. _____

A GORILLA:

2. An ugly or brutal man might be referred to as a *gorilla*. _____

PART III One of the challenging things about understanding animal-based metaphors is that the same animal can be the basis for dozens of different metaphors. And from the other direction, a whole variety of animal-based metaphors can be used to communicate similar ideas. The metaphors in the following sentences relate to five basic concepts: **Age, Gluttony, Power, Size,** and **Sneakiness.** Figure out which meaning is intended and write the italicized phrase in the appropriate part of the pie chart in Figure 2.1.

1. She's no *spring chicken.*

2. You need to *beef up* your argument.

3. Concrete barriers placed at irregular intervals to stop tanks are called *dragons' teeth.*

4. When the ice cream was brought in, the kids went *hog wild.*

5. She's a *mousy* little thing, isn't she?

6. Our new teacher is such a *shrimp.*

7. After the earthquake, *bulldozers* were flown in to help in the cleanup effort.

8. Even at formal dinners, she *wolfs down* her food.

9. He's a *snake in the grass.*

10. *Battering rams* were some of the first big weapons.

11. The *Flying Tigers* were famous World War II fighting planes.

12. I can't control the *kids* in the 4-year-olds' class.

13. There was something *fishy* about his insurance claim.

14. I'm jealous that my big *horsy* cousin got an athletic scholarship.

15. Have you read Frederick Forsyth's *The Day of the Jackal?*

16. She is such a *chameleon* that you can't count on what she says.

17. In a similar way to how children were given the name of *kids* from young goats, more ragged children were given the name of *urchins* based on their similarity to young hedgehogs.

Figure 2.1 Pie Chart

Write the metaphors in the appropriate sections of this pie chart.

Practicing with Analogies

Name: _____ **Period:** _____ **Date:** _____

Animals are a good practice topic for seeing how analogies work. With these comparisons, choose from the following words and write one of them in each of the appropriate spaces. Then identify the Common Feature (CF) that is being shown through the analogy.

buck   claws   crow   hive   mutton   pride   school   stallion   tadpole   tortoise

COMMON FEATURE

_____ **1.** A bull is to a cow as a _____ is to a doe.

_____ **2.** Fish are to a _____ as sheep are to a herd.

_____ **3.** Venison is to deer as _____ is to sheep.

_____ **4.** A caterpillar is to a butterfly as a _____ is to a frog.

_____ **5.** A billygoat is to a nannygoat as a _____ is to a mare.

_____ **6.** A flock is to birds as a _____ is to lions.

_____ **7.** Horses neigh in the morning almost like roosters _____.

_____ **8.** Fingernails are to people as _____ are to animals.

_____ **9.** At an Italian restaurant, a worm is to vermicelli what a _____ is to tortellini.

_____ **10.** A web is to a spider as a _____ is to a bee.

An Animal Crossword Puzzle

Name: _____ **Period:** _____ **Date:** _____

Use the clues to fill in the blank spaces. The allusions are to animals that
live in or around water.

Across

1. John _____ under his seat to use his cell phone.

3. The Miami _____ are a football
   team in Florida.

5. To work like a _____ is to
   accomplish more than seems possible.

6. Someone who _____ around is
   struggling and thrashing about like a fish out of
   water or like a sinking ship.

7. _____ are blank circles of metal
   like those pushed from electrical connection boxes.
   The word comes from a Middle English word for
   mud, which is where the namesake animals are
   usually found.

10. A red _____ (a sardine) is a false
    clue laid in the path of an investigation.

11. To _____ up is to close one's
    mouth and suddenly quit talking.

12. Band _____ are named after
    the shelters of many sea creatures.

Down

2. _____ get tears from opening their
   jaws, rather than from feeling sad.

4. Because e-mail is so fast, people have started calling stamped letters _____ mail.

6. To _____ for compliments is to hint
   that something deserves praise.

8. When people talk about jumbo _____, they
   are using an oxymoron (a contradictory term).

9. A building _____ is named after its
   similarity to the long legs and the long necks of a
   tropical birds.

Workshop 2.1: 1. a. from the horse's mouth, **b.** long in the tooth, **c.** to look a gift horse in the mouth. **2.** horse sense. **3. a.** horseplay, **b.** horsing around. **4.** horse laugh. **5.** to beat a dead horse. **6.** horse feathers. **7. a.** horse mackerel, **b.** horseradish, **c.** horsy, **d.** horse-faced. **8. a.** hold your horses. **9. a.** one-horse town. **10. a.** pommel horse, **b.** rocking horse, **c.** sawhorse, **d.** vaulting horse. **11. a.** dark horse, **b.** horse of a different color.

Workshop 2.2: A. 1. pork barrel legislation, **2.** hog wild, **3.** guinea pigs, **4.** hogwash, **5.** gas hogs. **B. 1.** bull market, **2.** beef, **3.** cash cow, **4.** bulldozers...bullies. **C. 1.** Dixie Chicks, **2.** cockeyed, **3.** chickens out, **4.** chicken feed, **5.** spring chicken. **D. 1.** lame duck, **2.** sitting duck, **3.** goose neck, **4.** goose egg, **5.** silly goose. **E. 1.** easel, **2.** donkey, **3.** mules, **4.** burro...burrito. **F. 1.** rat, **2.** mouse, **3.** the mice, **4.** muscles, **5.** Mickey Mouse. **G. 1.** dog trot, **2.** Canine, **3.** dog-tooth, **4.** hangdog, **5.** houndstooth, **6.** underdog. **H. 1.** cattail, **2.** cat-fish, **3.** catbird, **4.** cat out of the bag, **5.** kittenish...catty. **I. 1.** Rambo, **2.** goat, **3.** Dodge Ram, **4.** kidding, **5.** goatees, **6.** shepherd, **7.** black sheep, **8.** sheepskins, **9.** sheepish, **10.** lambs wool.

Workshop 2.3: A. 1. batter's cage, **2.** tellers' cages, **3.** playpens, **4.** Caged Bird, **5.** cooped up. **B. 1.** fend, **2.** corral, **3.** fence, **4.** fenders.

C. 1. shed, **2.** barn door, **3.** stables, **4.** barnstormer's, **5.** stable. **D. 1.** Den of Antiquity, **2.** burrow, **3.** nest egg, **4.** den of thieves, **5.** feather.

Workshop 2.4: Part I: 1. wolves or bears, **2.** birds, **3.** chickens, **4.** birds or poultry, **5.** fish, **6.** sheep, **7.** male sheep or goats, **8.** opossum, **9.** bears or large cats, **10.** birds, **11.** large cats, large birds, or bears, **12.** lions or tigers. **Part II: Bark: 1.** Accid, **2.** Meta. **Bridle: 1.** Accid, **2.** Meta. **Swallow: 1.** Accid, **2.** Meta. **Bear: 1.** Accid, **2.** Meta. **Deer: 1.** Accid, **2.** Meta. **Gorilla: 1.** Accid, **2.** Meta. **Part III: Age:** spring chicken, kids, urchins. **Sneakiness:** snake in the grass, fishy, jackal, chameleon. **Gluttony:** hog wild, wolfs down. **Power:** beef up, dragons' teeth, bulldozers, battering rams, flying tigers. **Size:** mousy, shrimp, horsy.

Workshop 2.5: 1. buck (gender), **2.** school (grouping), **3.** mutton (meat product), **4.** tadpole (infancy), **5.** stallion (gender), **6.** pride (grouping), **7.** crow (sound), **8.** claws (body protection), **9.** tortoise (shape comparison), **10.** hive (self-made home).

Workshop 2.6: Across: 1. ducked, **3.** dolphins, **5.** beaver, **6.** flounders, **7.** slugs, **10.** herring. **12.** Shells. **Down: 2.** crocodiles, **4.** snail, **6.** fish, **8.** shrimp, **9.** crane.

End-of-Chapter Activities

Use these charts as the basis for small groups to work together in preparing lessons to teach to fellow students. Other animals with metaphorical extensions that you could explore by starting with a good dictionary include such canines as *dogs, wolves*, and *coyotes*, such wild animals as *bears, kangaroos, moles, turkeys, turtles*, and *weasels*, and such animals of the air as *bees, bugs, butterflies, blue jays, cardinals, eagles*, and *vultures*. Animal parts or products that you could explore, in addition to the ones given here, are *beaks, fur, claws, hives, webs*, and *wool*.

Table 2.1 Some Wild Animals

Animal	Lexical Extensions	Sample Metaphorical Sentences
buffalo	buff buffer	To *buffalo* someone is to be pushy and demanding. A *sports buff* is a person who is wildly enthused about sports. The idea may have come from the enthusiasm of volunteer firefighters in New York who wore *buffalo hide* overcoats. Someone *in the buff* is nude because their skin looks like the inside of a buffalo hide. To *buff* a floor or a brass railing, etc. is to polish it with something soft, as with a piece of *buffalo hide*. A *buffer* is something soft (like a *buffalo hide*) that will absorb sound or protect something from damage. The *buffer* in a computer "softens" the transfer of information from the computer to the printer. Real estate *buffer* zones separate different types of property.

lion	dandelion	A *sea lion* is big and strong, but does not have the kind of agility that *mountain lions* and *jungle lions* have.
		Circus audiences like to see women *lion tamers*, but actually neither men nor women have the strength to fight a *lion*.
		The French name for *dandelions* means "tooth of lion" based on the shape of the petals and the bright yellow color.
		Someone who always expects the *lion's share* expects to get the biggest and the best.
		Woody Allen said that "The *lion* and the lamb will lie down together, but the lamb won't get much sleep."
leo = Latin *lion*	leonine leopard	By knowing that *leo* is Latin for *lion*, we can figure out that a *leopard* is a kind of lion.
		The saying "A *leopard* can't change its spots" is usually meant to say that people cannot change their personalities.
		Parents who name a son *Leo* probably want him to be strong.
		Both the *leopard frog* and the *leopard seal* have spots.
		A *leonine* hairstyle resembles a lion's mane.
monkey	Monkees monkeying	Mechanics need long arms to be able to reach into tight spots with their *monkey wrenches*.
		A *grease monkey* is a mechanic.
		The Monkees singing group chose a unique spelling so they could protect their trademark.
		To *throw a monkey wrench* into something is to dramatically interrupt whatever is going on.
		To *monkey around* is to play around with no serious purpose— that is, to engage in *monkey business*.
rabbit		A person who is a *scared rabbit* might also be described as a *chicken*.
		In John Updike's novel, *Rabbit Run*, readers keep wondering if the hero is scared.
		To *pull a rabbit out of a hat* is to suddenly come up with a magical or unexpected solution to a problem.
		Rabbit ear antennas are named both for rabbits and for insects.
		Welsh rarebit is made of cheese sauce poured over toast. English speakers first called it *Welsh rabbit* as an insult to people from Wales, who were too poor to have real rabbits.
hare harrier	harelip	*Hare* is an old word for *rabbit*.
		A *hare-brained* scheme is foolish.
		A *harelip* is an older term for a congenital deformity in which the two parts of someone's upper lip have not joined. Hares naturally have this kind of a split lip.
		Harrier hounds are a breed of hunting dogs, while *Hare and Hounds* is an old-fashioned game of chase.
snake	rattlesnake snakeskin	A *snake charmer* is a charismatic person who might charm more people than snakes.
		Someone described as selling *snake oil* is being accused of running a fraudulent business.
		If you are rolling dice and you get *snake eyes*, you have one and one.
		A *snake in the grass* is a hidden danger of some kind.
		A *plumber's snake* is a flexible tool that helps clean out pipes.
		The *Arizona Diamondbacks* are named after a kind of rattlesnake indigenous to local deserts.

serpent	serpentine	*Serpent* is related to a Greek word for something that creeps.
		Ancient speakers used *serpent* for poisonous animals that creep and hiss and bite people. The term then became another name for Satan or the Devil.
		Today a person called a *serpent* is being labeled as treacherous or evil.
		Something described as *serpentine* might be evil or tempting.
		Another meaning alludes to the physical appearance of serpents as with *serpentine* rocks or a *serpentine* road.
		Serpentine barbed wire is loosely coiled to keep out trespassers as on the top of chain link fences or spread on the ground around a military camp.

Animals of the Air

Animal	Lexical Extensions	Sample Metaphorical Sentences
avis= Latin *bird*	aviary aviation aviator	*Avis* is the Latin word for *bird* or *flying*.
		The *aviary* at the zoo is where birds are kept.
		The whole field of *aviation* is thought to be named from this word.
		The *Avis* rental car company is hinting with its name that people who rent from them will feel like they are flying.
		Aviator glasses have big, tinted lenses to help pilots see all around.
		In the early 1900s, it was considered so unusual for women to be pilots that they were given the specialized name of *aviatrix*, which is now considered obsolete or quaint.
eagle	eagles eagle-eyed	The Greek word for *eagle* is *aetos*, related to the Latin *avis*.
		When U. S. astronauts landed on the moon, they announced, "The *eagle* has landed," because the eagle is the symbol of the United States.
		An *Eagle Scout* has earned the highest honor in the Boy Scout program.
		Charles Lindberg was known as *The Lone Eagle* because he was the first person to fly solo across the Atlantic Ocean.
		An *eagle-eyed* person has unusually good eyesight.
		An *eagle* in golf is a better score than a *birdie* because it is two points under par.
butterfly	butterflies	If you have *butterflies in your stomach,* you are nervous about something.
		A *social butterfly* flits from one party or activity to another.
		The *butterfly ballot* in Florida caused problems in the 2000 Presidential election.
		A *butterfly valve* is easy to turn because it has two wing-shaped handles.
		The *butterfly stroke* in swimming is good for developing upper body strength.
dove	dovetail	*Doves* are a kind of pigeon that for centuries have symbolized peace as opposed to *hawks*, which symbolize war based on the way they scoop down from the sky to grab smaller animals.
		A *dovecote* is literally a small house or pen for domestic pigeons or other birds. Metaphorically, a *dovecote* is a harmonious group of people.
		The word *columbine* comes from a Latin word meaning *like a dove* because columbine flowers resembled a peaceful flock of doves. However, after the tragedy at Columbine High School in Colorado, the word developed almost opposite connotations.
		Based on the way that *dovetails* fan out, carpenters make *dovetail joints* when they want to be sure that two pieces of wood will not come apart.

| fly | flies
flit
flighty
shoofly | *Houseflies* may not be the most dramatic animals that *fly*, but they
    are the most common.
Shoofly pie is made with lots of molasses and brown sugar, which
    naturally attracts flies.
A *flighty* person irresponsibly *flits* from one interest to another.
Dr. Seuss's first job was drawing funny advertisements for *Flit* bug spray.
The *flyweight* level in boxing is for people who weigh less than 112 pounds. |
| pigeon | pigeon-toed | *Pigeon-hole* desks were popular in the early 1900s.
The victim of a *pigeon-drop* gets fooled by a con artist into giving up money
    in hopes of making a big profit.
Everyone in her family is *pigeon-toed*.
It is tempting to *pigeon hole* (or classify) people according to some visible
    characteristic such as their ethnicity, their addresses, or how expensive their
    clothes are, etc.
Clay pigeons are just round disks of red clay. |

Animal Parts

Item	Lexical Extensions	Sample Metaphorical Sentences
feather	feathering	A *feather in your cap* is an accomplishment. When a union *featherbeds*, it protects jobs that are not really essential. Blow drying is usually good for *feathered* haircuts. A *featherweight* boxer weighs less than 126 pounds. Women buy *anti-feathering* cream to keep their lipstick from spreading into wrinkles around their mouths. The *featherstitch* in embroidery is good for filling in wide spaces since the design goes first to the right and then to the left. When young couples *feather their nest*, they are saving money or making things comfortable for the future.
plume	plumage plumate plumed plumule	These words are related to the Latin word *pluma,* meaning *feather.* A *plume* of smoke or of water looks like a big feather. People who are *all plumed out* are dressed in a showy fashion, regardless of whether their clothing includes feathers. The soft, first budding of a plant is called a *plumule* because it resembles a small feather. *Plumates* are animals with full, bushy tails such as squirrels.
wings	wingback wingtip	*Wing* is related to *wind,* probably because of the way feathers moving through air enable birds to fly. The *wings* of a stage or of a building stretch out on both sides. Hardly anyone wears *wingtip* shoes any more. There's a big difference between a *wingback chair* and a *wingback* on the football field. People who all their lives have been under an older sibling's *wing* will probably have trouble being on their own. People who *wing it* are trusting to luck, like World War II pilots who brought their crippled planes in on *a wing and a prayer.*

		A *left-wing* Republican politician might work to get votes from the *right wing* of the Democratic party.
		If a bullet *wings* someone, either literally or metaphorically, the damage is not serious, based on a comparison to a bullet going through the feathers of a bird rather than through its body.
horn	greenhorn horned hornet	*Hornets* are insects with stingers shaped like little *horns*.
		A *greenhorn* is an inexperienced person—one's whose horns have not had time to grow.
		Horn books contained printed materials, such as the alphabet, covered for protection by pieces of opaque horn that had been flattened.
		Before people knew how to make plastics or celluloid, they carved buttons and rims for glasses out of horns. Today's *horn-rimmed* glasses resemble the earlier ones, but they are not really made from horn.
		To *blow one's horn* is to brag about oneself.
		To *horn in on something* is to intrude, much like an animal with horns might do.
		To *lock horns* over something is an allusion to the way fighting animals sometimes come to a hostile standstill when their horns get entangled.
		The *Hornbook* magazine is about books published for children.
cornu= Latin for *horn* or *corner*	capricorn corner coronet cornucopia	A *coronet* is a kind of horn.
		Capricorn, the name of the tenth sign of the Zodiac, literally refers to a *goat's horn*.
		A *cornucopia* is a *horn of plenty* often used for Thanksgiving decorations.
		To *cut corners* on something is to take the easy way out.
		When someone *turns the corner* on an illness, the person is getting better.

CHAPTER THREE

The Human Body

Teachers' Preface

Linguistic principles being illustrated in this chapter include:

1. The more speakers consciously interact with a body part, the more likely is its name to serve as the source for lexical extensions. However, this does not hold true for those body parts connected to bodily functions.

2. Synonyms and related words often reveal metaphorical relationships that are not obvious when words are looked at separately.

3. The names speakers give to technological innovations often reflect how their invention or development was inspired or at least influenced by the human body.

4. Learning the Latin names for body parts enables speakers to appreciate many previously unrecognized metaphors.

The sophomore class we taught at McClintock High School enjoyed making poster presentations about body metaphors and comparing English and Latin names.

5. One reason English speakers continue to use both Latin and Germanic words for body parts is that the Latin words add a tone of formality and respect to ordinary concepts.

6. Because bodies work in a limited number of ways and people are so familiar with what their bodies do, body-related words provide good illustrations for analogies.

As we have worked with the hundreds of metaphors we collected for this book, we were surprised to realize that it isn't always easy to decide whether a usage is metaphorical or nonmetaphorical. We began placing our examples along a continuum that contained four different points moving from what most people would describe as nonmetaphorical toward what people would clearly recognize as metaphorical. We try to illustrate this concept for students in Workshop 3.2, where we lead them through a discussion of the word *back* and then provide them with practice in deciding whether a term simply points to an association, whether it is a term used for convenience (what people often call *dead metaphors*), or a term that most likely inspires listeners or readers to get a dramatic picture in their minds. You may want to skip this concept with younger students because it is not necessary for speakers to figure out whether a particular usage is for "convenience" or "dramatic imagery" to get the meanings of the words. However, our college students had sensed some of these differences and were comforted to see them charted as:

Nonmetaphorical			**Metaphorical**
Association Terms	Convenience Metaphors	Dramatic or Visual Image Metaphors	Literary Metaphors

Because writers create literary metaphors to inspire unique feelings toward unique situations, we spend relatively little time with them in this textbook, which is designed to build students' skills with words they are likely to meet in repeated situations. However, when Don taught a semester-long college course on metaphor in the fall of 2002, the class used the material in this textbook for the first three-fourths of the class. Then, for the last one-fourth, the students presented their individual research where they were free to focus on literary metaphor. Both the teacher and the students were pleasantly surprised to see that after working with basic kinds of metaphors, the students were more skilled at finding and analyzing literary metaphors and that when students made their end-of-semester class presentations, the ensuing discussions were livelier and fuller than in other classes.

One of the findings presented in this workshop is that metaphors based on internal parts of bodies are fairly limited in number, partly because most people no longer butcher their own animals for food and so they are not as familiar with the insides of bodies. Nevertheless, speakers still say that a coward is *lily-livered* or *chicken-livered,* and they talk about *kidney beans*, which resemble the shape and color of kidneys. *Venting one's spleen,* meaning to express anger or ill will, has been in the language for 500 years. However, since so few speakers know much about their spleens (a small, vascular organ near the stomach that helps filter blood), the metaphor does not mean very much and so speakers shorten it and simply refer to someone as venting. The image is of an angry person *letting off steam* or *blowing out hot air.* When people *hyperventilate,* they breathe so fast that they lose carbon dioxide from their blood and so feel woozy or faint. When people jokingly tell a friend to *hyperdown!,* they are probably not worried about the person fainting, but instead are simply telling the person to calm down.

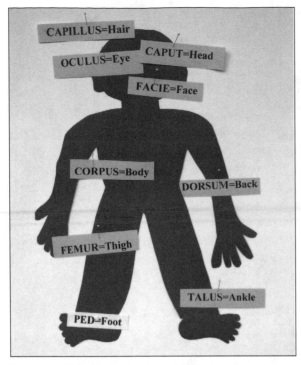

This paper doll shows only a few of the Latin roots that students can learn for body parts.

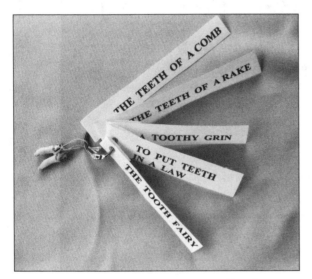

An old animal's tooth made a fascinating visual aid for metaphors related to teeth.

One reason so many metaphors are based on *hearts* is that speakers can hear and feel their hearts beating. They also observe the relationship between how fast their hearts are beating and what else they are involved in, either physically or emotionally. A person suffering *heartache* is probably suffering emotionally, while people suffering *heartburn, heart disease,* or a *heart attack* are suffering physically. When people talk about the *heart of a city,* they are trading the image of arteries and veins for that of roads and streets and mean the more important or central part of the city.

Synonyms and related words often reveal metaphorical relationships that are not obvious when words are looked at separately. For example, most speakers have not thought much about the fact that the main part of the human body, the *torso,* is called the *trunk* and the upper part of the trunk is called the *chest.* But if they think about such terms as *a treasure chest* and *grandmother's trunk,* then they might recognize their chests and their trunks as holders of such valuable parts of their bodies as their hearts, their lungs, and their digestive and reproductive systems.

In general, metaphors find their way into languages because they present dramatic images. For example, a *teardrop* pendant is a necklace with a hanging stone shaped like a drop. If shape were the only thing that mattered, it could just as easily be called a *raindrop* pendant. However, the idea of a *teardrop* is more dramatic in suggesting that the jewel might have just fallen from the wearer's eyes.

The *underbelly* of something is a side that is usually kept out of sight because it is somehow distasteful or unseemly. In a similar way, talking about *kicking butt* or being the *butt of a joke* is not considered refined speech since the allusion is to someone's *buttocks.* Successful speakers walk a fine line between being dramatic and not offending their listeners by using metaphors based on parts of the body that are considered vulgar and therefore to be avoided in polite company. Saying that someone *has guts* or *intestinal fortitude* is about as close as cautious speakers will come to publicly alluding to processes of digestion.

As a way to get students interested in looking beyond the simple fact that metaphors are connected to particular parts of the body, you might talk about *heads* as the basis for metaphors. Some of these metaphors are based on the shape of people's heads (a *head of lettuce* and a *head of cabbage*), others on the position of people's heads (*headlines* or *headings* on a printed page), others on the position of animals' heads (*headlights* on a car and a *head-on collision*), while still others are based on the importance of people's heads (a *headquarters building* and the *head of a company*). An interesting example of a metaphor that mixes these latter two ideas is the name of the government-sponsored *Head Start* program for preschool children. The idea is to give children an intellectual boost (to improve their brainpower) by sending them to school early. However, the name also alludes to a race in which the runners crouch like animals. The one who gets the *head start* is the one whose head is farthest out front, as with an animal.

CONVERSATION STARTERS

The following sentences are based on the internal workings of people's heads, but even here the allusion can be to either an intellectual or an emotional response. Talk about these sentences with students to see if they can decide whether the allusion is to EMOTION or INTELLECT. Several of the sentences could allude to both.

- She was *head over heels* in love. _____ (emotion)

- The *headmaster* makes all decisions about which classes will be offered. _____ (intellect)

- The generals are meeting right now in the *headquarters tent*. _____ (intellect)

- Ever since the news announcement, she's been *out of her head* with worry. _____ (emotion)

- When the national census is taken, people used to be asked to identify the *head of the household*. _____ (emotion and intellect)

- I mistakenly got put in a class way *over my head*. _____ (intellect)

- Even his mother says he's *headstrong*; I say he's *pigheaded*. _____ (emotion and intellect)

- Ever since graduation, he's been trying to set up a dot.com company, but I think he's just *knocking his head against a wall*. _____ (emotion and intellect)

Workshop 3.4 focuses on relationships between Latin and English names for body parts. We chose to work with Latin because of its wealth of contributions to English, but you might want to also talk a little about Greek contributions through such root words as *derma* for *skin* (*hypodermic, dermatitis, dermatologist,* etc.) and *rhino* for *nose* (*rhinoceros, rhinoscopy, rhinovirus,* and *rhinoplasty,* an operation that reshapes people's noses). A confusion that especially needs clearing up is that the Greek word for *foot* is *pod,* hence a foot doctor is called a *podiatrist* and speakers stand at a *podium.* A Greek word for *boy* or *child* is *ped-* or *pedo-,* and it is from this that English gets the word *pediatrician* for a doctor of children. A news story that came out of England in the late 1990s was about a vigilante gang that had sacked the home of a *pediatrician* because they were confused by a story they read on the Internet. They thought she was a *pedophile,* which is a person who has a warped kind of "love" for children and abuses them.

The Grounding of Eye Metaphors

Name: _____ **Period:** _____ **Date:** _____

Hundreds, if not thousands, of English words are lexical extensions that have grown out of the names for body parts. Because eyes are so important in allowing people to see, they are the source for dozens of metaphors, but the grounding of the metaphors—that is, what the source and the targets have in common—can be quite different.

Eyes attract attention because they have coloring unlike any other part of the body. This unusual coloring inspired the obvious comparison to the patterned *eyes* in the tail feathers of peacocks. The multiple colors in eyes and their translucent nature also inspired the poetic saying that people's *eyes* are *windows to the soul.* This is a metaphor that has come full circle because the word *window* literally means *wind eye* or *wind hole.* The first windows were simply holes left in walls. Their name is based on the same shape-based metaphor that named the *eyelets* in shoes and embroidered cloth and the *eyes* in needles, bolts, and hurricanes.

An office worker might be asked *to eyeball something,* meaning to look it over and take its measure informally. If the request comes marked *for your eyes only*, it is meant to be private, even if it turns out to be an *eye-popper* or an *eye-opener*, meaning something surprising or unexpected. If the same office worker is told to *keep an eye on someone* or *something*, she is supposed to watch for suspicious behavior, while if she is told to *keep an eye out for someone,* she is either watching for the person to appear or is expected to protect the person's interests. An office worker who *has his eye on* a particular position is hoping to get the job for himself.

The mother in a family might complain to teenagers that their rooms are *eyesores,* while they might complain to her that she left the *eyes in the mashed potatoes* or that she always cooks ground beef instead of the more expensive cuts such as the *eye of the round.*

A teacher in a literature class might talk about *eye rhyme* and *eye dialect. Eye rhyme* occurs when two words look like they rhyme but don't really, as with *move* and *love.* Authors use *eye dialect* (phonetic, nonstandard spelling) when they want to indicate that a character speaks nonmainstream English as with *ole* for *old, tell 'em* for *tell them*, and *wuz* for *was.* In casual speech, these words are pronounced the same by standard and nonstandard speakers, but the misspellings communicate to readers that the speaker is not part of the mainstream.

In a court of law, an *eye witness* is someone who actually saw the event that is being talked about. The expression *in the eyes of the law* implies the existence of differing points of view just as does the old saying, "Beauty is in the eye of the beholder." It is saying that someone might legally be judged either guilty or innocent, but according to some other standard (religious, community, or personal) the situation could be reversed.

Some artists specialize in *trompe l'oeil* (French for fool the eye) paintings, while less ambitious artists might hope to make greater profits by specializing in *eye candy*, which is anything beautiful or pleasing. Artists often use eyes as symbols for the unknown or the supernatural. Symbolic uses vary from the idea that "God is watching over all," to the idea that people need protection from *the evil eye.* The eye on the top of the pyramid that is part of the Great Seal of the United States printed on U.S. dollar bills is supposedly seeing in all directions. In Egyptian symbolism, the eye on the pharaoh's cobra is in the middle of its forehead, showing that it never sleeps.

Because eyes are such a crucial part of people's ability to defend themselves, they are sometimes used in metaphors relating to strength. During the Cold War in the 1960s people talked about John F. Kennedy and Nikita Khrushchev *staring each other down* to *see who would blink first* over the Cuban missile crisis. The saying of *an eye for an eye and a tooth for a tooth* comes from the Law of Moses in the Old Testament of the Bible. The message is that people should receive punishment equivalent to the damage they have done.

Here is an alphabetical list of twelve eye-related metaphors. Ponder on their meanings and the ways in which they relate to a person's eyes. This relationship is called the grounding. Three sources of grounding are shown in Figure 3.1. Try to match the examples with the concepts by writing four items in each section.

A window	Eyelets in shoes
An eye for an eye	In the eyes of the law
Eye dialect	The evil eye
Eye of a hurricane	The eye as a window to the soul
Eye in a peacock feather	To eyeball something
Eye witness	To keep an eye out for something

Figure 3.1 A Pie Chart of Eye Metaphors

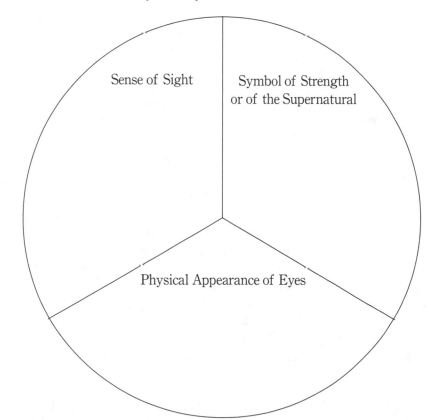

Sense of Sight

Symbol of Strength or of the Supernatural

Physical Appearance of Eyes

Metaphors from Literal to Literary

Name: _____ **Period:** _____ **Date:** _____

In this workshop, we will use words related to *back* to illustrate the different levels of lexical extensions that speakers have created. *Back* is such an all-purpose word that it can be used as a noun (My *back* is sprained), as an adjective (Take the one in the *back* row), as an adverb (Don't talk *back* to me), and as a verb (*Back* it up). But even when speakers know *back* is being used as a verb, they still have to look at the situation to decide whether it is being used in a basic or a metaphorical sense. For example, it is fairly basic when a neighbor knocks on the door and asks a guest to *back* his truck out of the driveway, but it is metaphorical when a teacher asks students to find some facts or examples to *back up* a point they are making. Common metaphors such as those based on names taken from body parts can be looked at in the following four ways.

ASSOCIATION TERMS

At the simplest level are the related words naming items that are in some way associated with the root word. We call these *association terms* as with *backpack, backache,* and *backwards*. Some association terms are purely literal, while others hover close to being metaphorical as in these sentences.

1. Julie could improve her tennis by developing a *backhand* stroke.

2. Some people try to stay in the *background* whenever TV cameras are around.

3. It sounded like a shot, but it was only a car *backfiring*.

4. The audience should never hear actors waiting *backstage*.

5. Please copy these pages *back-to-back*.

CONVENIENCE METAPHORS

A little more complex are words and phrases that are clearly metaphorical but still on a fairly simple level. We call these *convenience metaphors* because they allow speakers to make efficient comparisons. For example, we classified *backwards* as an *association word* when used to describe a car going *backwards*, but we would classify it as a *convenience metaphor* if it were applied to a shy child who is slow in developing social skills. Other examples of *back* being used as a convenience *metaphor* include:

1. Uncle Dan is a real *backslapper*.

2. Mark did not expect to be *stabbed in the back* by his own brother.

3. There is such a *backlog* of work that we never have free time.

4. She said she wouldn't take a *back seat* to anyone.

5. Her plan to come early and leave early *backfired* because she was asked to stand at the door and take tickets.

These are metaphorical sentences because Uncle Dan probably does not really slap people on the back. He is just an overly friendly person who might also be described as a *glad-hander*. And in spite of what happened to tennis player Monica Seles, who was literally *stabbed in the back* by a man who wanted to lessen her effectiveness as a player, the term does not usually apply to an actual stabbing. Nor does a *backlog* of work include a real log, nor does *taking a back seat* necessarily include sitting down, nor does a plan that *backfires* have to include a real fire.

DRAMATIC VISUAL IMAGES

The boundaries between convenience metaphors and those that present dramatic visual images are fuzzy because how metaphors are interpreted depends to a large extent on what the listener knows. Most people recognize the word *backlog* as an allusion to work that needs to be done—perhaps something that has been *logged in*. But for people who know the origin of the word, it might present a strong visual image. Historically, it comes from the time when homes were heated with fireplaces and people kept a great log smoldering at the back of the fireplace while smaller sticks and branches burned in front. The log was there as a *backup* to be used for lighting kindling and to serve as the main heat source only when there were no smaller pieces available. For people who know this story, the word *backlog* may trigger a dramatic visual image, but for most speakers it will not. They will be more apt to get a mental picture from such sentences as these, which, because of their imagery, would be fun to illustrate:

1. Politicians are notorious for *scratching each other's backs*.

2. I have *bent over backwards* to be a good employee, but my boss is never satisfied.

3. I'm surprised that she showed so little *backbone*—she was absolutely *spineless*—in the matter.

4. Taking a *back-door* or a *back-stairs approach* to something is similar to doing it *under the table*.

5. Sunshine laws were devised to keep politicians from making *backroom deals*.

LITERARY METAPHORS

We do not do very much in this vocabulary textbook with literary metaphors because authors create them with the intention of illustrating unique concepts rather than situations that occur over and over again. However, if a speaker or author creates an especially memorable metaphor, it may work its way into the public consciousness to be used as part of everyday language. Here are a few examples of *back*-related metaphors that might be considered "literary," partly because of their newness and partly because of their complexity. Notice how much more explanation is needed to explain their meanings.

1. The term *backlash* probably started as a literary metaphor. When today's speakers hear it, they might think of someone tied to a pole being lashed or beaten across the back. While these are *lashes* applied to someone's back, they aren't what is usually meant by a *backlash*. This concept is more metaphorical and relates to something like a bullwhip accidentally hitting the person who is doing the whipping or the people standing behind the person handling the whip. The meaning is therefore an unintended punishment or an unexpected adverse reaction to something. For example, if the leader of a group establishes such strict rules that followers rebel, then the leader or the institution suffers from a *backlash*.

2. *NIMBY* is another metaphor that might be considered "literary" because of its newness. It is an acronym standing for *Not In My Back Yard.* Journalists use it to describe situations in which people say they approve of such things as halfway houses and certain kinds of industrial plants or storage units, but only as long as they are located in someone else's neighborhood.

3. *Backwash* literally means a backward flow of water rushing in to fill a space that has been emptied by an expulsion such as that caused by a speedboat or a large wave. Figuratively, it is used to refer to the aftermath or the fallout from an event, as in "Our team was caught in the *backwash* when Jason tested positive for steroids."

4. A similar term is *back channeling,* based on the way water rushes in to fill an empty channel. Linguists use the term *back channeling* to describe the way listeners communicate to a speaker that they understand what the speaker is saying. In *back channeling,* listeners nod their heads and repeat short phrases and say things like, "Yes," "I agree," "Really," and "Uh-huh."

PART I Read the following paragraphs about metaphors based on various body parts. Each paragraph includes one or more examples of an Association Term, a Convenience Metaphor, and a Dramatic Image Metaphor. Fill in the lines following the paragraphs with at least one example taken from the paragraph:

A. *Skin* is what holds people together and protects their bodies so if speakers say someone *saved his own skin,* they are saying that the person saved his own life. Such allusions as *skin graft, skin tight,* and *skin test* are fairly easy to figure out. A person who is *skinny* might be described as *all skin and bones,* while someone who escapes danger *by the skin of her teeth* has had a close call because teeth do not have skin. *Going skinny-dipping* is swimming in the nude, while *getting the skinny* on someone means to get the facts or secrets about a person. It probably relates to the idea that a naked person cannot hide very much. A *skin game* is a swindle. The idea relates to the metaphor of *getting fleeced* (like a sheep being shorn) or of *losing your shirt,* so that you have nothing left but your skin. The popular maxim, "Beauty is only skin deep," is often countered with the comeback, "Yes, but so is skin."

I. Association Term: _____

2. Convenience Metaphor: _____

3. Dramatic Metaphor: _____

B. *Hair* is amazingly strong and durable for being so fine. The *hair trigger* on a gun will go off with only the pressure of a hair, while the cause of some airplane crashes has been traced to *hairline* cracks or fractures in key parts of the plane's shell. A person who is described as escaping danger by a *hairbreadth* has had a close call, while someone who *splits hairs* is overly concerned with tiny details. In *hairy* or *hair-raising* experiences, people's skin develops goose pimples so that their body hair stands up, although not as dramatically as cartoonists show it when they want to illustrate that a character is frightened. In the United States, taking care of people's hair is a billion-dollar business. It includes such services as *haircuts* and *hairstyling* and the selling of such products as *hair dryers, hair brushes, hair conditioners,* and *hairpieces. Camel hair* coats are a luxury and so are *camel hair* brushes for artists, even though most or them are really made from squirrels' hair.

1. Association Term: _____

2. Convenience Metaphor: _____

3. Dramatic Metaphor: _____

C. *Lips* have a distinctive shape, which is highlighted by the use of *lipstick* and *lip gloss*. Their shape also provides such metaphors as the *lip* on skateboards and the *lip* of a pitcher or a vase. A golf player who *lips a ball* gets it right to the edge of the hole, where it sits until the player takes an extra stroke to nudge it in. Because people kiss with their lips, the phrase *hot lips* is sometimes used to tease people for being sexual. Loretta Swit, playing the army nurse on the "M*A*S*H" television series, was known as *Margaret "Hot-Lips" Houlihan*. The role of the lips in speaking is shown in such phrases as *lipreading* for what deaf people do and *lip-synching* for what performers do when they move their lips to match the words on a previously recorded version of a song. If you are *tight lipped* about something, you are keeping it secret, while if you are *lippy* or if you *give someone lip*, you are being disrespectful by talking back. If you *give lip service* to an idea, you are also being disrespectful but in a different way. This metaphor, which has been used since the 1500s, means that you are offering insincere agreement, which is only on your lips rather than in your heart or your soul.

1. Association Term: _____

2. Convenience Metaphor: _____

3. Dramatic Metaphor: _____

D. *Teeth* (either human or animal) obviously underlie such comparisons as when people talk about the *teeth* in rakes, combs, saws, and gears. Common terms referring to teeth include *toothache, toothpaste,* and *tooth doctor.* If something is *like pulling teeth*, it is difficult to accomplish. Strength is the grounding for such metaphors as naming anti-tank barriers *dragons' teeth* and for describing someone as *fighting tooth and nail*. When legislators pass a bill *with teeth* or *with bite*, it is a bill that includes strong enforcement measures.

1. Association Term: _____

2. Convenience Metaphor: _____

3. Dramatic Metaphor: _____

E. *Shoulders* are all shaped pretty much the same so that obvious comparisons are made to the *shoulders* of a road and the *shoulders* of a bottle. Simple allusions are made to such things as *shoulder pads* and *shoulder straps*, while on a more complex level, *shoulders* are sometimes used to stand for strength, similar to the way *back* is used. We see this in such phrases as *to put your shoulder to the wheel* and *to shoulder a responsibility*. Someone who needs to use force to get somewhere might *shoulder* (or *muscle*) a way in. The implication is of using heavier force than when *elbowing* a way in and of being more purposeful than when *backing into something*, which sounds almost accidental.

1. Association Term: _____

2. Convenience Metaphor: _____

3. Dramatic Metaphor: _____

PART II Listed here in alphabetical order are terms or phrases taken from six different body parts. Copy the phrases in the appropriate column of the chart. When you have finished, you should have six items in each column.

bottleneck in traffic	footnote	skeletal remains
cut-throat competition	having your fingers in	throat lozenge
elbow macaroni	someone else's pie	throaty notes (on a horn)
elbow patches	kneehole desk	to elbow your way in
family skeleton	necklace	to put your foot in your mouth
fingernail	redneck values	
football	skeletal outline	

Association Terms	Convenience Metaphors	Dramatic Images

Up in Arms—An Extended Metaphor

Name: _____ **Period:** _____ **Date:** _____

The structure of the human body inspires inventions and technological developments that enable people to magnify and extend their power. Binoculars and telescopes extend humans' power of sight, while telephones extend their powers of speaking and hearing. Film and video recordings work for both hearing and sight. Even our sense of feeling has been extended by what NASA labels *telefactoring* and *telepresence,* as when a mechanical arm belonging to a robot placed in space is manipulated by a human scientist on earth and sends back messages letting the operators on earth experience the feeling of picking up a rock on the moon or repairing a gasket on a spaceship.

The whole concept of arms, as in weaponry, is a way of extending human reach, but first we will mention a few association terms, which include *armchairs, armrests,* and *armholes.* Convenience metaphors include *keeping someone at arm's length,* which can be said with either a literal or a metaphorical meaning; an *arm of the sea* or *an arm of* a political movement; or a child *nestling in the arms* of a tree. An *armature* on an electromagnetic device is a piece of soft metal that protrudes like an arm to relay electricity from one part to another, while the *yard arms* on a sailing ship are the horizontal bars that hold up sails.

But starting with the concept of *arm wrestling* or *twisting someone's arm,* most metaphors based on *arm* show how speakers have tied the concept of human *arms* into the idea of *arms as weapons.* Blank spaces are left in the following paragraphs. As you read them, try to figure out the appropriate words to write in the spaces from those listed above the paragraphs. Talk about the meanings and see if you can think of other examples.

arm	armaments	arms	firearms

In prehistoric times, people used their arms to protect themselves first with sticks and clubs and later with

knives and swords. Throwing stones extended the power of one's **1.**_____ even further and

inspired such inventions as slingshots, bows and arrows, catapults, guns and cannons, and today, rockets and mis-

sile launchers. This is why guns are called **2.**_____ and why a country's **3.**_____

include all of its military forces and equipment. To **4.**_____ a group means to provide its mem-

bers with guns, and perhaps other weapons, while to *arm a bomb* means to ready it for explosion.

| armed forces | armed services | armoires | armory |

In the United States, the *Army* is only one branch of the U.S. military, but it is the largest and has given its name as a cover term to the **5.** _____ _____ or the **6.** _____ _____. An **7.** _____ is a storehouse for weapons and ammunition. The word is related to a French word for large ornate chests called **8.** _____. These chests were used to hold tools and later weapons, but today, decorators use them as hideaways for television sets and clothes.

| alarm | armed | Armistice Day | armless | armored |

November 11th is now known as *Veteran's Day* to honor all U.S. veterans, but it used to be called **9.** _____ _____ in honor of the ending of World War I. An *armistice* is the end of a conflict, or literally "the standing up of the arms." The second part of the word comes from a Latin word meaning "to stand" as seen in the *Summer Solstice* and the *Winter Solstice* when the sun appears to stand on a central plane with no southward or northward motion. Since the middle ages, soldiers have worn *armor* to protect their bodies. Today's armies have **10.** _____ *tanks,* while in civilian life *armored trucks* are used to transport money. They are made from heavy steel with bulletproof windows; they also have **11.** _____ *guards.* We are so accustomed to thinking of *arms* as weapons that we interpret the phrase *an unarmed man* to mean "a man without a gun." A disabled man who actually has no arms will be called **12.** _____. Even the word **13.** _____ is related. It comes through French from the warning given when an enemy attacks: *Al arms!*

| armadillos | Armada | long arm | up in arms |

An *armada* is a fleet of armed warships. When the *Spanish* **14.** _____ brought explorers and conquerors to South America, they saw a new animal with an armor-like cover waddling across the deserts. Because this animal reminded the sailors of their own armored ships sailing across the ocean, they combined *armada* with a Spanish suffix *-illo* meaning "small" and named these picturesque animals **15.** _____.

If a group is **16.** _____ _____ _____ about something, the people are agitated and ready to fight, but probably with tools of persuasion other than weapons. The phrase *the* **17.** _____ _____ *of the law* also implies more than just weapons; it is the whole infrastructure of crime-fighting organizations, including such agencies as the FBI and state and local police, along with help from an interested public.

| arms | coat of arms | family arms | hugging |

A heraldic design used to represent a country or a family is called a **18.** _____ _____

_____ or **19.** _____ _____. In the Middle Ages, these designs served as

heralds to identify families or tribes. They were carried on flags in front of battalions and were posted on the gates

of a family's estate. The idea may be that family or group members are wrapped in and protected by the *arms* of

their extended family.

The title of Ernest Hemingway's famous 1929 novel, *A Farewell to* **20.** _____

is especially powerful because it alludes to two meanings of arms. A young American, disillusioned with war,

deserts the crumbling Italian army and also loses his lover, who dies in childbirth. This same double meaning of

arms is what caught the public's fancy with this 1960s slogan protesting the Vietnam War: *Arms are for*

21. _____ .

Latin and Related English Words for Body Parts

Name: _____ **Period:** _____ **Date:** _____

While English includes words from many languages, the reliance on Latin is unusually heavy. One reason is that the Roman Empire reached into what is now England and its Latin language influenced French, Italian, and Spanish, from which English later borrowed words. For example, English speakers took the names for *pince nez* glasses and the *Nez Perce Indians* from French. But these words are really from Latin because French speakers had adapted the Latin *nasus,* meaning nose, into *nez.* The *Nez Perce* Indians pierced their noses, while *pince nez* glasses pinch the wearer's nose.

A second reason that English has so many borrowings from Latin is the worldwide influence of the Catholic Church, which continued to use Latin long after it was no longer spoken indigenously. A difference between Latin and English is that Latin is an inflected language, meaning that the ends of words are changed to match the parts they play in a sentence. English speakers do some inflecting as with possessives and plurals, but in general, the English system does not match the Latin system, thus the tendency for English speakers has been to drop the endings of Latin words. This is why the beginnings rather than the endings of the words usually carry the meanings.

When the Romans departed from England in about 450 A.D., they left behind such words as *stomachus*, which became *stomach*, and *spina*, which became *spine*. *Viscus* refers to an internal organ as with the heart, the lungs, or the intestines. *Viscera* is the plural form and is used in such English allusions as a *visceral reaction* to something, meaning that it is more deeply felt at an emotional than an intellectual level. *To eviscerate* something is *to gut* it as when a program is *eviscerated* by having its funding taken away. Other body-related words developed specialized meanings as when *talus* (*ankle*) became *talon* to mean the claws of a bird and *femur* (*thigh*) became the specialized name of the *thigh bone* instead of the whole thigh. *Supercilium* for *eyebrow* became *supercilious* to refer to people who are haughty, or who raise their eyebrows at other people.

Read the paragraphs below about Latin words that have made several contributions to English. Try to figure out which word to write in the blank spaces of the sentences that follow.

A. Corpus is the Latin word for body. It is easy to recognize its Latin roots in the legal term, *corpus delecti*, which refers to the material evidence or "the body" in a homicide case. *Habeas corpus* is a writ presented to a court demanding that it release "the body," meaning that the court must either release or bring a prisoner to trial. The terms given below are so common that most speakers do not think of their connection to the Latin *corpus*. One reason is that the terms have undergone small changes, but recognizing their relationship to *corpus* will give you insight into the meanings. In Part I, the words are used in a more basic sense, while in Part II they are more metaphorical.

| corporal | Corps | corpse | corpsman | corpulent | corsets |

1. A dead body is a _____.

2. The Marine _____ is a fighting body, while the Peace Corps is an alternative to military ventures.

3. In the military, a medical assistant who works with bodies is called a _____

4. Schools cannot administer bodily or _____ punishment.

5. A euphemistic way of describing someone who is fat (who has lots of body) is to say the person is _____.

6. It used to be more fashionable than it is now for women to shape their bodies by wearing _____.

PART II

| corporation | corpus | Corpus Christi | corsage | incorporated |

1. A business group joining together to act as one body is called a _____.

2. Once people have joined like this, their company is said to be _____.

3. When scholars work with a body of material, they call it a _____.

4. A feast in the Catholic Church as well as a city in southern Texas are named _____ after the body of Christ.

5. A small body of flowers that a girl might wear to a formal dance is called a _____.

B. *Caput* is the Latin word for *head*. In English *capital punishment* literally means to deprive people of their heads, but the term has been generalized to mean execution by any means including lethal injections. Because heads are so important to the body, *capital* appears in several words designating something as important. Before people can start a business they must raise *capital*, meaning they gather money and other capital goods. The leader in a military unit is called the *Captain*, as is the headwaiter in high-class restaurants. Cities that serve as the *capitals* of states are the governmental headquarters. The buildings themselves are called *capitols*, spelled with an *o* in honor of the Temple of Jupiter, which was built on the *Capitoline Hill* in Rome.

| capitalizes | capital letters | capitals | decapitating |

1. _____ someone is the Latin-based equivalent of *beheading* a person.

2. In sentences, we use _____ for the important words, including any *headings*.

3. In ornate buildings, the columns have _____ or *heads*, which are flat coverings that help to bear the weight of the roof.

4. A person who _____ on something takes full advantage of an opportunity.

C. *Capillus* is the Latin word for *hair*. Because the most outstanding feature of hair is its fineness, speakers have adopted *capillary* as a name for things that are fine or thin. The *capillaries* in your body are the small blood vessels that form a network throughout your body. An extended metaphor based on how these blood vessels work has given us the word *capillarity* to describe a process in physics involving the elevation of liquids in tubes.

capillaries	capillary	leaves

1. Any tube with a very small hole through it might be referred to as a _____.

2. Capillary _____ are long and slender so that they look more like hair than like part of a plant.

3. When you get a hypodermic injection, the little bit of blood that might be seen comes from where the needle has gone through one or more _____.

D. *Facie* is the source for the English word *face*. English has kept it in its original form in the legal phrase that lawyers and judges use to talk about *prima facie evidence*, which *on the face of it* or *at first appearance* seems true. In nonlegal language, the meaning is similar to something being judged at *face value*. Carpenters talk about the *fascia* or *facing* that they nail around the eaves to protect the roof of a house. A person trying to *save face* is taking steps to keep from being embarrassed.

façade	face the music	face-time	facings

1. To _____ means to acknowledge blame or accept punishment.

2. The _____ of a building is its outer covering or *face*.

3. In today's world of high-tech communication, the phrase _____ has developed to refer to one-on-one meetings of real people.

4. Tailors often sew _____ into the fronts of jackets to give them more "body."

E. *Oculus* is the Latin word for *eye*, as in the name of *oculist* or *ocularist* for an eye doctor, who works with not only the eyeball, but also the *ocular muscles*. In the *Harry Potter* books, J. K. Rowling invented *omnioculars*, which allow the boys to see *all* kinds of things including reruns and forecasts of the Quidditch games.

binoculars	monocles	oculus

1. Modern builders are returning to the old-fashioned idea of including an _____, a round window, as a decorative item in houses.

2. _____ help people see with two eyes.

3. _____ are those lenses made to be held by the wearer in only one eye.

F. *Nasus* is the Latin word for *nose*. Most speakers know what a *nosepiece* is on glasses and what a *runny nose* or a *nosebleed* is, but they might not know that a *nostril* is a *nose hole* or that *nozzle* literally means *little nose*. To *nuzzle* is to prod and sniff with one's *nose*. *To follow your nose* might mean either to go straight ahead or to go in the direction of a strong smell. The *nosing* on a stairway sticks out like the *nose* of an airplane, while *nosy* people stick their noses into other people's business.

nasal	nose	nose dive	nosy	nozzles

1. The _____ at gas stations are as big as elephants' noses even though the word means *little nose*.

2. If a boxer takes a _____, he falls face forward, while if the same thing is said about the stock market, it goes down suddenly.

3. To win by a _____ is a dramatic description of a horse race, but it can also be said about other competitions.

4. When _____ people try sniffing out the facts, they often find the dirt on others.

5. If you have sinus problems, your _____ passages will probably get infected.

G. *Lingua* is the Latin word for *tongue* or *language*. A person who is *bilingual* speaks two languages, while a *linguist* is a person who takes a scientific approach to studying languages. The term *lingua franca* was coined to name a common language sort of like *Esperanto*, but it has now developed the meaning of anything resembling a common language among particular groups.

lingos	linguine	linguistic atlas	monolingual

1. Computer programmers, short-order cooks, and coaches and players all have their own _____ that probably won't be understood by outsiders.

2. A _____ might also be called a *dialect atlas* or a *linguistic geography* because it delineates the areas where people speak different dialects; for example, where they talk about *cokes* versus *sodas* versus *pop*.

3. The Italian pasta named _____ is shaped like long, flat tongues.

4. The United States is chided for being such a _____ country.

H. *Dent* is the Latin word for *teeth*, as seen in *dentist*, *dental hygiene*, and *dental care*. *Dentyne*® chewing gum was named to give the impression that it would clean people's teeth as they chewed. *Dent corn* is a kind of Indian corn whose kernels develop a *dent* as they ripen. The word *dandelion* is a borrowing from French *dent de lion* meaning *tooth of lion*. As with many metaphors, this one is more entertaining than accurate. The yellow color reminded speakers of lions while the shape of the individual petals reminded them of teeth.

dentated	dented	dentures	indented

1. A _____ fender looks like a giant has bitten into it.

2. An _____ paragraph also looks like someone has taken a bite out of it.

3. A _____ leaf looks as if it has teeth.

4. On Australian beaches, the lifeguards used to have a system for returning people's _____ because the surf is so strong it sometimes knocks them out of swimmers' mouths.

I. *Cor* for *heart* transfers directly into English when we describe a *cordial* greeting as being *hearty* or *heartfelt*. The original meaning of *record* was to memorize something, that is to learn it *by heart*. A *cardiograph* is an instrument that measures the movements of the heart and prints out *cardiograms*. These instruments are used to study *cardiovascular* problems (the heart and blood vessels), *cardiorespiratory* problems (the heart and the respiratory system), and *cardiothoracic* problems (the heart and chest).

cardiologist	cardiopulmonary	courageous	heartened

1. Someone who is _____ has a lot of heart.

2. If someone is *encouraged*, they are _____ by receiving good news.

3. A _____ is a heart doctor who specializes in *cardiopathy*, which means diseases of the heart.

4. _____ resuscitation is a procedure designed to restore breathing to a person who has suffered a heart attack.

J. *Manus,* meaning *hand,* is another word that transfers directly into English when speakers refer either to a *manual* or to a *handbook* and when they talk about *manual laborers* as those who work with their hands. A *manuscript* is handwritten, while the *manual* alphabet is the spelling system designed in the 1860s to allow deaf people to "speak" with their hands. The term *manufacture* came into English in the 1500s to describe things *made by hand* as opposed to things grown by nature. Because of the industrial revolution, today we think of *manufactured* things being machine-made rather than *handmade*, but we still realize that manufactured items were not grown by nature.

manacles	manager	manicurist	manual

1. Handcuffs are also called _____.

2. A _____ is a person who takes care of people's hands.

3. A _____ is someone who knows how to *handle* people.

4. If you take a class in _____ arts, you are learning to work with your hands.

K. *Digitus*, meaning *fingers* or *toes* for either humans or animals, has come out of relative obscurity because of computers. Because people count on their fingers, the numbers from 1 to 9, plus the sign for 0, have been called *digits* since the 1300s. In the late 1940s when scientists first starting envisioning computers, they described them as *digital* because they work strictly on the basis of numbers in contrast to the more flexible systems based on words, which are described as *analog* or *analogous* (comparative) systems. Within the last decade, people around the world have been introduced to *digital TV sets, digital cameras, digital recording devices*, and *digital telephones*.

| digital | digital watches | digitalis | digitally |

1. Because of people's overwhelming reliance on computers, some people describe the present period as the _____ age.

2. _____ is a heart stimulant extracted from the *foxglove* plant, whose leaves must have made some speakers think of the paws of foxes.

3. Movies that are available in *DVD* formats have been _____ recorded.

4. Now that _____ and clocks are so common, people worry over whether kids will feel motivated to learn to tell time on traditional clocks.

L. *Pedis*, meaning *foot,* is more common in English than most people realize because it is tucked inside words such as *expedition* and *expedite*, which both allude to people setting out with their feet. If you are an *impediment* to progress, you more or less *trip people up* by stopping their feet from moving. A *pedestal* provides *footing* for a statue, while the *brake pedals* and the *gas pedals* on cars are used by the drivers' feet to control the car. Through French, English speakers inherited the unusually colorful word of *pedigree*, which literally means "feet of crane." The allusion is to the long and the short lines typically shown on genealogy charts. Another influence from the way French speakers use the Latin *pedis* is the place name of *Piedmont*, which in ordinary English would simply be *foothills*.

| peddlers | pedestrian | pedicab | pedicure |

1. A _____ lane is a kind of footpath.

2. A _____ is to feet what a manicure is to hands.

3. _____ go on foot to sell things.

4. A _____ cab is an oversized tricycle where the operator furnishes the power by *pedaling.*

M. *Dextr* means *on the right* as in right-handed, while **Sinistr** means *on the left* as in left-handed. *Dextral* creatures tend toward the *right* as with humans and some other animals. Spiral shellfish that are *dextral* will form their coils clockwise or *to the right*. *Sinistral* creatures do the opposite. Because for the majority of people their *right hands* are more skilled than their left hands, *dextr-* took on positive connotations as when smart and skilled people are described as *dextrous* or as having *dexterity*. The names *Dexter* and *Poindexter* are meant to communicate that their bearers are capable and intelligent. *Sinistr* developed negative connotations because around the world left-handed people are a small minority. Primitive societies have many superstitions about left-handedness, and even today in some countries left-handed children are forced to use their right hands. The word *sinister,* taken directly from this word for *left* is used to describe someone who is evil or who presages ill fortune. It is even more negative than the French word for *left*, which is *gauche*, and which means *awkward*. Perhaps the negative connotations were helped along by the coincidence of the word beginning with the same sound as *synn*, an Old English word we now have as *sin* to refer to serious moral lapses.

ambidextrous	Dexedrine®	dextrous	sinister

1. A person who is _____ is equally skilled with both hands, or according to the term, literally has two *right* hands.

2. The idea of being _____ started as a description of physical skill but was then generalized to intellectual skill as when someone is praised for *adroitly* (French for *right*) answering questions in court.

3. _____ is a registered trademark that takes advantage of the positive connotations of being *right*.

4. In English when we talk about a *left-handed compliment* or about someone having *two left feet*, we are expressing milder versions of the attitude shown in the word _____.

N. Here is a list of body-related words with Latin roots. Write the appropriate words in the spaces by the English words with similar meanings, then create a sentence for each pair of words showing how they relate. You may change grammatical details. For example, if you should join the words *two eyes* with *binoculars,* you could write. "Binoculars increase people's ability to see long distances with both of their eyes."

Army Corps of Engineers	a corpse	femur
a capital blunder	decapitated	a pedestrian lane
a cordial greeting	digital	prima facie

1. A crucial mistake = _____

_____

_____

2. A body of engineers = _____

_____

_____

3. Run by numbers = _____

_____

_____

4. A foot path = _____

_____

_____

5. The upper leg bone = _____

_____

_____

6. Beheaded = _____

_____

_____

7. On the face of it = _____

_____

_____

8 A dead body = _____

_____

_____

9. A hearty greeting = _____

_____

_____

Workshop 3.1: Sense of sight: eye dialect, eye witness, to eyeball something, to keep an eye out for something. **Symbol:** an eye for an eye..., the evil eye, the eye as a window to the sun, the eyes of the law. **Appearance:** a window, eye in a peacock feather, eyelets in shoes, the eye of a hurricane.

Workshop 3.2: Part I: Possible answers include: **A. 1.** skin graft, skin test, **2.** skin tight, skinny, skin and bones, skinny dipping, **3.** getting the skinny on someone, a skin game. **B. 1.** haircuts, hair-styling, hair brushes, camel hair brushes, hair dryer, **2.** hair trigger, hairline crack, **3.** splitting hairs, a hair-raising experience. **C. 1.** lip-stick, lip gloss, lipreading, lip-synching, **2.** the lip on a skateboard or a pitcher, to lip a golf ball, **3.** to give lip service or be lippy. **D. 1.** toothache, toothpaste, tooth doctor, **2.** the teeth in rakes, combs, saws, and gears, **3.** like pulling teeth, fighting tooth and nail, a bill with teeth in it. **E. 1.** shoulder straps, shoulder pad, **2.** shoulders of a road or a bottle, **3.** to shoulder a responsibility or to put your shoulder to the wheel. **Part II: Association:** fingernail, football, necklace, throat lozenge, elbow patches, skeletal remains.

Convenience: bottleneck in traffic, footnote, skeleton outline, elbow macaroni, throaty notes on a horn, kneehole desk. **Dramatic:** family skeleton, cut-throat competition, having your fingers in someone else's pie, redneck values, to elbow your way in, to put your foot in your mouth.

Workshop 3.3: 1. arms, **2.** firearms, **3.** armaments, **4.** arm, **5.** armed services, **6.** armed forces, **7.** armory, **8.** armoires, **9.** Armistice Day, **10.** armored, **11.** armed, **12.** armless, **13.** alarm, **14.** Armada, **15.** armadillo, **16.** up in arms, **17.** long arm, **18.** coat of arms, **19.** family arms, **20.** arms, **21.** hugging.

Workshop 3.4: A. Part I: 1. corpse, **2.** corps, **3.** corpsman, **4.** corporal, **5.** corpulent, **6.** corsets. **Part II: A. 1.** corporation, **2.** incorporated, **3.** corpus, **4.** Corpus Christi, **5.** corsage. **B. 1.** decapitating, **2.** capital letters, **3.** capitals, **4.** capitalizes. **C. 1.** capillary, **2.** leaves, **3.** capillaries. **D. 1.** face the music, **2.** façade, **3.** face-time, **4.** facings. **E. 1.** oculus, **2.** binoculars, **3.** monocles. **F. 1.** nozzles, **2.** nosedive, **3.** nose, **4.** nosy, **5.** nasal. **G. 1.** lingos, **2.** linguistic atlas, **3.** linguine, **4.** monolingual. **H. 1.** dented, **2.** indented, **3.** dentated, **4.** dentures. **I. 1.** courageous, **2.** heartened, **3.** cardiologist, **4.** cardiopulmonary. **J. 1.** manacles, **2.** manicurist, **3.** manager, **4.** manual. **K. 1.** digital, **2.** digitalis, **3.** digitally, **4.** digital watches. **L. 1.** pedestrian, **2.** pedicure, **3.** peddlers, **4.** pedicab. **M. 1.** ambidextrous, **2.** dextrous, **3.** Dexedrine, **4.** sinister. **N. Possible sentences: 1.** A capital blunder is so big it could cost the person his head. **2.** The Army Corps of Engineers works as a body to solve structural problems. **3.** A digital society relies on computers that work through numbers. **4.** A foopath is made for more leisurely walking than is a pedestrian lane crossing a busy street. **5.** The upper leg bone, the femur, is the biggest bone in the human body. **6.** Someone who is beheaded is decapitated. **7.** Prima facie evidence makes sense on the face of it. **8.** It sounds more respectful to talk about a corpse than about a dead body. **9.** Cordial people give hearty greetings.

End-of-Chapter Activities

1. Choose one of these proverbs or clichés to illustrate either through a poster or a brief write-up.

- ☐ A friend is someone who reaches for your hand and touches your heart.
- ☐ Absence makes the heart grow fonder.
- ☐ Home is where the heart is.
- ☐ Heads I win; tails you lose.
- ☐ You scratch my back and I'll scratch yours.
- ☐ Two thumbs up!
- ☐ They charged an arm and a leg.
- ☐ Sam has a leg up on the competition.
- ☐ Put your shoulder to the wheel.
- ☐ Don't be so spineless!

2. Think about the word *body* and how many ways it is used with different meanings, including as part of the indefinite pronouns *anybody, everybody, nobody,* and *somebody*. You might act out or illustrate the famous Greek legend of Ulysses and the Cyclops, in which *Nobody* played an important role. When Ulysses and his men found that they were trapped in the cave of the one-eyed giant, the quick-thinking Ulysses offered the Giant wine and when the Giant asked Ulysses what his name was, he said *Nobody*. After the giant fell asleep, Ulysses and his men blinded the Cyclops with the tip of a long pole that they had sharpened in the fire. When the Cyclops roared for help and said he had been blinded, the other Cyclops asked him who had done such a thing and who they should search for. When the Cyclops said *Nobody*, they assumed he was joking and shrugged and went on their way so that Ulysses and his men were able to escape—at least partially. Choose one of the following *body* words to illustrate either with pictures from magazines or ones that you draw yourself.

Body bags	Body language
Embodiment	Body block
A body of land or water	Full-bodied hair
Body blow	The body politic
A legislative body	Body building
A body shirt	The student body
Body check	A body suit
A wide-body plane	Body count
Body surfing	Body guard
Celestial bodies	

3. For lack of space, the following body parts were not fully discussed in this chapter. Choose one of them to explore and teach to your classmates. Perhaps your teacher will let you work in groups of two or three. You can start finding information by looking in several good dictionaries. However, you will also want to brainstorm because, as you have seen, many times the root will be in the middle or the end of a word so that your examples will come from different pages of a dictionary. Try to create a visual aid or to figure out a class activity that will help your fellow students remember what you say.

Beard (also check *bard)*
Blood (also check *sangria)*
Bone
Brow
Cutis (Latin for skin as in *cuticle* and *cutaneous*)
Ear
Finger
Foot
Guts
Hand
Heel
Knee
Leg
Mouth
Neck
Ops (Greek for *eye* as in *optical* and *myopic*)
Skeleton
Thumb
Toe
Tongue

CHAPTER FOUR

Communication

Teachers' Preface

Linguistic principles being illustrated in this chapter include:

1. The kind of communication that humans do is believed to be unique to their species in that a limited number of sounds enables people to talk about ideas and concepts, even those not in their immediate vicinity, not in the present time, and not even in the real world.

2. When new words are needed for new discoveries or developments, the most likely source for the new words is an adaptation of words already in the language.

3. Color words tend to exaggerate and streamline categories as when people are identified as *white, black, yellow, brown,* or *red.*

On the left, 16-year-old Brandon demonstrates *BOOTING UP* for his little sister. *Pulling yourself up by the bootstraps* (also called a *bootstrap operation*) is the source of the metaphor describing how computers *boot up* or pull themselves together to start work. Above, in what we describe as a *crab grass approach* (it moved sideways), this presentation on the difference between piping and fluting led to another student making a model of a *fluted column*, and another student making a poster comparing different kinds of columns, including newspaper columns and columns of numbers.

4. The most basic color names are the ones with the most metaphorical extensions, but when authors want to bring attention to a title, they are likely to choose less common colors or to make them "special" in some way as with Fred Gipson's *Old Yeller* and Toni Morrison's *The Bluest Eye*.

CONVERSATION STARTERS

Our students had fun talking about how words associated with colors and paint are used to communicate other ideas. Here are some incidents and ideas that might serve to start such discussions.

ASU students drew these pictures for a game they devised. The class was divided into teams. Team captains drew out one of the pictures the presenters had drawn and taped it up near the root word it illustrated. The team was then given 60 seconds to see how many related words they could write on the chalkboard.

- Because English now has words for most color terms, "recently" borrowed words are used in specialized ways. The French *rouge* (red) is reserved for the coloring that some women put on their cheeks, but younger women are more likely to refer to this as *blush* than as *rouge*. *Khaki* is a Persian word for dust or dirt. While English speakers sometimes describe things as *khaki*-colored, more often the term is used to talk about men's tan pants. *Jaundice* (yellow) is borrowed from the French *jaune* and is reserved to talk about people being *jaundiced* (having yellowish skin and eyes) when they are unhealthy. More often the term is used metaphorically to refer to someone's attitude of distaste or hostility.
- *Paint* is a word that gets used metaphorically as when someone "*paints* himself into a corner," or when someone is overly optimistic and "*paints* a *rosy* picture." Basketball players *in the paint* are near the basket, while *to paint the town red* is to go out and celebrate. *Pinto beans* and *pinto ponies* both have spots on them, based on the Spanish word *pintado*, which means *paint*. This is why *Old Paint* is a popular name for spotted horses.
- Stanford University has a hard time keeping the name of its athletic teams singular. They want to be known as the *Stanford Cardinal*, after the color, not the animal. The color name, in fact, honors Cardinals in the Catholic Church, who wear bright red robes. Stanford used to be the *Redskins*, but changed when Native Americans explained that they felt insulted by the term *Redskins*. Stanford did not want to change its color scheme, along with their name, and so chose *Cardinal* as a more interesting name than something like *The Reds*.
- *Harvard beets* are also named after a color, even though most people do not realize it. The chef who invented the recipe named them because he thought they resembled the uniforms of Harvard football players.

Even more interesting to students is how computer scientists have provided the world with a whole new vocabulary. You can get additional ideas for working with computer language from "Literary Metaphors and Other Linguistic Innovations in Computer Language" (Kelvin Don Nilsen and Alleen Pace Nilsen, *English Journal,* October, 1995: 65–71). The important point to help students understand about computers is that because they are such a recent invention, they have mostly been the receivers of metaphors, rather than the source. But even though they are a fairly recent development, they are making such a profound impact on culture that computer-related terms are already being given additional meanings. For example, the name of the television news program "Hard Copy," which suggests both *hard line* and *hard core*, was undoubtedly influenced by the computer term *hard copy* for something printed on paper (i.e., "documented") compared to soft copy for something in the machine. As a comparison to *e-mail* and the *Internet*, people refer to the U. S. Postal Service as *U.Snail, snail mail*, or *papernet*. Speakers are also beginning to use such terms as *glitch, bug* and *debug, user-friendly, protocol, input, zap*, and *programming* or *de-programming* to refer to things other than computers.

- According to David Crystal in his book *Language Play*, The custom of calling unwanted e-mail *SPAM* comes from a funny Monty Python skit where a man enters a cafe and asks what's on the menu. The waitress replies, with help from a Viking chorus singing in the background:

  Well, there's egg and bacon; egg sausage and bacon; egg and spam; egg bacon and spam; egg bacon sausage and spam; spam bacon sausage and spam; spam egg spam spam bacon and spam; spam sausage spam spam bacon spam tomato and spam; spam spam spam egg and spam; spam spam spam spam spam baked beans spam spam and spam . . .

  The Python troupe was capitalizing on the familiarity that people already had with *SPAM®*, an acronym from SPiced hAM, for a relatively inexpensive canned meat known around the world.

- Because so many new names were needed, computer pioneers adopted an almost playful attitude. Steve Jobs was into health foods and so chose *Apple* as a name for the computer he designed to appeal to ordinary people instead of to highly trained engineers. *Lotus* software for spreadsheets got its name because of a comparison to the way lotus flowers open out and float on water.

- Other names were taken from science fiction and fantasy. Rebooting by pressing on the control, alternate, and delete keys, is called the *Vulcan Nerve Pinch* from the original "Star Trek" television series. An *Obi-Wan* error (named after *Star War's* Obi Wan Kenobi) refers to something that is off by one as when programmers start with zero when they should have started with one or vice versa. In an *Obi-Wan* alphabetical code, messages are written one letter off as when in the movie *2001: A Space Odyssey*, the producers are suspected of making a sly allusion to IBM through naming the giant computer HAL. *UTSL* is a play on "Use the Force Luke" and is a playful way to tell someone who is asking too many questions to "Use the Source"— that is, to look it up in the source manual.

- Competition among companies is fierce as shown by the creation of such names as *WordPerfect* and by the way early users had to type *WIN* to get into Microsoft's *Windows* program. In the 1960s, people talked about *IBM and the Seven Dwarves* (Burroughs, Control Data, General Electric, Honeywell, NCR, RCA, and Univac). In a fairly recent example of IBM's trying to take back its leadership position, it named a new computer software *Eclipse*, as a sly allusion to what it hoped to do to the highly successful *Java* program invented by *Sun* Microsystems.

The Power of Communication

Name: _____ **Period:** _____ **Date:** _____

One of the prime differences between the Neanderthals and the later Cro-Magnon prehistoric peoples is thought to be a slightly different placement of the larynx and the tongue so that it was easier for the latter group to make the wide variety of sounds that are crucial to human speech. This change also made it easier for people to choke, which is one of the reasons that we are cautioned against talking when our mouths are full.

The chart below illustrates some lexical extensions—many of them metaphorical—that are based on common procedures of voice communication. In the column to the left, the basic word is boldfaced in a sample sentence. Other words and phrases are given in italics. Think and talk about these lexical extensions. Write a sample sentence using one of them in the column on the right. Or you may use a different lexical extension of the same word if you can think of one. By sharing some of your own sentences aloud, and listening to those of your classmates, you will get a feel for how important these concepts are.

Illustrations	Your Sample Sentences
Communicating with family and friends is considered the first step to understanding. *Communicable diseases* *Taking communion* at church *To commune* with nature *A community* of scholars	
Talking parrots do not really talk in the sense of connecting sounds to thoughts. *To talk something up* *To get a talking-to* *A walkie-talkie* *To talk* (to reveal secrets) *To give a talk* (a speech) *A talking head* (a TV commentator)	
Edgar Allan Poe's "The **Tell-Tale** Heart" is a spooky story. *A teller's cage* at a bank *A telling detail* in a story *A tattletale* *A folktale*	

He felt that his **calling** in life was to be a writer.
A cat call
To be called on the carpet
A telephone call
To call out (to identify in print or to phone
   for food or some other service)

At most any zoo you can see **chattering**
   monkeys.
A chatterbox
Chatty
Chattering teeth
A computer chatroom

People who are not **speaking** to each
   other are estranged.
A speakerphone
A loudspeaker
A speakeasy (an illegal bar during prohibition
   where people had to be quiet to keep from
   attracting the police)
A speech
Something *unspeakable* (horrible)
A spokesperson
The Speaker of the House

Listening is a big part of communication.
To listen in
A listening post
A good listener

Laughing often communicates more than words.
Laughing gas
A laughing stock
Laughing hyenas, gulls, and jackasses
A laughing brook
To laugh all the way to the bank
To laugh off a suggestion

The company that advertises its cleaning solvent
   with "Shout It Out!" is using **shout** to stand
   for strength.
A shouting match
Within shouting distance (neighbors)
A shout song
To shout down the opposition

The title of Mildred Taylor's book, *Roll of Thunder, Hear My Cry,* uses **cry** as a symbol of strength or rebellion. *To cry out* (to call out) *A cry for help* *A crying shame* *A far cry from . . .* *A crybaby* *To cry off*	
The **sighing** of the wind in the trees and around the corners made us think of winter. *To sigh* (for someone or something) *A sigh of relief*	
The book *The Horse* **Whisperer** is about a gentle way of training horses. *A whispering campaign* (a semi-private spreading of rumors) *A whisperer* (a rumormonger)	

As you have seen, it is fairly easy to understand lexical extensions and metaphors based on common English words about communication. However, it is not so easy to understand those that are based on Latin or Greek root words. Following are explanations of some of these words that have been further developed in English. Read the sentences that follow the general explanations and choose the most appropriate words to write in the blank spaces. Talk about how the extended meanings relate to the basic meanings and see if you can think of other examples.

A. *Vox* is the Latin root for *voice*. Sometimes politicians will refer to the *vox populi*, meaning "the voice of the people." If you are *equivocal* about something, you hear equal voices or you have equal feelings for both sides of a question. Several English words stemming from this root relate to calling someone. For example, the jobs that are referred to as *vocations* are usually jobs that might also be described as someone's *calling* in life as when a person is a teacher, a minister, or a doctor. If your driver's license is *revoked*, it is called back by the agency that granted it. At a religious service, the *invocation* is a prayer that calls on a higher being to bless the people who are in attendance.

avocation	evokes	invoke	provokes	revoking

1. When a movie _____ strong emotions, people in the audience will probably laugh, cry, or get angry.

2. _____ a law is similar to *recalling* an elected official.

3. Your _____ is not your job; it is a hobby or something you do for fun.

4. A person who _____ you calls forth negative feelings.

5. When officials are worried about crowd control they are more likely to _____ (call on) the harshest rules they have.

B. *Dicere* is the Latin word meaning *to speak*, which is closely related to the word *dictare*, meaning *to assert* or rule, as when a *dictator* expects every word that he says to be obeyed. A *dictum* is a noteworthy statement, or in legal terms, a judicial opinion that is rendered on an issue peripheral to the main case that the court is deciding.

Dictaphones®	dictatorial	diction	dictionary

1. Today people invent new words almost faster than _____ editors can record them.

2. Now that we have computers and _____, fewer secretaries are learning to take dictation.

3. People are universally judged by their _____, which includes their choice of words and their pronunciation.

4. It is funny that in the same family, some members will be _____, while others are very casual.

C. *Lexis* is Greek for *word*. A *lexicographer* is a person who studies words and edits dictionaries. *Lexicography*, in fact, is the subject of this textbook, as when we write about *lexical extensions*. A *lexeme* is any meaningful linguistic unit—in other words, it is a word that is part of a language. The branch of linguistics that studies words is called *lexicology*, while the branch that studies *morphemes* (the smallest units that carry meaning, which may or may not be whole words) is called *morphology*.

lexical	lexicology	lexicon

1. A dictionary might also be called a _____.

2. The _____ meaning of a word is its semantic or root meaning as opposed to the grammatical clues that might be part of the word.

3. Because words are spoken before they are written, _____ of course has to be combined with phonology, the study of sounds.

D. *Jocus* is Latin for joke, from which English gets such words as *joking* and *jesting*. Even the word *juggler* is related, having come from the French *jogler*, which in turn came from the Latin *jocus*. When writers are being formal, or when they want to communicate that something happened long ago, they will stay closer to the Latin root and will refer to a *jocose* mood, or to a *jocund* speech or a *jocular* gathering.

joker	joking	The Joker

1. In the *Batman* movies, a character named _____ was pretty important.

2. When people say something that hurts another person's feelings, they will often apologize by saying something like, "I was only _____."

3. A _____ in a legislative bill is something added on as an amendment that may not be noticed but that will have the effect of drastically changing the outcome.

E. **Onyma** is the Greek root for *name*. English speakers have adapted it into such words as *anonymous*, meaning without a name; *patronym* meaning to be named after one's father; and *synonym*, meaning a word that has almost the same meaning as another word. If a person suffers *ignominy*, the person has been disgraced and has ruined his or her reputation or "good name." When you *nominate* someone, you name the person. In English grammar, the *nominative case* is usually filled by nouns because these are the words that name things. When men write romances and when women write adventure stories, they sometimes use *pseudonyms* (false names) to appear to be of the opposite sex. *Eponyms* are words taken from someone's name as when the *sousaphone* was named after John Philip Sousa.

anonymous	antonym	homonym	metonymy	nominal

1. _____ requirements are pretty basic; they are requirements *in name only.*

2. _____ occurs when something gets a name associated with a part of it as when people call cars *wheels* or refer to their television as the *box* or the *tube.*

3. An _____ names something that is the opposite, while a *synonym* names something with a similar meaning.

4. A _____ is a word that is spelled or pronounced the same but has a different meaning.

5. It is much easier to be _____ in a big city than in a small town.

F. **Parabolare** is a Latin root cognate with *parable*, as in the stories told in the Bible. French speakers borrowed the word from Latin and shortened it to *parlé*, meaning *to speak*. From this English speakers developed such words as *Parliament*, meaning a place to talk out problems, and *parlor*, meaning a room in a family's home where people could meet and talk.

parley	parliamentary	parlors	parse	parseltongue

1. If people gather for a _____, they are gathering to talk and negotiate as when in Western history the European settlers and the Native Americans would meet to draw up treaties.

2. Most problem-solving meetings could benefit from following _____ procedures.

3. To _____ a sentence is to analyze and describe its parts of speech.

4. Harry Potter communicated with snakes through _____.

5. Visiting hours at funeral _____ are usually in the evening before the funeral.

G. *Lingua* is Latin for *tongue* in both the literal sense of a person or an animal's tongue, and in the more metaphorical sense of someone's language as in, "English is my *mother tongue.*" It is this latter sense that is the root of such words as *linguistics, language,* and *bilingual. Linguine* is an Italian pasta that is shaped like the long tongues of snakes. A *lingua franca* is a common language that groups of people from different areas, either geographical or academic, have worked out to communicate with each other. The first *lingua franca* was a blend of Italian, French, Spanish, Greek, and Arabic that traders used in Mediterranean ports in the 1600s. Today, in the Caribbean, *pidgin* (business) English is a similar kind of *lingua franca.*

| language arts | lingua franca | linguist | monolingual |

1. A _____ person knows only one language.

2. The _____ in school include reading, writing, speaking, and listening.

3. A _____ is a person who studies languages.

4. Computer engineers have developed their own _____.

H. *Loquere* is Latin for *speak*. Related words include *colloquial,* to refer to informal or casual speech, and *eloquent,* to refer to formal and persuasive speech. A *colloquium* is a kind of formal gathering in which presentations are made and discussions are held. A *loquacious* person always has something to say, while people who suffer from *logorrhea* talk to themselves in an incoherent fashion. *Circumlocution* refers to using too many words as when someone talks *all around* the subject instead of getting to the point. Literally, the word *ventriloquist* refers to someone *speaking from the stomach.*

| colloquies | elocution | eloquent | grandiloquence |

1. Children used to take _____ lessons.

2. Our principal is an _____ speaker.

3. In some colleges, students have _____, which are oral examinations in which faculty members and students converse about the students' work.

4. When people are accused of _____, they are being accused of *grandstanding* with overly pompous language.

I. *Plangere* is a Latin word for *lamenting*. English speakers most often use it in the word *complain*, but it also appears in the legal terms *plaintiff* and *plaintive*.

| complainant | complainers | plaintiff | plaintive |

1. In court, the _____ is the one on the opposite side from the defendant.

2. In less formal proceedings, this person might be called the _____.

3. If someone has a _____ tone, the person is almost begging.

4. People who are tired of _____ can put up a bumper sticker that reads "No Whining!"

J. *Quere* is the Latin word for *ask*. If you are *queried* about something, you are asked a *question*. *Quere* is also the root for *inquire* and *inquest*. In the case of suspicious deaths, an *inquest* is usually ordered so that *questions* can be asked and answered.

| inquiries | query | quest | questionable |

1. It is best to send a _____ letter before mailing off the whole manuscript of a book to a publisher.

2 It is _____, if not illegal, for a coach to bet on games in his own league.

3. One way to measure the success of an advertisement is to keep track of all _____.

4. When someone goes on a _____, the person is usually looking for answers to some of life's big *questions*.

Nonvoice Communications

Name: _____ Period: _____ Date: _____

Even in ancient times, when people were too far away to hear each other speak, they communicated with drums and with horns. Depending on the sense of sight instead of sound, they stacked up rocks and sticks and scratched directions or even ornate pictures on cave walls. They also sent smoke signals and, as the ability to make fur, leather, and cloth developed, they began carrying banners and flags. These were forerunners to the idea of written languages, which enable people to communicate not only across space, but also across time.

If we were to draw a timeline of people's existence on earth, we would have to place a mark in the fairly recent past to show when the majority of the earth's citizens took written language for granted. There are still many people in the world who can neither read nor write, but in all but the most isolated areas, people know and accept the idea that written marks represent spoken language. The connection between the word *spell* to refer to *the spelling of words* versus the *casting of a magic spell* is more than a coincidence. In the Middle Ages, and even later, the general population was suspicious of those who could make marks and then interpret those marks. On one hand, they thought that the priests and the monks who could read and write had divine help. On the other hand, they were suspicious that wizards and witches might use such marks to cast spells or communicate with the devil. Remembering that both meanings of the word *spell* have a long history, look at the following sentences and on the blank space by each one write either MAGIC or WRITING to identify the source of the italicized word.

_____ **1.** She had him *spellbound* for the longest time.

_____ **2.** You need to *spell out* your wishes more carefully to get the results you want.

_____ **3.** *Spelling bees* are fun but they aren't very educational because the kids who need the practice are the first ones who have to sit down.

_____ **4.** My grandfather is a *spell-binding* storyteller.

_____ **5.** President Kennedy was known for his poor *spelling*.

_____ **6.** "Lumos!" is a *spell* that Harry Potter uses to create light.

Someone who asks you to sit *for a spell* is probably not going to test your spelling nor enchant you in some way. That *spell* is a different word that comes from Old English *spala*, which meant substitute. The *spell* that has to do with letters and words comes from *spel*, an old High German word that is cognate with *tale* and *talk*.

Although there are not as many Latin and Greek root words related to writing, there are some. As you did with the voice concepts, read about these nonvoice concepts and then see if you can figure out which of the listed words is most appropriate to write in each of the blank spaces. Talk about the meanings and see if you can think of other related words.

A. *Scribere* is the Latin word for *write.* English speakers have made full use of this word in such terms as *inscribe, inscription, script,* and *describe.* An old-fashioned word for a copier is *scrivener,* as used in Herman Melville's story about *Bartleby, the Scrivener.* When you *subscribe* to a magazine you, in effect, write your name on the bottom line. This is similar to someone being *inscribed* as a charter member of a club. If you are *conscripted* into the army, you are drafted through a written order of some kind. *Manuscripts* are "written," as distinguished from something that has been published. When you add a *P.S.* to a letter, you are adding a *postscript,* a written note that comes afterwards.

prescriptions	scribblings	scrip	scripted	scripture

1. Doctors have such bad handwriting and they are in such a hurry that they are now being asked to computerize their _____.

2. According to Holy _____, killing another human being is a sin.

3. Because the man's testimony appeared to have been _____, the jury was not convinced.

4. It's cute when parents frame their children's _____ and hang them on their office walls.

5. At school carnivals, it is safer to distribute _____ that can be used only at the event than to have all the kids going around with real money.

B. *Graphein* is the Greek word for *writing* or *drawing.* It relates to the concept of scratching or cutting into something because the first communication marks that people made were scratched into rocks or pressed into mud or clay tablets. It is in this sense that a movie or a newscast that *cuts* into people's sensibilities, might be described as *graphic. Graphs* are charts that usually illustrate some kind of comparison. A *polygraph* shows many different measures of a body's reaction, which when viewed together reveal things about a person's emotions that may indicate whether the person was lying. *Cartography* is the drawing and labeling of maps, while *graffiti* are written messages placed on walls and the sides of trains, etc. *Graphemes* are the units that make up a writing system as with the ABCs for English.

autograph	demographics	graphite	graphologist	monograph

1. A _____ is easier than a whole book to get published because it is a shorter piece of writing devoted to a single (*mono*) subject.

2. Kids write some funny stuff when they _____ yearbooks.

3. The _____ of a group of people are records charting their characteristics.

4. A _____ uses people's handwriting as the basis for analyzing their personalities.

5. _____ is a lustrous form of carbon that is used in lead pencils.

C. *Signum* is a Latin word for *mark,* from which English speakers developed the verb *sign* as in, "You'll need to *sign* your name in three places," and the noun *sign* as in "A speeding car knocked down our street *sign.*" A person *assigned* to do something is marked for a particular job. If that person *resigns,* he or she is in effect taking back a *signature*, or at least an agreement to do something. A matter considered *significant* is viewed as a *sign* of important things to come, while if you *signify* something to your friends, you give them some kind of a *sign* even if it is only rolling your eyes or looking meaningfully in a particular direction.

| designing | ensign | insignia | signals | signet |

1. In Arizona, Native Americans used to send smoke _____ from the tops of Signal Butte and Signal Peak, which are now homes to communications towers installed for the convenience of cell phone users.

2. TV sitcoms often feature_____ women who are aiming to put their mark on some man.

3. People can get arrested for impersonation if they wear the official _____ of a military unit or a police department when they are not members.

4. A _____ ring has an emblem on it based on the old custom of kings wearing rings that could be used as their mark or *signature* when pressed into the daub of wax that sealed written messages.

5. An _____ is now a particular rank in the navy. The name was adapted from the old custom of having certain people *assigned* to carry the emblems or *insignia* of military groups.

D. **Stizein** is the Greek word for *tattoo*. From this the Greeks developed the word *stigma* to name the brands that were given to runaway slaves and criminals. English speakers began using the word in the 1500s. Because such brands were considered a disgrace, the word soon developed more general meanings as when people talk about someone being *stigmatized* by being publicly humiliated for shoplifting or for cheating.

| stigmas | stigmata | stigmatize |

1. Some people develop_____ resembling the wounds or scars of Jesus.
2. Different generations _____ different sets of activities.
3. Many plants have_____, which are the small parts of the pistil on which the pollen grains fall.

E. **Rhetorica** is a Latin word meaning *oratory*, a word for elegant speech. *Rhetorical principles* guide people to make effective use of logic and to devise persuasive statements and arguments. Most modern speakers use the word to allude to writing because this is where people can take the time to develop rhetorical principles. In a kind of backlash against overly eloquent speech or writing, in some contexts *rhetorical* is used as a put-down, as when people dismiss something as *academic* or *rhetorical*.

| rhetoric | rhetorical | rhetorician |

1. A _____ is either a teacher or a practitioner of rhetoric.
2. A _____ question is one that is asked more for form than for its content.
3. Someone might dismiss a politician's argument as nothing but _____, meaning that it was mostly for show but lacking in substance.

Music and Performance

Name: _____ **Period:** _____ **Date:** _____

The word *band*, as in references to *bands of criminals, bandages*, and *headbands*, was in the language before it was connected to the performance of music. But because the music-related meaning appeals in a dramatic and pleasing way to both our senses of sound and sight, it is likely to be the meaning that comes to the minds of most people when they hear the word *band*. The metaphor of *jumping on the bandwagon*, meaning to climb aboard some popular idea or movement, comes from circus parades where the band was carried on a wagon.

Conduct and *conductor* also have nonmusic meanings, as with the *conductor* on a train or with someone *conducting* research. Nevertheless, people often think of these words in relation to music because it is so impressive to see how one person can tell the members of a band what to play and when to march or stand still. This idea of a *conductor* is at the root of the verb *to orchestrate,* which means to put something complex together. The allusion is to challenge of achieving *harmony* from thirty or forty different people playing different parts with different instruments.

Stage is related to the words *stand* and *step*. People can perform either from a *stand* or from a larger, more formal *stage.* The relation to *step* is shown in the word *stage-coach.* Trips on a *stagecoach* are conducted one step at a time. At each step (or *stage*), the coach stopped for a change of horses and perhaps drivers. Metaphors based on the theater idea of a *stage* includes the idea of *stageplays* in which actors *play* with people's emotions and with words. To *upstage* someone is to grab the credit, as when an actor stands in front of another actor. To do something *offstage* can mean doing something behind the scenes or in private life, while a person accused of being *onstage* all the time is thought to be showing off or living just to impress other people.

Here are some Latin- or Greek-based root words that have been given extended meanings. Talk about the root words and write the most appropriate terms in the blank spaces of the sentences that follow the basic explanations.

A. *Phone* is the Greek word for *sound* and from this English speakers took their words for *telephones* and *phonographs*. When children learn to read, they study *phonics*, meaning they learn the various sounds that are made by the different letters and letter combinations. *Symphony* orchestras make sounds that are harmonious or in sync.

cacophonous	euphonious	microphone	phonology

1. It is not very often that a junior high orchestra sounds _____.

2. _____ sounds are the opposite of *euphonious* sounds.

3. _____ is the study of the sounds of a language.

4. Billy Crystal said that when he was a kid watching the Academy Awards, he would use his toothbrush as a _____ and pretend he was a winning actor.

B. *Sonus* is a Latin word referring to *sound*. It gives English speakers such high-tech words as *sonic boom* for when an airplane breaks the speed of sound and *sonogram* for a medical procedure, which uses *ultrasound* waves to chart what is inside a body. *Resonance* describes sound that is rich in tone and variety, while if something is described as being *consonant* with your ideas, it is in harmony with your beliefs.

| resonates | resounding | sonata | sonnets | sonorous |

1. A _____ is a musical composition.

2. If an idea _____ with you, it "sounds right."

3. A person who speaks in _____ tones has an imposing and effective voice.

4. _____ are poems that sound almost like music because of their rhythm.

5. All speakers long for their ideas to be met with _____ applause.

C. *Cantare* is a Latin word for *singing*, from which English derived such words as *chant* and *enchantment*. Cheerleaders are good at getting crowds to *chant* encouraging messages, while auctioneers have their own kind of unique *chanting*. In old-fashioned stories, you might read about the *chanteys* of sailors who sing while they work to help them stay together. This is similar to the way soldiers sometimes *chant* songs as they march.

| cantor | Encanto | enchantments | incantations |

1. In the 1920s, people in Phoenix chose to name their *enchanting* public park _____, which they took from the related Spanish word, *Encantado*.

2. In Jewish religious services, the _____ plays an important role.

3. Shakespeare starts Macbeth with _____ from the three witches.

4. Fairy tales would not be nearly as interesting without the possibility of _____.

D. *Tonus* is the Latin word for *tension*. From this, English gets the word *tone*, which with speech or singing refers to how tightly the vocal cords are stretched. An alternate form is the word *tune*. When people *tone up* their muscles, they are stretching them and getting them in shape. Their goal for their bodies is similar to the goal of a mechanic when he *tunes* up an engine. When you *tune* in to a radio station, you are reaching to make a good connection much like when you try to get *tuned in* to a friend or to a program. If you *tune someone out*, you are breaking off the connection.

| intonation | monotone | tone | toned down | tonettes |

1. The _____ of the meeting did not bode well for a happy ending.

2. If they _____ their rhetoric, they would probably be more successful.

3. Children in elementary school used to play _____ (simple plastic flutes), but now that people are so afraid of communicable diseases, they have pretty much disappeared.

4. Someone who is a _____ can appreciate music but probably should not try to sing for other people.

5. Studies have shown that mothers use different _____ patterns when talking to their children than when talking to adults.

E. *Paroida* is a Greek word made from *vide* (song) and the prefix *para*, to mean *alongside* or *fake*. In English we spell the word *parody* and use it with a similar meaning. A *parody* is an imitation of something as when children at summer camp sing parodies of "Row, row, row your boat" or make up new versions of nonsense poems. While the first parodies were of other people's songs, today people make parodies of all kinds. Related words include *ode*, *melody*, and *comedy*. Today, *melodies* are still restricted to music, but *odes* are usually lyric poems that tell about heroic actions, while *comedies* can be anything from the *sitcoms* we see on television to performances by *standup comedians* or the sit-down television hosts on late-night TV.

| comedy | melodies | parody |

1. Questions about whether something was a _____ or a ripoff of intellectual property have gone all the way to the Supreme Court.

2. It is amazing how many _____ from classical music are reconfigured into popular tunes.

3. _____ is the usual reason for creating parodies.

F. *Oper* or *Opus* is Latin for *work*. If you have ever seen an *opera*, with its elaborate stage settings, its many singers, its beautiful costumes, and its accompanying orchestra, you can understand why it was given a name alluding to work. Related usages include the kinds of *operations* that doctors do as well as the work of *operating* construction equipment. When people make *operational* plans, they are figuring out what will *work*.

magnum opus	opera glasses	operant	operatic

1. A person's _____ is the person's great work.

2. A person described as doing everything in an _____ fashion is theatrical or overly dramatic.

3. People are going to think you are funny if you take _____ to the stadium to watch a football game.

4. _____ conditioning is the training of people or animals to expect things to work in a certain way as when cows learn they will get water if they press their noses on a lever.

G. *Laud* is a Latin word meaning *to praise or acclaim*. A person who is *lauded* for an accomplishment might be given a prize or honored at some kind of a ceremony. Students who graduate *magna cum laude* are graduating with "great honors," while those who graduate *summa cum laude* are graduating with "highest honors." Either way, their families will *applaud*. When people are given a *standing ovation*, the audience stands up to *applaud* a *laudatory* performance. *Ovation* comes from the Latin word *ovare*, meaning to exult.

applause	laudable	lauded

1. Former President Jimmy Carter has been _____ for his peace efforts, including being given the Nobel Peace Prize.

2. Even though many people died on September 11th, there is universal agreement that the New York City police and firefighters made a _____ rescue effort.

3. _____ is recognized around the world as a way to praise performances.

Musical Instruments

Name: _____ **Period:** _____ **Date:** _____

The musical instruments whose names have been given extended and metaphorical meanings are the basic instruments that people have played for hundreds of years. The ancient Greeks had such stringed instruments as *harps* and *lyres*. What started out as the simplest of *pipes* have now evolved into instruments as different as bagpipes, clarinets, French horns, piccolos, and flutes. As you read about these basic musical instruments, talk about the extended meanings that are illustrated in the sample sentences. Then try to write three examples in each of the appropriate parts of the pie chart (Figure 4.1), outlining the most common features that are highlighted in music-based metaphors.

Item	Lexical Extensions	Sample Sentences
drum	brake drum drum brake drumhead drum major/ majorette drummer drumstick eardrum	They will do anything to *drum up* business. He was *drummed out of office* after the scandal broke. My *brake drums* need new linings. At Thanksgiving, I let others eat the *drumsticks*. She's always *beating the drum* for some cause. The teacher works hard *to drum* grammar into the heads of her seventh graders. Eric suffered a broken *eardrum* in the accident. The restaurant used surplus *oil drums* as snack tables.
fiddle	fiddler fiddler crab fiddlesticks	Nero *fiddled* while Rome burned. She just *fiddles away* her time. When I complain, my grandmother says "Oh, *fiddlesticks!*" *Fiddler crabs* look like one arm is raised to play a violin. It makes me nervous when people *fiddle with* my computer.
flute	flauta fluted fluty fluting flutist	*Fluted collars* were popular in the middle ages. *Fluted columns* seem more elegant than plain ones. I hate washing our *flute glasses* because I'm afraid they will break. She has a *fluty voice*. At Mexican restaurants, I always order *flautas*. The architect deleted the *fluting* to save money.
harp	harp seal harpsichord	I wish she would quit *harping* about it. The *harp* on a lamp is what holds up the lampshade. *Harpsichords* are the forerunners to pianos. The *harp seal* has markings on its fur in the shape of a harp.

horn	horned horning horny	It takes more skill to get a sound to come from an animal's *horn* than from a *horn* manufactured for musical purposes. Some people like to *horn in* on other people's business. Drivers in the United States do not honk their *horns* as often as do drivers in many other countries. Someone who is *horny* is feeling sexual. The *horned owl* has tufts of feathers that only look like horns. A *horn of plenty* is also called a *cornucopia* because *cornu* is the Latin word for *horn*. Today, *horn-rimmed* glasses are likely to be made from plastic.
lyre	lyrate lyrebird lyrical lyricist lyrics	The horns of the impala are *lyrate*, meaning they are *lyre* shaped. The tail feathers of *lyrebirds* are also *lyrate*. I can't remember whether Rodgers or Hammerstein is the *lyricist*. A lot of people are upset about the *lyrics* in today's rock music. Maya Angelou uses a *lyrical* style for both poetry and prose.
pipe	piper piping	Some people worry that the Internet is a *pied piper* leading young people astray. When you are sewing, it is a bother to put *piping* around a pocket or a collar. An old adage preaches, "You've got to pay the *piper*." *Organ Pipe National Monument* is in Arizona.

Figure 4.1 A Pie Chart of Musical Instruments

Using Colors for More than Decoration

Name: _____ **Period:** _____ **Date:** _____

One of the first things that parents try to teach their children is the names of the basic colors. Even infants recognize the difference between *black* and *white*, which has inspired some parents to abandon the traditional pastel colors and to decorate their babies' nurseries in *black* and *white*. Before children go to kindergarten, many of them have learned the primary colors (*red, yellow,* and *blue*) and have also moved into *orange*, *green*, *purple*, and *brown*. They are slower to learn about such mixtures as *grey, pink, tan*, and *lavender*.

Artists, designers, and interior decorators probably know and use over a hundred different names for colors, but it is the basic colors shown in the tables on pages 96 through 99 that are used as a way of communicating more than just the color of something. Working in groups of three or four, choose one of these sets of color words to teach to the rest of the class. Prepare a presentation that will take about ten minutes. Besides presenting the sample sentences that are given here, try making up some new ones of your own. When our students did this, some of them dressed in colors to match their presentations. Others brought artwork made in the appropriate colors, while the group that had *orange* passed out candy orange slices.

Some things to talk about are whether your color is a *hot* color (red, yellow, orange, or fuscia) or a *cool* color (blue, green, gray, purple). You might conjecture on why people consider some colors to be hot and others to be cool. Do the metaphorical extensions lean toward *hot* or *cool* items? You might also talk about the prestige of certain colors and how the same color can have both positive and negative connotations. For example, *blue* is connected to winners as with *blue ribbons, blue chip stocks,* and *bluebloods*, but it also has negative connotations as when someone feels *blue* or has been beaten until *black and blue*. *Black* has negative connotations, probably inherited from primitive times when people were afraid of the dark, but it also has some positive connotations as was shown by the "Black IS Beautiful!" campaign sponsored by African Americans during the 1960s. People wear *black* at funerals based on an ancient belief that *Death* might still be hanging around and will take whoever else catches his eye. In western cultures, *white* is considered a sign of purity and innocence, so brides wear white gowns, however, in some cultures brides dress in red. See what you can find out about the connotations in different cultures of the color you are teaching.

The most common color words are the ones that have the most lexical extensions, but when authors or artists want to draw attention to their work, they are likely to choose a less common color, as Alice Walker did for the title of her *The Color Purple* and Anthony Burgess did for his *A Clockwork Orange*. See if you can find titles of movies, plays, or novels that include your color word. If so, why do you think the author chose it?

Here are descriptions of some common processes of language change. See if you can apply them to some of the words in the section you are teaching. You can also ask around or look in books presenting the origins of idioms to see if you can find the stories behind some of the lexical extensions in your set of words.

- **Generalization** takes place when color words start out as accurate descriptions, but then the item is changed or the category is enlarged as with today's *blackboards*, many of which are actually *green boards*. A related process is when the name is based on a dramatic example, as with the species called *black bears*, which in actuality can range in color from very dark to almost white.
- **Association** is sometimes the basis for a name, as when an unethical businessman is called a *white-collar criminal*. Even though the man might wear pastel-colored shirts, he is associated in people's minds with business suits and white shirts and ties. Another example is how in the 1950s Communists were called *Reds* by association with the red flag of the Soviet Union.
- **Comparative** terms are often created as extensions of well-known association terms. For example, in the 1950s, moderately radical people were called *pinkos*, meaning they were "almost" communists. This is similar to talking about an electrical *brownout* being not quite a *blackout* because such protected areas as hospitals and police stations are allowed to remain on or the power merely fades instead of going completely out. And in a comparison to *white-collar* workers, men who do physical labor are referred to as having *blue-collar* jobs, while women who work in service-oriented positions are talked about as *pink-collar* workers.
- **Literary** terms are those that get known either from literature or from folklore. For example, most Americans have never seen a real *white elephant* but they have heard about the custom in India where Hindus believe that white elephants are sacred and therefore take good care of them even though they do not contribute to the local economy. From this we view a *white elephant* gift as something big and showy but not really very useful.

Color	Lexical Extensions	Sample Metaphorical Sentences
black	blackball blackbird blackboard blacked out blacken blackjack blackmail blackness blacksmith	The *Black Panthers* were influential in protesting the Vietnam War. I wonder if people ever feel comfortable at *black tie* events. Halloween decorations can be made more exciting with a *black light* and bits of fluorescent material. In spite of modern medicine, *black lung* disease still kills coal miners around the world. During almost any war, dealers in *black market* goods make unfair profits. There's something cheerful about the flowers called *Black-Eyed Susans*. Many *blackboards* are in fact green. Since 1968 when physicists described a *black hole* in space, people have joked about such *black holes* as the Chicago post office and the U. S. deficit. *Black bears* range in color from very dark to almost white. His reputation was *blackened* by rumors released on the Internet. He *blacked out* from shock as much as from the hit.

		People in the entertainment field are still angry about having been *blackballed* because of the Communist scare in the 1950s. Local fans always complained about the games being *blacked out* on television because not enough tickets had been sold. The people investigating the plane crash were relieved to recover the *black box* apparently undamaged. In trying to keep us from oversimplifying everything, our debate coach frequently cautioned us against making our arguments *all black and white*. He says he doesn't know why he gets treated like the *black sheep* of the family.
blue	bluebird Bluecoat bluegrass blues bluing blueprint	She *feels blue* every holiday season. The announcement came *out of the blue* and caught all of us by surprise. *Blue jeans* have become the uniform of choice for a whole generation. In the anthrax scare, *blue-collar* workers did not feel they got treatment equal to that given to Congressional employees. *Bluecoats* in the Civil War were Union soldiers. Investigators hate to reveal what they have learned about certain crimes lest the information become a *blueprint* for copy cats. I could hardly recognize my article after the editor's *blue penciling*. The photographs shown in court revealed several *black-and-blue* marks, but the jury wondered if they had been retouched. At first he was happy about being appointed to such a *blue ribbon* task force, but then all the work started. *Kentucky bluegrass* music was made famous by the *Blue Grass Boys*. You would never know from looking at him now that he was a *blue baby*. Her grandfather got rich with *blue chip* stocks.
brown	brown out brownstone	The helicopter was thought to have crashed because in such a dusty area its own blades caused a *brown out*. Don't disturb Uncle Milton; he's in a *brown study*. I feel silly actually eating my lunch at *brown bag* presentations. She grew up in a *brownstone* in the Bronx. Don't expect anything chocolate if you order *Brown Betty*.
gray grey	graying grayish grey beard greyhound	The *graying* of the baby boomers is bringing about some changes in social attitudes. Though you wouldn't know it at a first meeting, he has a lot of *gray matter*. Coming from Arizona, I had a hard time getting used to all the *gray* winter days in the upper Midwest. *Greyhound* busses don't have the monopoly they used to have. Today we hear more about AARP than about the *Gray Panthers*, but both organizations were founded to work against age discrimination. It's easier to argue if you classify everything as black and white and ignore all the *grays*. In *Lord of the Rings,* Gandolf the Grey is not as powerful as is Gandolf the White.

green	greenbacks
	greenery
	greengage
	greenhouse
	greenlight
	greens
		This must be his first time sailing; he looks *green around the gills*.
		We were surprised to get the *green light* from the parents' committee.
		Practically everyone is concerned about the *greenhouse effect* and what it is doing
		    to the atmosphere.
		When we came to help on my grandfather's ranch, he didn't hesitate to let us
		    know that he thought we were all *greenhorns*.
		The *greens fees* are so high that he can afford to golf only one or two times a year.
		That city has stringent zoning requirements so that all new housing developments
		    must incorporate *greenbelts*.
		Independent *green grocers* have mostly been replaced by the produce
		    departments in the chain stores.
		Their friendship is an off-and-on affair because Zachary gets *green with
		    envy* whenever Tom has a success.
		People say he just married her because his *green card* was about to expire.

orange	orangeade
	orangery
	orangish
		Tourists are disappointed to find that many of the *oranges* they see hanging
		    on southwest trees are not edible.
		In 1796, the *Orangeman* society was secretly founded to protect the Prince
		    of Orange in the north of Ireland.
		An *orange peel* surface on something like porcelain has a rough finish.
		Anthony Burgess's *A Clockwork Orange* is a scary look at what might
		    be the future.

pink	pinkeye pinkie pinko	*Pink-collar* workers are in service jobs generally held by women. The idea of calling moderately radical people *pinkos* got a boost during the Communist scare of the 1950s when really radical people were called *reds*. She's *tickled pink* over getting to go with the band. The *pink bollworm* is highly feared in cotton-growing areas. Practically every child in the nursery school class developed *pinkeye*. Baby fingers are often called *pinkies*.

purple	purplish	Veterans who were awarded the *Purple Heart* can get special license plates
		    in some states.
		My creative writing teacher was always describing my best paragraphs
		    as *purple passages*.
		Alice Walker's *The Color Purple* was made into an unusually good film.

red	red cap
	Redcoat
	redden
	reddish
	red-eye
	redneck
		Now that airports are so crowded, people are asking for more *red-eye specials*
		    to spread the traffic over 24 hours.
		Red baiting was a national sport in the 1950s.
		His accusation was nothing more than a *red herring*.
		It will be a *red-letter day* if he ever graduates.
		The company has been operating *in the red* ever since the accident.
		The *Red Cross* has been assisting not just the victims' families but also the survivors.
		How he dares to claim innocence when he was caught *red-handed* is beyond me.
		Halfway through the season, the coach was sorry that he had agreed
		    to *red shirt* Brian.
		After the September 11th tragedy, all airports were on a *red alert*.

		When she discovered that she had sent her private e-mail to the whole bulletin board, she turned *red with embarrassment*. It would be great if we could book that band while their record is still *red hot*. We plan to *roll out the red carpet* if they agree to come. During the Revolutionary War, the word *turncoat* was frequently used to refer to British *Redcoats*, who decided to defect and become Americans. *Red-light districts* have mostly gone out of fashion in U.S. towns. People will give you many different definitions of what it means to be a *red-blooded American*.
white	whitening white out	Every Christmas we have a *white elephant* gift exchange that is as much fun as our real gifts. She can't keep from telling *white lies*. The cook burned the lemon filling, but covered it up with the beaten egg *whites*. I was amused at the advertisement for the "most colorful *white sale* ever." *White-collar crime* is harder to investigate than ordinary robberies. The turnpike was closed because the storm was causing a *white out*. In Persian a *safid riysh* (a *white beard)* is a term of respect for what English speakers might call "a wise old man." *White lightning* is a euphemism for moonshine whiskey. Especially in poetry books it is nice to have lots of *white space* on the pages. Every white house is not *The White House*. He was in a *white fury* about the whole affair.
yellow	yellowed yellowing	I still cry when I read *Old Yeller*. *Yellow journalism* has now moved to the Internet where if reporters guess wrong they can erase the story without a trace. The *Yellow Pages* are so thick ours had to be divided into two volumes. Even though the pages are *yellowed* with age, my grandmother insists that all of us use the family Bible for special events. *Yellow fever* is transmitted by mosquitoes so one wouldn't expect to find the disease in cold or dry climates. After Jake called Sam a *yellow dog*, there was no way to make peace.

Using Colors for More Than Decoration

A COLORLESS BUT COLORFUL CROSSWORD PUZZLE

Although all the spaces in this crossword puzzle should be filled in with color words, the allusions are actually not to these colors but to things that are in some way associated with the colors and have therefore been given a *colorful* name. Here are the clues you will need to fill in the blanks.

ACROSS

2. Our debate coach encourages us to acknowledge the _____ areas rather to focus only on *black-and-white* issues.

3. Before girls are old enough to be Scouts, they are _____.

5. People call their baby finger a _____.

6. _____ jokes are pretty popular, maybe because people in this group are not considered an ethnic minority.

7. British soldiers during the American Revolution were known as _____.

8. An almost sure way to start a fight is to say that a gang member is _____.

10. Many _____ actually have brown-colored feathers.

11. If you get the _____ on a project, you are authorized to go ahead with it.

DOWN

1. A greenhouse built so that oranges can be grown in cold climates is called an _____.

2. Sailors and cowboys call beginners or novices (those who have not yet ripened) _____.

3. Some devious people who offer to protect a victim are really planning _____.

4. She is really good at singing the _____.

9. Little _____ lies sometimes keep people from getting their feelings hurt.

Computer-Assisted Communication

Name: _____ **Period:** _____ **Date:** _____

This workshop is based on a different principle than most of the others, which have as their subject a semantic area so important to English speakers that it has given rise to many extended uses. For the most part, computers are too new to have done that, but they are also so important to modern-day life that we did not want to leave them out. In at least one way, the nature of computers has brought a fundamental change to English. To a computer, an empty space indicates a new unit, which means that computers do not know to keep two word units together. Computer engineers solved this problem by inventing *bicapitalization*. This is when two words are joined as a single word, with a capital letter being used to indicate the new word. Trademarks were the first to do this as in *PowerPoint®, CompuServe®,* and *WordPerfect®.* The custom caught on so fast that noncomputer companies are following suit as with *Harper-Collins®* book publishers, *DreamWorks®* media, and *Project NExT®* (New Experiences in Teaching).

A word that was saved from almost extinction by computers is the word *icon,* which used to be used mostly in religious contexts to talk about religious images. Today, when most computer-literate people hear the word *icon,* they think of the little pictures on computers that stand for such things as *file, print, cut, paste, save,* etc. The word is such a big part of computer technology that one company named itself *Ikon®.* It changed the *C* to a *K* so that it could protect the word as its own trademark.

Computer technology provides a wonderful illustration of how speakers adapt words they already know to new uses. For example, read the sentences on the left side of the following chart and notice the words or phrases that are in boldface. These sentences are written to illustrate the "old" meanings of some basic English words that have been given new meanings in relation to computers. Talk about the older meanings and what they have in common with the new computer-related meanings. Write a sentence for each one that will illustrate the newer meanings. Feel free to change the grammatical markers that show things like parts of speech and plural versus singular.

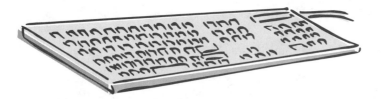

Sentences Illustrating Basic Meanings	Your Sentences Illustrating New Computer-Related Meanings
1. When she travels, Aunt Natalia always brings me a souvenir **bookmark.**	
2. At the Chatterbox Cafe, one room is set aside as a **chatroom** with no music or TV.	
3. Every teenager needs to have a **bulletin board** to post reminders.	
4. Starting with kindergarten, children learn how to **cut and paste**.	
5. If you **default** on a loan, chances are you will lose whatever you gave as collateral.	
6. After a summer of returning **files** to their drawers, my fingernails are ruined.	
7. Sandra is a **flaming** redhead and has a temper to match.	
8. It is better to have separate **recycle bins** for paper, plastic, and glass.	
9. Restaurants need to redo their **menus** every few months to give customers more choices.	
10. The first books were **scrolls** rolled from one stick to the next.	
11. She has some kind of a **virus** and was told to stay in bed for the next three days.	
12. Babies are happier when mothers **wrap** them up.	

Another way that computer users create new words is to clip and blend established words into new combinations. In each of the following sets of alphabetized words, choose a word from the right to match with a word from the left. Put them together to form a new computer-related term. Notice that they follow different principles. Some you will need to hyphenate others you will need to clip off endings or beginnings, while still others will blend together in the same forms as the original. Talk about what the new term has in common with the older words. Then use the new terms in sentences to illustrate their meanings.

Set One

cyber	friendly
desk	sheets
spread	space
technology	top
user	world

Set Two

de	board
emotion	bug
mother	etiquette
net	icons
plug	ins

Workshop 4.1: A. 1. evokes, **2.** revoking, **3.** avocation, **4.** provokes **5.** invoke. **B. 1.** dictionary, **2.** Dictaphones, **3.** diction, **4.** dictatorial. **C. 1.** lexicon, **2.** lexical, **3.** lexicology. **D. 1.** The Joker, **2.** joking, **3.** joker. **E. 1.** nominal, **2.** metonymy, **3.** antonym, **4.** homonym, **5.** anonymous. **F. 1.** parley, **2.** parliamentary, **3.** parse, **4.** parseltongue, **5.** parlors. **G. 1.** monolingual, **2.** language arts, **3.** linguist, **4.** lingua franca. **H. 1.** elocution, **2.** eloquent, **3.** colloquies, **4.** grandiloquence. **I. 1.** plaintiff, **2.** complainant, **3.** plaintive, **4.** complainers. **J. 1.** query, **2.** questionable, **3.** inquiries, **4.** quest.

Workshop 4.2: 1. Magic, **2.** Writing, **3.** Writing, **4.** Magic, **5.** Writing, **6.** Magic. **A. 1.** prescriptions, **2.** scripture, **3.** scripted, **4.** scribblings, **5.** scrip. **B. 1.** monograph, **2.** autograph, **3.** demographics, **4.** graphologist, **5.** graphite. **C. 1.** signals, **2.** designing, **3.** insignia, **4.** signet, **5.** ensign. **D. 1.** stigmata, **2.** stigmatize, **3.** stigmas. **E. 1.** rhetorician, **2.** rhetorical, **3.** rhetoric.

Workshop 4.3: A. 1. euphonious, **2.** cacophonous, **3.** phonology, **4.** microphone. **B. 1.** sonata, **2.** resonates, **3.** sonorous, **4.** sonnets, **5.** resounding. **C. 1.** Encanto, **2.** cantor, **3.** incantations, **4.** enchantments. **D. 1.** tone, **2.** toned down, **3.** tonettes, **4.** monotone, **5.** intonation. **E. 1.** parody, **2.** melodies, **3.** comedy. **F. 1.** magnum opus, **2.** operatic, **3.** opera glasses, **4.** operant. **G. 1.** lauded, **2.** laudable, **3.** applause.

Workshop 4.4: Possible answers: A. (People's actions) drum up business, drummed out, fiddle away, fiddler crabs, horn in on, a pied piper. **B.** (Sound) eardrums, fluty voice, harping about, lyrics. **C.** (Shape) drumsticks, oil drums, fluted collars, fluted column, harp on a lamp, lyre birds, Organ Pipe National Monument.

Workshop 4.5: Across: 2. gray, **3.** Brownies, **5.** pinkie, **6.** redneck, **7.** redcoats, **8.** yellow, **10.** blackbirds, **11.** green light. **Down: 1.** orangery, **2.** greenhorns, **3.** blackmail, **4.** blues, **9.** white.

Workshop 4.6: Possible answers: 1. When you find a good website, **bookmark it. 2.** You have to be careful about who you meet through Internet **chatrooms. 3.** Internet **bulletin boards** are a good way to keep informed. **4.** I like to **cut** something from one document **and paste** it into a different document. **5.** When I get too many toggles, I reboot so as to reestablish the **default** values. **6.** People who leave all their **files** in the same directory are not very well organized. **7. Flaming** on the Internet is easy; just use all capital letters. **8.** Usually when I mistakenly delete a file, I can find it in the **recycle bin. 9.** Some computer **menus** are available in the form of icons. **10.** Most computers have a **scroll** bar on the right side of the screen. **11.** Trojan horses are tricks that introduce **viruses** into a computer disguised under some kind of a game or offer. **12.** In most computer programs a word at the end of a long sentence will be **wrapped** down to the next line. **Possible sentences: Set One:** The world inside of a computer is known as **cyberspace.** Writing and printing newsletters on a personal computer is called **desktop publishing.** Computerized accounting can be done on Lotus **spreadsheets.** Allowing ordinary language to be used for computer commands is one way that companies try to be **user-friendly.** Computers are everywhere in today's **technoworld. Set Two:** Special programs are needed to **debug** infected computers. **Emoticons** are those kinds of funny faces made mostly from punctuation marks. A **motherboard** takes care of a computer like a mother takes care of a family. Good manners on the Internet are referred to as **netiquette.** A basic computer can be expanded by adding **plug-ins.**

End-of-Chapter Activities

1. If you play a musical instrument, do some research to find out how it got its name. Report to the class. Also, see if you can teach your fellow students five musical terms that they might not know because they have not had the same music lessons that you have had.

2. Choose a color-related expression to illustrate either for a bulletin board or for your *Changing Words* book. Here are some possibilities:

- ☐ Green around the gills
- ☐ A greenbelt around a city
- ☐ A greenhorn
- ☐ Green with envy (the green-eyed monster)
- ☐ A green thumb
- ☐ A blacksmith
- ☐ The black market
- ☐ To paint yourself into a corner
- ☐ Out of the blue
- ☐ To whitewash something
- ☐ A white elephant gift
- ☐ A jaundiced attitude
- ☐ She didn't paint a very rosy picture

3. Think some more about computer terminology and see if you can find some new words that were not talked about in this chapter. Make a report on three such terms. Try to describe the process through which they were developed. Are any of them metaphors? Were they created as a comparison? Or was it through clipping and blending? Which terms developed informally, like slang? Which were purposely coined for commercial interests? You could start by asking yourself such basic questions as why people talk about both the *World Wide Web* and the *Internet.* What do webs and nets have in common, and how do they relate to computers? For centuries, people have known that *hardware* is the kind of thing they buy at a *hardware* store. How does this term relate to *software*? *Links* in chains have been around for centuries. How do these *links* relate to *links* on a computer?

CHAPTER FIVE

Plants and Food

Teachers' Preface

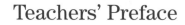

Linguistic principles being illustrated in this chapter include:

1. The more dramatic an action, the more memorable a scene, or the more often an event is experienced, the more likely it is to inspire metaphors.

2. Plants and food serve as both the sources and targets of metaphors. Well-known concepts (*grass, trees, bread, eggs*, etc.) are sources from which other things are named, while smaller individual items (*foxtail, cattail, lady fingers, shoestring potatoes*, etc.) are metaphorical targets that have received their names from better-known concepts.

3. Terms can provide examples of both generalization and specialization. Such terms as *grow, plant, harvest, feed,* and *swallow* are applied to a wide range of human activities. A good example of linguistic specialization is the way that plant names are adapted to become the names of towns, streets, and colors.

4. Just as with many other categories of words, food terms have varying degrees of prestige. Such terms as *mush* and *porridge* are being replaced by *cereal*, but the old words do not completely disappear.

Our ESL class poses with their plant posters (*A branch railroad, To plant suspicions, A budding genius, A table leaf,* and *A family tree*).

5. When English speakers borrow words from other languages, they often anglicize the pronunciation and lose the original metaphor as when the French *l'oeuf* (egg) was changed to *love* for a score of zero in tennis.

6. Using *apple* to represent the concept of fruit and *salt* to represent the concept of spice illustrates prototypicality. This is when people think of particular items as most completely or most perfectly illustrating the concept of particular categories.

7. Food names are often used as euphemisms or as substitutes for words that are considered vulgar or prejudicial. They allow people to talk in code so that only those who know the allusion will understand the speaker's intent.

One of Don's ASU students drew him *branching out*.

In two classes of high school seniors, we started this workshop by giving a mini-lesson on metaphors related to apples and to milk. Then we passed out apples and *Milky Way* candy bars and, while students were eating, asked them to work in groups of four or five to jot down all the food metaphors they could think of. At the end of ten minutes, each group chose a speaker to share their best ideas.

We were surprised at how many of the groups presented "edgy" metaphors. They giggled and acted embarrassed, yet they chose to test the situation by not just writing down, but presenting orally, metaphors usually considered crude—for example, *wiener, banana, to cut the cheese,* and *to pop the cherry.* They hinted that the proverb *The blacker the berry, the sweeter the juice* was a sexual allusion, and while they lowered their voices and made apologetic murmurings, they also presented the terms *cracker* for a white

The most interesting of these food metaphors is the Milky Way® candy bar named after the Milky Way Galaxy, a repetitious metaphor taken from the Greek word for milk, *galactose.*

person, *beaner* for a Hispanic, *rice burner* for a small car imported from Asia, and *cottage cheese thighs* for someone overweight.

How a teacher chooses to handle this kind of creativity, of course, depends on the class and the community, but in some ways it worked well for us to have a discussion of such terms early on so that students could move forward. We tried to help them understand that food is so ubiquitous and comes in so many varieties that food-related metaphors can be used to represent almost any human emotion. Even a 16-year-old has eaten over 17,000 meals, not to mention snacks. Since eating is a satisfying, multisensory experience, it stands to reason that speakers will extend their experiences with food to many other aspects of their lives.

CONVERSATION STARTERS

• One way to encourage students to begin thinking of the symbolism that speakers assign to plants is to talk about or show parts of the 1979 movie *Being There* from Jerzy Kozinski's novel. The film starred Peter Sellers as a mentally deficient man raised in the home of a wealthy eccentric, where he worked as the gardener. The man, who becomes known as *Chauncey Gardener*, dresses in his wealthy employer's cast-off, but still very fine, clothing. From a lifetime of watching and imitating television, he has developed a style of speaking that makes him sound calm and wise. Through a series of coincidences, he is catapulted into a celebrity role where he makes such solemn pronouncements as, "It is possible for everything to grow strong and there is plenty of room for new growth, but first some things must wilt and die. Some plants do well in the sun and some do well in the shade. As long as the roots are not severed, all is well and will be well in the garden…In the garden we have spring and summer, but then we get fall and winter." While this "chancy gardener" is speaking literally about the only thing he knows, the listening world interprets his *down-to-earth* pronouncements as wise and wonderful metaphors about the state of the U. S. economy and its political future.

- Talk about how prestige is associated with particular kinds of food as when a *soufflé* is considered fancier than an *omelet,* and an *omelet* fancier than *scrambled eggs.* In another example, *cereal* is more prestigious than *mush, pablum,* and *gruel.* Talk with students about how modern advertisers have created names for cereal to counterbalance the negative connotations of *mush, gruel,* and *pablum. Rice Krispies* are guaranteed to "Snap, Crackle, and Pop," while such names as Corn *Flakes,* Sugar *Pops, Crispy* Critters, and Cocoa *Puffs* counteract the idea of a heavy and soggy mass sitting at the bottom of a bowl.

- *Grub* is a Western frontier word for any kind of humble food, probably based on the idea that when people were about to starve to death they were reduced to eating grubs (worms and bugs) that they would find under rocks and logs. During the Gold Rush days, people would offer to provide a *grubstake* for a prospector, meaning they would pay for his food and basic supplies if he would give them a share of whatever gold he found. Today, we talk about people looking *grubby* and about getting a *grubstake* to support almost any endeavor.

- *Scuttlebutt* is an interesting word that relates to the community aspects of drinking water as when today people refer to *water-cooler talk.* On sailing ships, the water barrel or the *water hole* was called a *scuttlebutt.* As sailors gathered here to get a drink, just as modern office workers gather around water coolers, they would exchange gossip. From this, *scuttlebutt* developed the meaning of a rumor or some kind of underground information. To *scuttle a ship* means to put holes in its bottom—upside down water holes—so it will sink. The meaning has been extended so that almost any project can be *scuttled.*

- On the left are some food-related terms, while on the right are some metaphorical extensions. Lead students in talking about the grounding of the two items. What do they have in common?

   1. a meat roast … a celebrity roast (both get hot and change colors)
   2. chocolate mousse … mousse for your hair (consistency)
   3. gravy … riding the gravy train (something extra on top, a luxury)
   4. grease … a greaser (both are slimy and unappealing)
   5. honey … a honeymoon (both are sweet and desirable)
   6. red herring (sardine) … a red herring in a mystery story (they smell bad; red herrings used to be thrown down to confuse dogs following a trail)
   7. pasta … paste (same coloring and consistency)
   8. hash … to hash out, or rehash, a problem (a mixture of things being stirred up)
   9. spice … a spicy movie (both are tasty and exciting)
   10. parched corn … parchment (both are very dry)

Farming and Gardening Metaphors

Name: _____ **Period:** _____ **Date:** _____

Farming and gardening metaphors are among some of our oldest usages. The Biblical scripture, "Whatsoever ye sow, that also shall ye reap," says in the literal sense that if you plant wheat, that is what you will harvest. In a more metaphorical sense, it says that if you are dishonest with other people, they will be dishonest with you or that if you spread discontent and unhappiness, your own life will be filled with these same negative emotions. On a more prosaic level, farms are filled with *sticks* and *straw*, both of which have given English many different metaphors. From *straw* we get allusions to *straw man* arguments, to *straw bosses* or *straw votes* (they are unofficial), to people *grasping at straws*, and to something that is *the last straw* or *the straw that breaks the camel's back*. From *stick* we get such shape metaphors as *lipstick, glue sticks,* and *sticks* of gum. The idea of paper *stickers* is an action metaphor. It comes from the kinds of little *stickers* that grow on plants and seemingly reach out to grab onto animals and people who happen to be passing by. When you are *stuck* with a job you don't want or at a place you would rather not be, you are like an animal that has been entrapped by thorns and *stickers*.

The following terms related to farming and gardening are explained mostly in their literal senses. Following these explanations are sentences that use the terms in more metaphorical senses. Choose the most appropriate terms and write them in the blank spaces. As you do this, think about what action or characteristic is being highlighted in each metaphor.

A. *Hay* is a word adapted from *hew*, meaning "to cut," so technically the name is accurate only after the alfalfa or wild grass has been cut; nevertheless people talk about *hay fields*. *To make hay while the sun shines* is usually offered metaphorically, but it is based on the fact that wet hay will rot and sometimes catch on fire.

hayseeds	haywire	hit the hay

1. To _____ is going off to bed, based on the image of someone sleeping on a pile of hay in a barn.

2. _____ are rustic and unsophisticated people, based on the idea that they probably have hayseeds and bits of straw in their hair from sleeping in a barn.

3. The image behind the term _____ for things that are going badly is of a broken hay baler with loose wires flying in one direction and clumps of hay flying in another.

B. *Muck* is the mixture of mud, manure, and straw that typically collects in the stalls and pens of barns and barnyards, especially in rainy or snowy weather. *Muck-raking* or *mucking* literally refers to the unpleasant task of cleaning out such places.

We know that this has been considered on odious task for thousands of years because in Greek mythology, one of the most memorable tasks assigned to Hercules was cleaning out the Aegean Stables.

mucking around	muckrakers	muckraking

1. Metaphorically, _____ is messing with anything low-based or vulgar.

2. Politicians who use negative campaign tactics are sometimes accused of _____ or mudslinging.

3. The people who put out tabloid newspapers are often described as being _____.

C. *Grain* is a cover term for the edible parts of such plants as rice, wheat, barley, oats, and rye. The word can be used as both a count noun as in "a few *grains* of rice," or as a mass noun as in "a worldwide shortage of grain." Metaphorically, *grains* can refer to anything small, while *ingrained* can refer to something that is worked into the very fiber of something or into the smallest parts. Doctors talk about *granules* forming on the surface of wounds or about *granulated eyelids*.

a grain of	grainy	granulated	ingrained

1. Her feelings of family superiority are so _____ that she will have a hard time finding someone to marry.

2. Sometimes I wonder if my cousin has even _____ common sense.

3. When pictures are photocopied, they often turn out _____.

4. _____ sugar dissolves faster in coffee than do cubes.

D. *Harrows* are wider than plows and have several rows of sharp spikes or disks. Farmers, with the help of a tractor or a horse, drag harrows through fields to loosen the soil, dig up old roots, and work leftover foliage into the ground to act as fertilizer for the next year's crops. While the previous crop was growing, small creatures such as mice, rats, rabbits, and gophers are likely to have made their homes in the fields, burrowing under roots and stones to create nests for their young. At harrowing time, these safe havens, which had been homes of peace and plenty, suddenly turn into gruesome scenes of panic, massacre, and bloodshed.

harrow	harrower	harrowing

1. Robert C. O'Brien's book *Mrs. Frisby and the Rats of NIMH* opens with the rats helping Mrs. Frisby move her babies to a new home because they know that the farmer is coming with his

_____.

2. A _____ experience can be any terrible experience, as when a child is kidnapped.

3. A _____ is the person who torments or vexes someone.

E. *Cultivating* a garden is making sure that the plants have an ample supply of water, sunlight, fertilizer, and whatever else is needed for their best growth. Farmers have *cultivators* to help with the job of *weeding*, but common metaphorical uses of *cultivating* relate to the image of a farmer giving individualized care to the growth and development of plants.

cultivate	cultivated	cultivating	cults	culture

1. When a baseball player is in a *bush league* or on a *farm team*, the idea is that the experience will help _____ his talents.

2. The _____ of a society is made up of the things the society values and promotes and has therefore *cultivated*.

3. A person who knows and appreciates classical music is said to have _____ tastes.

4. _____ are groups whose leaders are considered to have been intrusive in *cultivating* the thinking of their followers so that they will blindly do whatever the leader instructs.

5. Someone who wants to be a popular singer will try _____ contacts with people in the recording business.

F. *Threshing* or *Thrashing* is the process of separating the grain from its hulls and stalks. Before the machine age, *thrashing* was done by flailing or flogging the grain, which is why people refer to a beating as a *thrashing*. Hard-working swimmers, as well as a particular species of sharks, are called *thrashers*. *Threshing* is also the source of the cliché *to separate the wheat from the chaff*, which alludes to any process of sorting between valuable and almost worthless things. Literally, *thresholds* are the raised platforms on the floor beneath doors leading to the outside of a building. In farm buildings, this raised platform serves to keep the valuable grain from being dragged outside along with the chaff.

at the threshold	high threshold	on the threshold	over the threshold

1. Grooms carry their brides _____ as a symbol of entering a new life.

2. In a similar way, we might talk about a well-prepared and talented person as being _____ of a wonderful career.

3. Something just entering your mind is _____ of awareness.

4. People with a _____ for pain can bear more pain than someone with a low threshold.

G. Straw is the chaff, or the leftovers, after barley or wheat has been threshed. Although it is not good for eating, it is kept around farms to provide bedding and insulation. *Strawberries* got their name because the plants they grow on spread out to resemble the way straw looks when *strewn* about. A *strawberry birthmark* is a second-generation metaphor, named because of its reddish color and the fact that it is slightly raised from the surrounding skin.

> draw straws   soda straws   straw vote   strewn

1. When people _____ for something, they are more likely to do it with pieces of paper or matches because straws are not as available as they used to be when the United States was basically a rural society.

2. _____ are modeled after real straw, which is hollow.

3. Her clothes and books are always _____ across the floor of her bedroom.

4. A _____ is an informal or unofficial vote based on the image of people having a straw and putting it down by the name of their favorite candidate.

H. Trees inspire a feeling of reverence and awe because of their size, their beauty, and their usefulness. Throughout history, people have ascribed magical powers to trees and have sometimes thought of them as home to the spirits of special beings. Evergreen trees were part of midwinter festivals long before the holiday developed its association with the Christian religion. As days grew shorter and shorter and most plants lost their foliage, *evergreen* trees provided hope by symbolizing everlasting life. *Limb* is an alternate name for *branch*; however, *limbs* can refer to human arms and legs whereas *branches* cannot.

> branch   branching   on a limb   tree

1. Grammarians draw upside down trees to show the _____ relationships among the words and phrases in a sentence.

2. The shape chosen for a family _____ depends on whether the person making it wants to focus on ancestors or descendants.

3. You would not expect a _____ library to have as many books as the main library.

4. The warning against going out _____ comes from tree climbing where the further out someone goes the greater is the chance of the limb's breaking and the climber's falling.

I. Tree Trunks hold trees up and serve as conduits for water and nutrients to travel from the earth to the branches and the leaves. British speakers make *trunk calls* whereas Americans make *long distance phone calls*. The difference in terminology reflects the fact that telephones were invented after the United States had separated from England, and so each group of speakers came up with its own terminology. The British metaphor is based on the idea of a main telephone line with *branches* extending out to separate phones. Before someone at the tip of one branch can talk to someone at the tip of another branch, the call has to be routed back to the trunk and then connected to another branch where it can be sent out.

| elephant trunks | human trunk | steamer trunks | trunks |

1. Nearly everyone uses the _____ of their cars for storage.

2. However, few people have what used to be called _____ because they have been replaced by suitcases, footlockers, and duffel bags.

3. _____ are more flexible than tree trunks, but they have a similar texture and also help to guide nutrients into the body.

4. The _____ includes the *chest*, which holds such valuables as the heart and lungs.

J. *Log* is thought to be a Scandinavian word related to *lie* because it refers to a tree trunk that is lying down. Technically, logs must be at least six feet long, but the owners of fireplaces call anything bigger than a *stick of wood* a *log*. The term *logrolling* comes from American frontier days when neighbors who were clearing their fields or getting ready to build log cabins would assist each other in rolling huge logs to wherever they were needed. Another meaning of *logrolling* is the guiding of logs through water as a way of moving them downstream. This work is now a competitive sport, but in frontier America, it was a serious, yet precarious, business to balance oneself on floating and rolling logs while using a pole for prodding and guiding the logs around barriers and around each other. Since the 1600s, ships have kept *logbooks* of their daily speeds. A floating block of wood (a *log*) was hauled behind the ship and run out on a reel. The speed of the ship dictated the pull on the reel and how much rope it would feed out. *Knots* were tied in the rope at regular intervals and so the number of exposed *knots* would be the figures written in the daily *log*. Today's equipment for measuring speeds is much more sophisticated, but nautical miles are still referred to as *knots* and recordkeeping books as *logs*.

| as easy as rolling off | logbooks | logjam | logrolling |

1. Metaphorically, _____ refers to situations so big they cannot be stopped, as with a bill in Congress where different individuals have promised to support each other's bills.

2. The phrase _____ *a log* comes from the frequent duckings that frontier lumbermen got when trying to guide logs down a river.

3. A _____ is an impasse or a deadlock grounded in the image of logs getting tangled together so that all forward movement is stopped.

4. Today, all kinds of businesses keep _____, which is why *logging onto a computer* sounds like such a natural part of the workday.

K. *Foliage* is the collective name for the leaves on trees and bushes. It is related to the word *leaf* and, like *leaf,* is used metaphorically to stress the thinness of something as when statues are covered in *gold leaf* or *foil. Foil* is thicker than *leaf* and so can be used as a separate covering.

foil	foils	foilage	foliated

1. In fiction, the _____ are "thin" characters put in a story for the purpose of highlighting or bringing attention to the qualities of more important characters.

2. Aluminum _____ has mostly replaced waxed paper as an all-purpose wrap for kitchen use.

3. Something that is _____ is shaped like a leaf or is layered (as with rocks) to give the appearance of stacked up leaves.

4. Interior decorators rely mostly on _____ plants because they are more interested in greenery than in flowers or produce.

L. *Being Fruitful* is a literal description of trees that produce apples, pears, plums, and peaches, but farmers hope that their walnut, pecan, and almond trees, and even their vegetable gardens, will also be fruitful.

fructose	Fruit of the Loom®	fruitful	fruition

1. When a discussion proves productive, people might describe it as _____.

2. Because fruit has positive connotations, an underwear company chose _____ as a trademark to imply that something wonderful comes from its weaving looms.

3. _____ is a technical name for a particular kind of sugar that occurs in fruit juices and honey.

4. When a project comes to _____, it is at the stage where benefits are accruing.

Plants as the Source of Shape and Action Metaphors

Name: _____ **Period:** _____ **Date:** _____

At fairly simple levels, things are named because they are in some way associated with a plant, as when speakers took the name *paper* from *papyrus*, the plant first used to make paper. The easiest kind of association to demonstrate is that of shape as when *light bulbs* were named after the shape of tulip bulbs or garlic bulbs and when people talk about *mushroom clouds, bushy hair,* and *stemware glasses.*

More complex names are taken from the natural actions of plants, as when plants *sprout, put down roots, bud, bloom, flower, branch out, produce fruit* and *seeds,* and *wither* and *die.* The verb *to nettle,* which means to irritate or bother someone, is based on how *stinging nettles* prick the skin of animals and people. In the 1980s when computer engineer Mitch Kapor developed a way to computerize spreadsheets, he named his software *Lotus* as a comparison to the graceful way that lotus flowers spread out and float. In another example, while farmers value rich, *fertile soil,* creative people value *fertile minds* and *fertile imaginations.* Couples who have a difficult time conceiving a child go for help to *fertility clinics.*

The other common grounding is based on people's actions in relation to plants. The image of gardeners carefully making choices about what should stay and what should be removed as they *weed* their gardens is the basis of the metaphor about librarians *weeding* their book collections and discarding worn and out-of-date books. The image of a farmer *cutting out the deadwood* from (*pruning*) apple trees is the basis of the metaphor about company executives getting rid of (*firing*) the *deadwood* (people who are not *productive*) in their companies as they *prune expenses.* In other examples, a comedian might *plant* a stooge in the audience, while a detective might *plant* a listening device in a suspect's office. *Snowplows* are named because they are put to work in much the same way that farmers use their plows for soil. Allusions to *ships plowing through the waves* and to a speaker *plowing through* a long and boring speech are more abstract or metaphorical. When people say they are *bushed,* they are saying that they are as tired as if they have been making their way through heavy bushes. If they have been *bushwhacked* or *ambushed,* someone has hidden in the bushes and attacked them.

Here are a few examples illustrating these three kinds of groundings. Talk about what the italicized words in these sentences have in common with the plant or part of a plant that is mentioned.

Shape or Characteristic	Innate Plant Action	Human Interaction with a Plant
For Thanksgiving dinner we will have to put a *leaf* in the table.	When *leaflets* are passed out at school, they often end up as litter on the campus.	From *leafing* through the material, I judge it to be well done.
Ever since she was a child, her hair has been *bushy*.	*Bushings* in machines serve to soften the effects of abrasion.	Banks cut heavy foliage by ATM machines so that people will not be *ambushed* by thieves.
It is not wise to come to a final exam with only a *stump* of a pencil.	When people have an arm or a leg amputated, the *stump* has to be toughened before a prosthesis can be attached.	When politicians go *stumping for votes*, the image is of them standing on a tree *stump* so they can be seen and heard as they campaign.
The dentist had a hard time pulling her wisdom teeth because the *roots* were intertwined.	When families move to a new town, they *put down roots* by buying a house, joining a church, and getting to know their neighbors.	When people *root* for a sports team, they give it support.

The sentences below illustrate two kinds of metaphors: those based on innate plant actions and those based on humans interacting with plants. Try to figure out which is which. If the metaphor is based on a characteristic or an action that a plant does on its own, write the italicized words near the tree (Figure 5.1). If the metaphor is based on humans interacting with plants, write the italicized phrase near the farmer's clothing. The point is not who is doing the acting in the sentence (humans are responsible for all the actions), but whether the action is being compared to something a plant does naturally or to something that a human does while interacting with a plant. You will need to pay attention to the whole sentence because the same part of a plant could be the source for both kinds of metaphors.

1. My grandfather keeps *beating around the bush* when he talks about what he plans to leave his grandchildren.

2. Her hard work *bore unexpected fruit*.

3. There was nothing we could do against such organized *logrolling*.

4. She is always *going out on a limb* for her boyfriend.

5. As soon as she was on her own, she *blossomed* into a beautiful young woman.

6. Amazon.com *branched out* to sell more than books.

7. Contradictory campaign signs *sprouted on all the lawns* in our neighborhood.

8. It is too bad that she *planted such doubts* in his mind.

9. The company says it will be bankrupt if it does not *prune expenses*.

10. My grandfather's hobby is *caning chairs*.

11. Our plans for a protest march were *nipped in the bud*.

12. Even though there are still disagreements, we had a *fruitful discussion*.

Figure 5.1 Metaphors Based on Plant Actions versus Human Interactions with Plants

Metaphors based on the innate actions of plants

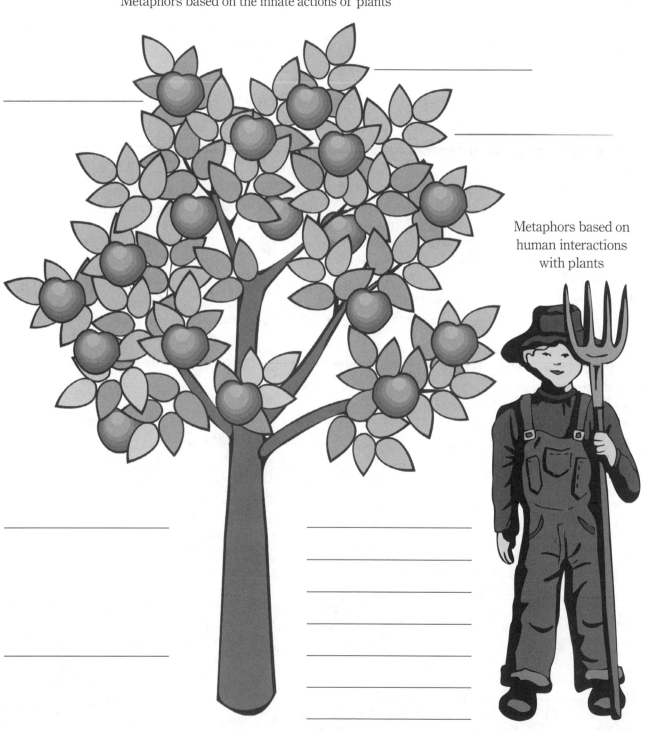

Metaphors based on human interactions with plants

Plants as the Source of Color Words

Name: _____ **Period:** _____ **Date:** _____

All speakers need to do to understand why so many color words relate to plants is to look at the vibrant colors in a flower garden or in a fruit and vegetable market. Before paints and dyes became commonplace, these natural colors must have seemed even more miraculous.

Although plants do not provide many names for dark tones, there is the *Black Forest* in Germany, which we know mostly through *Black Forest cake*. Pieces of furniture made from particular woods naturally get the name of the wood: *cherry, walnut, ebony, mahogany, pine,* etc. That you can buy varnishes and stains with such names shows that they are also used as color words. While the surface structure of the term *spring green* does not contain the name of a plant, the allusion is to the vibrant color of new leaves.

A slightly different kind of plant name is that associated with the food that comes from the plant, as when kitchen appliances are labeled *almond* or *avocado*, leather products are identified as *oat, wheat,* or *coffee*, and fabrics are identified as *peach, plum, celery,* or *apricot*. A *strawberry blond* has light red hair, while a *strawberry roan* horse is a darker red. Fashion and decorator magazines, along with paint charts and even big boxes of crayons, are good places to study color names. Look at some of these, or just brainstorm, and see if you can find color words to fit all around the color wheel in Figure 5.2.

Figure 5.2 A Color Wheel Based on Plant Names

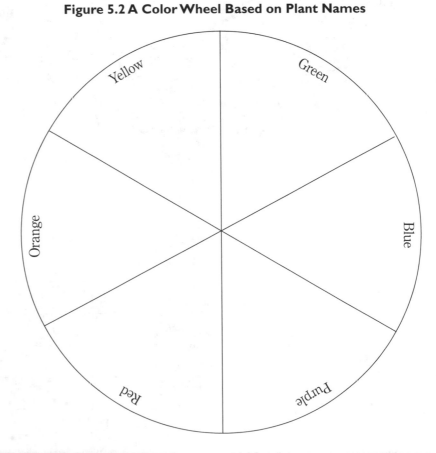

Good Food—Good Taste

Name: _____ **Period:** _____ **Date:** _____

The origin of the common English cliché *to give someone a cold shoulder* reflects the important role that food has played for hundreds of years in people's social relationships. It does not mean to turn away from someone but instead means being so inhospitable that when company arrives at a home, the hostess doesn't think enough of the person to go to the trouble of providing a hot meal. Instead, she goes to the cupboard and slices off a piece of cold meat from the shoulder of salted mutton, beef, or pork (most likely a ham) that affluent families kept on hand. It was the equivalent of serving someone leftovers. It has the same negative connotation as in the phrase *cold turkey* to describe the unpleasant situation of withdrawing from an addiction all at once with little or no emotional or medical support.

Another indication of how speakers relate to food is that the idea of taste has been extended to refer to a myriad of likes and dislikes. When people talk about someone having *good taste*, they are probably not thinking of the person being a food taster. Instead, they are thinking about what people wear, what they do for entertainment, how they decorate their homes, what books they read, and who their friends are. In the spring of 2001, when the Metropolitan Museum of Art in New York City devoted its major display to "Jacqueline Kennedy: The White House Years," she was credited with changing, "the climate of *taste* in America." *Time* magazine said that "no mid-century woman in the English-speaking world influenced *taste* the way she did in the 1960s."

That the magazine article had little—if anything—to do with food illustrates how the meaning of *taste* has undergone linguistic generalization. But even when a word undergoes generalization, it retains its older, more specific meanings. In a literal sense, the human tongue has taste buds that sense four tastes: *sweet, sour, bitter,* and *salt.* The hundreds of different flavors that are associated with different foods come from the way these foods trigger unique combinations. After reading some basic information about these four tastes, choose the most appropriate words or phrases to write in the blank spaces of the more metaphorical sentences that follow.

A. *Sweet* is an obvious and pleasant taste so we should expect it to be the basis for many lexical extensions and metaphors. *Sweet potatoes, sweet corn,* and *sweet and sour pork* are lexical extensions, while such other terms of affection as *honey, candy,* and *sugar* are related because their prime feature is their sweetness, and such terms of affection as *sweetheart, sweetie pie,* and *sweet cheeks* are metaphors. *Nectar* is the sweet substance that bees collect from flowers and transform into honey, so its name was borrowed for a kind of newly developed, smooth-skinned peach (nectarine). Because of the sweetness of such fruits as peaches, cherries, plums, apples, and berries, they are often treated metaphorically as symbols for love or sexuality.

| sickeningly sweet | sweet peas | sweet spot | sweetheart |

1. The flowers called _____ are a sign of warm weather.

2. The _____ on a baseball bat or a tennis racquet is the best place to hit.

3. A _____ contract is designed to give someone a special advantage.

4. A saccharine movie or book is one that is _____.

B. *Sour* is in some ways the opposite of sweet. Lexical extensions include *sourball candies* and the *sour cream* that people put on baked potatoes. Lemons are the proto-typical sour fruit, which is why people describe a car that continually breaks down as a *lemon*. The cliché, "If life gives you lemons, make lemonade," is advising people to make the best out of a bad thing. This is slightly different from describing a *sweet lemon* situation, which occurs when something bad happens to a person and that person pretends that nothing bad has happened. The phrase developed through an analogy to Aesop's famous fable about *sour grapes*. In this 2000-year-old story, a fox wants desperately to eat the beautiful grapes he sees hanging from a vine. However, he can't reach them, nor can he knock them down with a stick. When he finally has to give up, he saves his pride by claiming that the grapes are sour and so he does not want them. The analogy is to the way people save their pride about losing something by claiming they didn't want it anyway.

| sauerkraut | sour | soured | sourpuss |

1. The German name for cabbage soaked in brine is _____.

2. It hurts to hear musicians hitting _____ notes.

3. We have a neighbor who is truly an old _____.

4. Negative campaigning has _____ many people on politics.

C. *Bitter* is the least common of the four basic tastes. It is acrid or disagreeable like the taste of hops, which give the bitter taste to malt liquors. Various plants are called *bitterweed, bitterbrush, bitter cress*, and *bitterroot*. One species of almond is called *bitteralmond* because the nutmeat tastes more like a peach pit than an almond. *Bittersweet chocolate* is one of the few positive food terms alluding to this taste. The fact that we avoid bitter food makes the word all the more tempting to use as a metaphor. *Acer* is the Latin word for *bitter*. A person described as *acerbic* or as having an *acerbic wit* is harsh or bitter. Someone who *acerbates* a situation makes it worse, thereby irritating or exasperating people.

| bitter battle | bitter end | embittered |

1. The phrase a _____ is so common that Dr. Seuss was making a joke when he wrote *The Butter Battle Book.*

2. Many couples who start out to have a friendly divorce end up _____.

3. Someone who hangs onto hopes until the _____ has perseverance.

D. *Salt* is the only taste that is also a basic food, and in its double role it has inspired many other words including *salad, salami, sausage, sauce,* and *salsa.* Salt is found in nature and is necessary to life. At hospitals, before some medicines are injected into patients' bodies they are dissolved in *saline* (salty) *solutions* that resemble the body's natural composition. In rural farming areas, if there are no natural *salt licks,* farmers and ranchers must put out *salt blocks* for their animals. *Salt flats* are formed when great quantities of salty water evaporate. At the *Bonneville Salt Flats* in Utah, the surface is so smooth that it is used for testing racing vehicles. Under the city of Detroit, Michigan, an old salt mine is preserved as a tourist attraction. Before modern machinery was developed, working in salt mines was such hard work that any difficult working environment might be described as *being in the salt mines.* This is why if someone tells you to *go pound salt,* that person is not wishing you well. Before the invention of canning or freezing, salt was used as a preservative as in beef jerky and in *salt pork.* A *saltcellar* was the cool, underground room where salted meat was hung, but then it developed the meaning of a small container holding table salt. Today most table salt is purchased in round boxes with a pouring spout at the top, but the *saltbox* architectural design for a house shows this was not always true. It is rectangular with two stories in the front and one in the back covered by a long sloping roof.

below the salt	earn one's salt	old salt	salt of the earth	salty

1. The phrase to _____ takes on added meaning when we realize that the word *salary* comes from *salarium,* meaning "salt allowance."

2. Salt used to be used as a divider at banquet tables with those seated _____ having less prestige than those seated *above the salt,* which was nearer to the head of the table.

3. The _____ describes a person who exemplifies the kinds of humble qualities that make the world a better place.

4. An _____ is an experienced sailor, someone who has sailed many salty oceans.

5. A _____ story is *earthy,* meaning that it deals with subjects that are rough or coarse—far removed from romantic or heavenly considerations.

   The following sections are about some other foods that are so basic that they have served as the grounding for several metaphors. Read the paragraphs and then again choose the most appropriate terms to write in the blank spaces of the more metaphorical sentences.

E. *Eggs* are both plentiful and nutritious and thus provide the grounding for several metaphors. In nature, the real purpose for eggs is to *hatch* into babies. From the image of a baby bird breaking out of an egg comes the metaphor of people *hatching* plans and the idea of cellar doors or the covers for *holds* on ships being called *hatches*. When sailors *batten down the hatches* to get ready for a storm, they are closing and fastening the horizontal covers that lead into the bottom decks or storage bins. *Having egg on your face* means to be embarrassed, while being an *egghead* means to be intellectual. *Egg beaters* are standard kitchen equipment. Because of the rotary action of the blades, people sometimes refer to helicopters as *egg beaters*, or in another cooking metaphor, as *choppers*. The phrase about *egging someone on* probably inspires an image of someone encouraging his or her friends to throw rotten eggs at an enemy, but it really comes from an Old Norse word meaning *edge*. It refers to people who stand on the edge while encouraging his or her friends to get in the midst of a fracas. The Latin word for egg is *ovum*, cognate with *oval*, which describes the shape of eggs. The words *ovary, ovum,* and *ovulate* all relate to the female reproductive system. The scorekeeping system in tennis was borrowed from French where *l'oeuf,* meaning *the egg*, was pronounced as *love* by English speakers. This playful use of *egg* to mean *zero* is also seen when people describe a score as a *goose egg*. It is more dramatic than just saying *egg* because geese lay bigger eggs than do chickens.

| egg carton | eggshell | hatchback | Oval | robin's egg |

1. _____ mattress pads and pillows give extra gentle support.

2. _____ blue is a pale color often used to symbolize spring.

3. When speakers talk about *The* _____ *Office* in the White House, they are talking about the egg-shaped office of the President.

4. _____ is the name of a slightly glossy, yellowish-white paint.

5. _____ cars open up sort of like birds hatching from eggs.

F. *Meat*, until about the twelfth century, was any kind of food, as opposed to drink. When speakers talk about *nut meats*, they are using the term in its old sense, but when they refer to a *meat-and-potatoes* restaurant, or a *meat-and-potatoes kind of guy,* they are thinking of animal flesh that has been prepared for food. When the French conquered England in 1066, one of the niceties they brought with them were new words for various kinds of meat prepared for the table: *venison* from deer, *mutton* from sheep, *pork* from pigs, *veal* from calves, and *beef* from cattle. *Carne* is the Latin word for meat and is seen in such phrases as *chile con carne* and the word *carnival*, which literally means "farewell to meat." The first *carnivals* were the feasts and festivals of *Mardi Gras* (Fat Tuesday) that some Christians hold before they begin Lent, a time when they make sacrifices. The traditional sacrifice was to refrain from eating meat.

| baloney | beef | carnivore | SPAM® |

1. A kind of inexpensive processed meat fashioned after recipes from Bologna, Italy, is now a metaphor for anything of little value as in "That's a lot of _____."

2. Computer users adopted _____, a trademark name taken from SPiced hAM, to refer to junk e-mail.

3. A _____ is a meat-eating animal, such as a lion or tiger.

4. Because _____ is considered a hearty meat, it is used as a symbol for strength as when weight lifters *beef up* their muscles, a school *beefs up* its offerings, and airports *beef up* their security.

G. *Apples* are the prototypical representation of fruit as illustated by such maxims as "an apple a day keeps the doctor away" and "as American as apple pie." Both French and Persian speakers call potatoes *apples of the earth*. New York City devised an unusually successful advertising campaign when it named itself *The Big Apple* with such advertising slogans as "Take a bite out of the Big Apple." Manhattan, Kansas, capitalized on the success of the New York slogan by advertising itself as *The Little Apple*. When Steve Jobs designed a computer to be marketed to ordinary people rather than to high-tech computer experts, he chose the name *Apple* because he was "into" health foods and wanted a short, easy-to-remember "natural"-sounding name. *Pomum* is the Latin name for apples. *Pommels* are the rounded (apple-shaped) knobs on the fronts of saddles and on the *pommel horses* used in gymnastics.

Macintosh	pomegranates	pomology	Pomona

1. _____ are something like apples with grains or seeds.

2. _____, California is named after the Roman goddess of fruit.

3. Later generations of Apple computers were named _____ after a kind of apple.

4. _____ is the science and practice of growing fruit.

H. *Bread* stands for more than *bread* in such terms as *breadwinner,* for the person who earns a family's money, and *breadline,* for a place where food is distributed to poor people. The Biblical advice to "Cast your bread upon the water and it shall return fourfold" is encouraging people to send their works out to do good in the world. The promise of an increase in size fits with how bread is made from flour, water, and yeast. The yeast causes the mixture to rise both before and during baking. Even the words *lord* and *lady* relate to bread. *Lord* comes from two Middle English words *hlaf weard* (loaf guard), while *lady* comes from two similar words *hlaf diga* (loaf giver). *Panis* is the Latin word for *bread*, as seen in *companion* (a person with whom you eat bread) and the *pantry* as the place in your house where bread is kept.

company	panatela	panniers	unleavened

1. One of the ways that Jews celebrate Passover is by eating _____ bread (*matzos*) in memory of the fact that their ancestors had to flee Egypt so fast that they did not have time for their bread to rise before they baked it.

2. _____ cigars are rolled so that they look like miniature loaves of bread.

3. Bakers used to deliver their bread in double-sided baskets called _____, a name still used for the side baskets on bicycles.

4. If you work someplace that has a _____ cafeteria, the workers are fulfilling the literal meaning of the name because they are eating their bread together.

Food-Related Clichés

Name: _____ **Period:** _____ **Date:** _____

Other evidence showing the important role that food plays is the number of proverbs
that relate to food. The proverbs on the left are all based on food, while those on the
right come from some other source. Figure out what the food-related proverb means
and then try to find one from the right column that expresses a similar idea. Write that
letter of it in the space before the number. Talk about the meanings and how such different visual images can communicate approximately the same meanings.

Food-Related Proverbs	**Other Proverbs**
_____ 1. You have to crack some eggs to make an omelet.	**A.** Straight from the horse's mouth.
_____ 2. Don't put all your eggs in one basket.	**B.** Everything but the kitchen sink.
_____ 3. From soup to nuts.	**C.** Going from bad to worse.
_____ 4. The proof is in the pudding.	**D.** Keep your options open.
_____ 5. To spill the beans.	**E.** It's just one thing after another!
_____ 6. Out of the frying pan, into the fire.	**F.** Nothing ventured; nothing gained.
_____ 7. To butter someone up.	**G.** To soft soap someone.
_____ 8. Easy as pie.	**H.** So it goes!
_____ 9. That's how the cookie crumbles.	**I.** To let the cat out of the bag.
_____ 10. Driving me nuts.	**J.** To each his own.
_____ 11. The upper crust.	**K.** Driving me crazy.
_____ 12. There's no accounting for taste.	**L.** Easy as rolling off a log.
_____ 13. Life is a box of chocolates; you never know what you're going to get.	**M.** A blue blood.

Cooking and Eating

Name: _____ Period: _____ Date: _____

PART I Because chefs know that in the cooking process significant changes occur to the same basic substances, they are able to appreciate what is meant when cheaters *cook the data* or *cook the books* (or the *numbers*) to come out with a more favorable result for themselves. They also know that once *your goose is cooked*, there is no way to go back to the original state of things. People who have *parched* corn can easily understand what is meant when they read that "Each year the *parched* desert welcomes the summer monsoons." In a similar way, someone who has made a Christmas punch by setting a pan filled with fruit juices on a back burner to *mull* for several hours while the flavors blend together and absorb the taste of various spices knows that *mulling over a problem* takes time. Here is a partial recipe for Shepherd's Stew. Use the boldfaced and italicized words in the recipe to fill in the blank spaces in the metaphorical sentences that follow the recipe. You will need to add *–ed* to several of the verbs because most of the sentences are in past tense, while the recipe is in present tense. Talk about what the cooking terms and the metaphorical uses have in common.

Shepherd's Stew

Broil, grill, or **fry** meat chunks **Dilute** the mixture with one quart of water.
Slice carrots. **Salt and pepper** to taste.
Peel potatoes Bring to a **boiling point.**
Mince onions. **Lower the heat** and **simmer** for two hours.

1. I won't _____ words but instead will tell you exactly what I think.

2. Investigators _____ him for hours about the whereabouts of his sister.

3. The police have promised to _____ if the gangs will keep to their own neighborhoods.

4. He pulled out a wad of bills and _____ off three twenties.

5. I never intended to get *em* _____ in their family quarrels.

6. I think a _____ beard looks distinguished.

7. The two brothers' resentment _____ for months, before coming to a _____ _____ on their stepfather's birthday.

8. The golfer lost when he _____ his ball into the rough.

9. The support for a woman governor was _____ when the Libertarians also nominated a woman.

10. Crime stories that still talk about someone being _____ are old fashioned now that most executions are done by injection.

PART II Whether families live in igloos on an ice field, grass huts in a jungle, tents in a desert, apartments in a crowded city, or suburban homes behind white picket fences, they all sit down and eat together. Even though drive-in restaurants and convenience stores are bringing changes to family life, it is still easy to understand why the custom of family dining is likely to remain. People who literally *eat on the run* are prone to choking, while virtually everyone agrees that food tastes better when it is freshly prepared.

While both animals and humans eat, speakers generally base metaphors on human eating. If a speaker makes a comparison to animals, then the speaker is insulting the human. For example, a speaker might accuse a girl of being gullible for *swallowing* her boyfriend's ridiculous explanations, but the speaker is being even more insulting by saying the girl *swallowed* his stories *hook, line, and sinker*. The second version is saying that the girl is as stupid as a fish.

A different fish comparison is being made—this time to piranhas—if a speaker describes a group of gossiping workers as participating in a *feeding frenzy*. The idea is that they are enjoying themselves to excess while bringing great harm to the person they are gossiping about. Less subtle allusions to the way that animals eat are such phrases as *pigging out*, *wolfing your food*, and *going hog wild*.

The following phrases can be interpreted both literally and metaphorically. Write two sentences using each phrase. On the left use the phrase in a literal or basic sentence; on the right use it in a metaphorical or extended sentence. It is fine if you need to change the wording a bit to make it fit the grammar of your sentences.

Literal or Basic	Extended or Metaphorical
1. a fine kettle of fish	
2. a bitter taste in her mouth	
3. all sweetness and light	
4. to bite off more than he can chew	
5. to have a lot on her plate	
6. to eat it up	
7. to be spoonfed	
8. slow to digest something	

A Crossword Puzzle of Plants and Farming Words

Name: _____ **Period:** _____ **Date:** _____

Use the blank spaces in these sentences as clues for the words in the crossword puzzle.
The words are at least one step removed from referring to actual farming and plants.

ACROSS

4. The _____ of my watch just fell off.

6. She's a beautiful _____ blond.

7. It used to be covered with gold _____,
which has long since disappeared.

8. My cousin is _____ through college
without having any extracurricular activities.

10. Her parents hoped college would help her
_____ new friends.

11. Many industrial _____ are moving
from the Northeast to the Sunbelt.

DOWN

1. He's always careful to _____ his bets.

2. Next summer, the librarian
will_____ the collection.

3. The first time I went to an opera, I felt like such a
_____ *seed*.

5. A _____ experience is fraught with
danger.

7. Diabetics have to be careful about keeping circulation in their lower _____.

9. A _____ spread sheet is easier to
make than I imagined.

Workshop 5.1: A. 1. hit the hay, **2.** hayseeds, **3.** haywire. **B. 1.** mucking around, **2.** muckraking, **3.** muckrakers. **C. 1.** ingrained, **2.** a grain of, **3.** grainy, **4.** granulated. **D. 1.** harrow, **2.** harrowing, **3.** harrower. **E. 1.** cultivate, **2.** culture, **3.** cultivated, **4.** cults, **5.** cultivating. **F. 1.** over the threshold, **2.** on the threshold, **3.** at the threshold, **4.** high threshold. **G. 1.** draw straws, **2.** soda straws, **3.** strewn, **4.** straw vote. **H. 1.** branching, **2.** trees, **3.** branch, **4.** on a limb. **I. 1.** trunks, **2.** steamer trunks, **3.** elephant trunks, **4.** human trunk. **J. 1.** logrolling, **2.** easy as rolling off, **3.** logjam, **4.** logbooks. **K. 1.** foils, **2.** foil, **3.** foliated, **4.** foliage. **L. 1.** fruitful, **2.** Fruit of the Loom, **3.** fructose, **4.** fruition.

Workshop 5.2: Human Actions: beating round the bush, logrolling, going out on a limb, planted ... doubts, prune expenses, caning chairs, nipped in the bud. **Plant Actions:** bore ... fruit, blossomed, branched out, sprouted, fruitful.

Workshop 5.3: Answers will vary, but here are the colors we found in the Crayola 64-pack box. **Yellows:** cornflower, dandelion, goldenrod. **Greens:** asparagus, spring green, Granny Smith apple green, olive green, forest green. **Blues:** periwinkle, thistle, blue violet. **Purples:** wisteria, violet, lavender, orchid, violet red. **Reds:** red violet, mahogany, bittersweet, carnation pink, strawberry, red orange. **Oranges:** burnt orange, orange, peach, apricot.

Workshop 5.4: A. 1. sweet peas, **2.** sweet spot, **3.** sweetheart, **4.** sickeningly sweet. **B. 1.** sauerkraut, **2.** sour, **3.** sourpuss, **4.** soured.

C. 1. bitter battle, **2.** embittered, **3.** bitter end. **D. 1.** earn one's salt, **2.** below the salt, **3.** salt of the Earth, **4.** old salt, **5.** salty. **E. 1.** egg carton, **2.** robin's egg, **3.** Oval, **4.** eggshell, **5.** hatchback. **F. 1.** baloney, **2.** SPAM, **3.** carnivore, **4.** beef. **G. 1.** pomegranates, **2.** Pomona, **3.** Macintosh, **4.** pomology. **H. 1.** unleavened, **2.** panatela, **3.** panniers, **4.** company.

Workshop 5.5: 1-F, 2-D, 3-B, 4-A, 5-I, 6-C, 7-G, 8-L, 9-H, 10-K, 11-M, 12-J, 13-E.

Workshop 5.6: Part I: 1. mince, **2.** grilled, **3.** lower the heat, **4.** peeled, **5.** embroiled, **6.** salt and pepper, **7.** simmered .... boiling point, **8.** sliced, **9.** diluted, **10.** fried. **Part II:** Answers will vary. Possible metaphorical sentences include: **1.** Her showing up three weeks late is a fine kettle of fish. **2.** The divorce left a bitter taste in her mouth. **3.** High school cannot be all sweetness and light. **4.** By getting a job with fake credentials, he bit off more than he can chew. **5.** Having married a man with three children has left her with a lot on her plate. **6.** She foolishly ate up all his flattery. **7.** Steve probably won't do well in college because his mother has always spoonfed him. **8.** I don't think speedreading is for me because I'm slow to digest what I read.

Workshop 5.7: Across: 4. stem, **6.** strawberry, **7.** leaf, **8.** plowing, **10.** cultivate, **11.** plants. **Down: 1.** hedge, **2.** weed, **3.** hay, **5.** harrowing, **7.** limbs, **9.** lotus.

End-of-Chapter Activities

1. Sharing food and drink has long been a symbol of mutual friendship and support as seen in dozens of old folktales, myths, and scriptures where people are blessed for sharing food with strangers or punished for being selfish. Choose a medium that you are already familiar with (folktales, myths, the Old or New Testament, popular movies, etc.) and find a story about the sharing of food. Analyze what the food symbolizes and try to figure out why the creator chose to include food as part of "the plot." Another idea is to look at different pieces of literature to see what you can observe about the symbolism that goes along with food. Do characters eat different kinds of foods in happy and light-hearted stories as opposed to solemn and heavy stories? Are there particular foods that go with particular seasons or holidays?

2. While this chapter has been about foods and plants as the *sources* of metaphors, you could do a presentation or write a paper on plants and food that have been the targets or the recipients of metaphors. A good source of information on plants could be the National Audubon Society's *Field Guides* published by Alfred A. Knopf. For example, while looking at only a few pages of the 2001 *Field Guide to Wildflowers: Western Region,* we found

such names as the *Teddybear Cholla,* the *California Pitcher Plant,* the *Bladderpod,* and the *Dwarf Bramble.* A more standard example is the name of *gladiolas.* These are tall spiky plants that florists like to put in funeral bouquets because they stand so tall and are fairly hardy. What do you think they are named after? For food, you can get ideas by wandering through grocery stores or looking on restaurant menus, but even easier would be to look at a cookbook or at what is in your refrigerator and your cupboards. Also, most large city newspapers have one day a week when they prepare features on food and carry advertisements for local grocery store weekly specials. You will probably find foods that were named from their place of origin (*Quiche Lorraine* and *Boston Baked Beans*) for what they do (*popcorn* and *popovers*) or for a chef or a celebrity who liked them (*Caesar salad* and *Melba toast*).

3. Look at a map or an atlas of an area. If you are looking at a metropolitan area, you can study street names. If you are looking at a map of your state or of the United States, you can study the names of towns. Find those that appear to be named after plants—for example, *Oak Park, Cedar Falls, Redwood City, Sage Brush Flat,* and *Cape Canaveral* (from *cane*). Make a list and then try to make observations about them. Answer such questions as whether they tell something about the vegetation of the area. For example, in what states are you likely to find towns named *Cactus?* What about towns named *Shamrock*, or a variation of *Pine* or *Bloom* or *Grove?* If you find Spanish names such as variations of *Alamo* or *Alameda* for *poplar tree* or *Las Vegas* for *meadows*, what does this tell you about the history of an area?

4. Symbols are more all-encompassing than metaphors. Talk about trees in relation to symbolism. A *mother log* is an example of something that is both a realistic description and a symbol. In forests, a decaying log may provide the seed materials as well as the nutrition for young saplings that grow up from the underside. What other things might trees or plants symbolize? Would the meaning differ depending on the situation? What about the dove, which in the Old Testament story brought a leaf back to Noah? What about O'Henry's story "The Last Leaf"? And what about the symbolism of *The Garden of Eden* in the Old Testament and *The Secret Garden* in the book by Frances Hodgson Burnett.

5. Choose a food-related idiom to illustrate with a poster or a story. Here are some ideas, but feel free to brainstorm and think of others. Several appear in the various exercises of this workshop.

☐ Apple pie order
☐ The cheese stands alone (from the nursery rhyme and from the title of Robert Cormier's novel)
☐ Going bananas or being the top banana
☐ Being in a pickle
☐ Having a bone to pick with someone
☐ Being full of ginger
☐ Being the cream in someone's coffee
☐ The cream rises to the top or the cream of the crop

6. Choose the name of a food or a plant that we did not have space to cover in this workshop and figure out a way to teach about it to your classmates. Lexical extensions for a few plant-related words are outlined in the following charts as an example of basic research. You might try to make your own charts similar to these for such foods as *beef, beans, cheese, ham, lettuce, milk, potatoes,* or *tomatoes,* or for such parts of plants as *flowers, blossoms, sticks, leaves,* and such *fruits* as *cherries, plums,* and *peaches.* You might make a poster, bring a three-dimensional visual aid, or even a snack to help your fellow students remember what you say. Your goal should be to illustrate how the name you chose has developed extended meanings and has been used as the basis for metaphors.

Item	Lexical Extensions	Sample Sentences
cane	caning	*Cane* is any fast-growing plant, such as rattan, bamboo, and sugar cane.
		Because the center stalks grow straight up, they make convenient walking sticks, hence the word *cane* for an aid to walking.
		Today we expect a cane to have a *shepherd's crook* or a curve at the top.
		The Kennedy Space Center used to be known as *Cape Canaveral,* because a major industry was growing cane.
		Even 3-year-olds know that for a stick of peppermint candy to qualify as a *candy cane,* it must have a curved top.
		Cane can be split into flexible strips, called *rattan,* that have historically been used for *caning* or beating people.
		Caning a chair is weaving a seat or a back from strips of rattan.
farms	farm team farmer farmhand farmhouse	In baseball, a *farm team* is in the minor leagues.
		Calling someone a *farmer* is sometimes intended as an insulting way to say that a person lacks sophistication.
		A family that has to *farm out* its children is too poor to support them and so sends them to live with relatives.
		People worry when good *farmland* is turned over to real estate developers for building malls and apartment houses.

fields	fielder	Someone who is *out in left field* is like a baseball player who is not in a position to become a hero. In another metaphor related to baseball, at press conferences, attorneys often *field* reporters' questions so as to protect their clients. Schools, as well as military units, have *field days* for athletic competitions. In the British military, a *field marshal* is the highest ranking military official. A *field of honor* is the place where a battle or a duel is fought. When adults ask each other what *field* they are in, they are referring to a person's occupation or profession.
hedges	hedgehog hedgerow to hedge hedging	*Hedges* or *hedgerows* are bushes or trees grown for protection as well as for marking divisions of land. *Hedgehogs* are various kinds of small spiny animals (porcupines) traditionally viewed as growing in hedges. Like the animal that can roll itself into a protected ball, military defenses, especially those made from barbed wire, are called *hedgehogs*. People who *hedge* their bets by not betting all their money on a single horse are spreading out their money to protect themselves. People who insert *hedges* (*maybe, perhaps, helps to*, etc.) in their statements are also building in protections. Baby *hedgehogs* are called *urchins*, from which English speakers took the name for poor and uncared-for children.
pine needles	pineapple porcupine	*Pine needles* are themselves named metaphorically because these *leaves* look like sewing needles. The *pine* part of their name has been passed on to *porcupines*, which have long prickly spines on their backs. *Pineapples* are covered with stickers, plus they grow on a plant with spiny leaves. In a third-generation metaphor, hand grenades are called *pineapples* because they are similar in shape and color, although not in size or purpose.
stems	stemware to stem	*Stems* are to flowers what trunks are to trees. Based on shape we get such metaphors as the *stem of a pipe,* the *stem* of a watch, and *stemware* glasses. Based on the way *stems* grow, people talk about various problems *stemming* from particular circumstances. When talking about ships, from *stem to stern* means from one end to the other. From the idea that a *stem* is crucial to development, linguists talk about the *stem* of a word. Biologists do research on *stem cells*, which are the general cells that give rise to specialized cells. *Stem-winder* is an old-fashioned term for a rousing oration, perhaps based on the image of a speaker winding up the audience in hopes of sending them forth to action.

CHAPTER SIX

Clothing

Teachers' Preface

Linguistic principles being illustrated in this chapter include:

1. Relatively large numbers of clothing-related metaphors came into English when most households spun thread and wove their own cloth, tanned their own leather, and sewed their own clothing.

2. Metaphors are more likely to develop from words that involve human action, as with such old examples as *spin* and *weave* and such new examples as *zippers* and *Velcro*.

3. The longer in history that people have worn a basic item of clothing, the more likely it is to be the source of lexical extensions and metaphors.

4. Recently developed, specific items of clothing, such as *tuxedos, anklets, T-shirts, boxer shorts,* and *tank tops,* are more likely to be the targets of metaphors. They receive their names as a result of comparisons with or connections to better-known concepts.

5. In similar semantic areas, people tend to develop new words that are in some way analogous as with the rhyming words *muff, cuff,* and *ruff;* the diminutives *corset, bracelet, anklet,* and *helmet;* and the male/female pair *shirt* and *skirt.*

6. Common words sometimes undergo lexical inversion in which they develop ironic meanings as when *crowning someone* can mean either to strike someone on the head or to make the person a king or a queen.

7. New technologies give new life to old clothing terms as with *lavalier microphones* and *bulletproof vests.*

If you know someone who weaves or who sews, try to arrange for a demonstration or bring in items from your own sewing basket. Such simple things as *warp* and *weft, loom, selvage/selvedge, bias tape,* and *on the seamy side* are much easier to understand if they can be seen and touched.

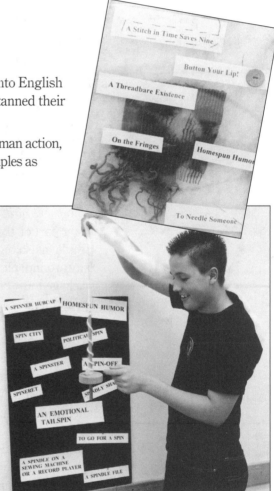

A worn piece of a Navajo saddle blanket is used as an attention-getter for such sewing metaphors as *A threadbare existence, On the fringes,* and *Homespun humor.* Below, a sophomore at Tempe High School succeeds in spinning yarn from raw wool.

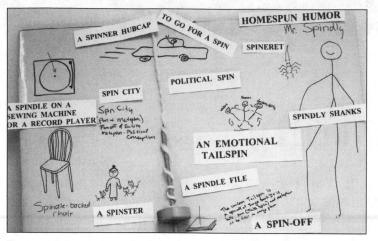

The poster on spinning metaphors was made by a college group preparing a learning center. Besides the word strips we provided, they observed that *Spin City* was a pun on *Sin City* at the same time that it was a metaphor for political corruption.

Reading Mark Twain's *The Prince and the Pauper* would fit nicely with this chapter because Twain's whole plot revolves around the way that people jump to conclusions based on a person's clothing. A good point to make with students is that the items of clothing that have the longest and the richest histories are the ones that were the easiest for people to make such as capes, hoods, robes, and free-flowing gowns. In such one-size-fits-all clothing, no one had to bother with linings, collars, sleeves, or buttons and buttonholes. Even today it is not unusual to see pictures of people in preindustrial countries wrapping themselves in blankets as protection from the cold.

CONVERSATION STARTERS

- A very old piece of wraparound clothing is the *girdle*, which today is a high-tech device worn mostly by women who want their bodies molded into more appealing shapes. However, the first *girdles* were simply bands of cloth wrapped around the body. For men, girdles were apparently used as loincloths as shown by the Biblical statement "He girded up his loins and ran" (1 Kings 18:46). In the New Testament (Peter 1:13), Peter was already using the term metaphorically when he advised, "Gird up the loins of your mind." The wraparound idea is shown in the modern term *pelvic girdle*, which refers to the hips and the related bones that surround the lower part of the human body. Related words include both *girth* and *girder*. When people take a big package to the post office, the clerk will measure its *girth* (all the way around) plus its length. For regular mailing, the length plus the *girth* of a package must be less than 108 inches. The *girth* on a horse is the band that wraps around its waist to keep the saddle in place. *Girders* form the steel cages that support modern skyscrapers.

- While the hook-and-loop fastener with the trademark name of *Velcro* is a much more recent invention than girdles, its name has already being extended. News photographers coined the term *Velcroids* for people who cling to celebrities in hopes of having their pictures taken. *Velcroid facts* are interesting bits of information that are independent enough that writers can tear them off from one article and attach them to another. Many of the statements about particular words in this book are examples of *Velcroid facts*.

- *Sabots* were originally heavy wooden shoes carved out of a single piece of wood and worn by European peasants. Today, a similar shape of shoe might also be made from leather, but it is the wooden ones that are metaphorically interesting because they gave us the word *sabotage*. As part of a revolt against industrialization and the machinery that was taking jobs, workers gathered at factories and threw their wooden shoes into the machinery. Ever since, *sabotage* has been used to name any deliberate destruction of equipment that is meant to bring down either a political, commercial, or educational institution. A *saboteur* is a person plotting or carrying out *sabotage*.

- *Pants* are circuitously named after St. Pantaleone, the patron saint of Venice, who in the fourth century was a Christian physician and martyr. His name literally refers to a *lion*, and as such was chosen as the ironic name for a cowardly but funny character in the Italian *commedia dell'arte* of the 1500s. This suave comic figure (not St. Pantaleone) always wore colorful trousers that were tight from the ankle to the knee and then exaggeratedly bloused out around the thighs and hips. The fashion began to be referred to as *pantaloons* and, as traveling troupes took the Italian comedies throughout Europe, the word came into widespread use.

To get more directly into the topic of literal versus metaphorical meanings of clothing terms, you might lead students to conjecture about the literal and figurative meanings of these sentences.

1. Let me stop by my house and pick up a few *rags*. (Someone might want real rags to use in a community cleanup project, while metaphorically someone might want to get some extra clothing before going away for the weekend.)

2. We always expect my uncle to have something *up his sleeve*. (Literally, the uncle might bring surprise gifts to children or he might be a cheater in cards, while metaphorically he might always have surprising ideas.)

3. It's easy to see who *wears the pants* in that family. (Literally, it is men who are traditionally pictured wearing pants, as on the doors to restrooms for males, so the phrase is alluding to a man. The more abstract allusion is to whoever is in control. This wouldn't even be a phrase in the language if not for the assumption that men are the ones in control. It may be that your students are young enough to have never heard this phrase.)

4. Cindy was surprised when they decided to *skirt* it. (Literally, people might put a skirt around a platform or a table, while metaphorically people skirt or go around issues that might be troublesome.)

5. The makers of Ben and Jerry's ice cream are known for their *shirtsleeve* approach to business. (Literally, everyone might be encouraged to come to work without suits, but metaphorically the allusion is to having an informal atmosphere at work.)

Clothes as the Source of Metaphors

Name: _____ **Period:** _____ **Date:** _____

Only someone like the fictional Amelia Bedelia would fail to realize that English speakers have several different meanings for *dress*. She is the funny housemaid who when her employer left her a note to *dress* the chicken, put ruffles and little pants on it. She was supposed to get the chicken ready for baking and to make the kind of *dressing*, or stuffing, that people serve with Thanksgiving turkey.

The secret to much of the humor in the *Amelia Bedelia* books is that she does not understand metaphorical processes. She tries to figure out literal interpretations when she hears people talk about such things as the *outskirts* of a city, the *hood* of a car, the *Cape* of Good Hope, *ragtime music,* and a *coat of arms* or a second *coat of paint*. She has not realized how the names for anything that people do on a daily basis, which includes getting dressed, will be enlarged and given additional meaning.

Except for the leather *car bras* that cover the fronts of sports cars and allusions to *jocks* from the *jock straps* worn first by the men who ride race horses and now by most athletes. English has relatively few metaphors based on underclothing. One reason is that in the history of the world underwear is a fairly new invention. Another reason is that items viewed as *unmentionables* will not be talked about and as a consequence will not lend their names to other concepts.

But as this chapter shows, several other pieces of clothing are surprisingly rich sources of metaphors. One such word is *vest*, which can be as different as the *pin-striped vest* worn by a well-dressed lawyer, the *hand-embroidered vest* worn by a country singer, the *bulletproof vest* worn by some police officers, the knitted under-shirts worn by some women, and the *life preserver vests* required on boats.

Vest comes from a word meaning *to clothe*. One of the metaphors it has given English is the verb *to invest*, as when you "clothe" or authorize a person to act on behalf of you or your money. At college graduations, the *hooding* of students earning master's or doctoral degrees is called the *investiture*. Church authorities wear *vestments* as a symbol of their authority. The *vestry* in a church used to be the place where the clergy put on their *vestments*, but the term has now expanded so that meetings might be held in the *vestry*. In law, when something has been *vested*, it has been fixed and settled so that it is not contingent on someone else's actions. Having a *vested* interest in something could mean that you are officially connected to the matter, or, more metaphorically, it could simply mean that you have taken it upon yourself to be interested as when an adult befriends a teenager and claims a *vested interest* in the young person's academic success.

We do not have space to explore all such clothing-related metaphors this fully, but you can get ideas from reading the following chart. As you read it, circle the usages that are metaphorical in communicating something beyond clothing. Talk about the words and see if you can think of other metaphors.

Item	Lexical Extensions	Sample Sentences
pants	pantaloons panties	Southern belles used to wear decorated *pantaloons* under their hoop skirts. The cliché about *who wears the pants in the family* is a leftover from the days when only men wore pants and so they stood for masculine authority. The cliché of *flying by the seat of one's pants* came out of World War II when pilots sometimes had to fly damaged planes and they felt were being held up by nothing but their pants.
dress	dresser dressing to dress	In Western culture, only females wear *dresses*, but everyone gets dressed. Men keep their clothes in *dresser* drawers. Mousse is a popular kind of hair *dressing*. In some businesses, the receptionists are hired as much for *window dressing* as for real work.
jacket	jacketed	*Jackets* are named for the common man, the *Jack of all trades*. *Book jackets* protect the book. In a similar way, *jackets* for records or CDs serve both as protection and as advertising. A new item on some restaurant menus is potatoes *jacketed* and mashed.
skirt	to skirt	*Skirt* as a slang term for a girl or woman is falling out of fashion because it is considered sexist. The idea behind beltways is to *skirt* inner city traffic. At the counseling sessions, she always *skirted* sensitive topics. The company prefers to rent office space in the *outskirts* of the city. People who early in 2000 sold their stock in the dot.com companies were lucky to *skirt disaster*.
shirt	shirttail	*Shirttail relatives* are either distant relatives or the kind you want to keep out-of-sight. A *shirtsleeves* atmosphere is casual and informal. *"Keep your shirt on!"* means to calm down. He *lost his shirt* in the stock market crash. He's such a good friend, I'm confident he would give me the *shirt off his back*.
sleeve	sleevelets	In an office, *sleeves* are open-ended tubular wrappings. In a machine shop, a *sleeve* might be a round metal covering. Cloth *sleevelets* used to be worn by newspaper editors and printers, and even store clerks, to keep their shirt cuffs from getting dirty. I get the feeling that he's *laughing up his sleeve*. He's got something *up his sleeve*.

From Head to Foot

Name: _____ **Period:** _____ **Date:** _____

HEAD COVERINGS

Hat is related to *hut* and *hood*, both of which are designed to protect people's heads from the elements. We see the idea of protection in the German word *fingerhut* for what English speakers call *thimbles*. We also see the idea of protection in the word *helmet*, which is the diminutive of *helm*, an old English word that means protection, as when the person at the *helm* of a ship is working in a protective role. The first *helmets* were part of medieval armor, but today people wear *bicycle* and *motorcycle helmets, football helmets, firefighters' helmets, space helmets, divers' helmets, soldiers' helmets,* and *pith helmets.* Construction workers call their helmets *hard hats.*

While the head coverings mentioned above were made for protection, other head coverings serve to make people more attractive. When ornate hats and bonnets were high fashion for women, Italian hat makers were especially skilled, thus the whole business of making hats was labeled *millinery* from the name of Milan, Italy. The *Mad Hatter* in Lewis Carroll's *Alice in Wonderland* was a *milliner*, and his personality may have been based on real-life milliners because many of them suffered from mercury poisoning. They held pins—which were poisoned from the dyes and other chemicals in the felt, fur, and feathers that they worked with—in their mouths.

You undoubtedly know the general meanings of such other words as *caps, hoods, veils,* and *scarves,* but you might not recognize some of the extended meanings of head coverings as shown in the following chart.

Item	Lexical Extension	Sample Sentences
cap	cape capelet capstone	The Latin word for head is *caput*, and these words all relate to something covering the head. A *cap* covers just the head, while a *cape* might cover the whole body and a *capelet* just the shoulders. A *capstone* is literally the topmost stone put on a building; figuratively, it is something important as when students write an honors paper for their *capstone experience.*

crown	crowned	The *crown prince* or *crown princess* is the person next in line for the throne. An ironic use of the term *crowning* is the hitting of someone on the head. We all wear *crowns*, because that is what the topmost part of our heads are called. Some of us also wear *crowns* on our teeth because a dentist has covered a damaged tooth with gold or porcelain. Even horses wear *crownpieces* because that is the part of the bridle that goes over the top of the head and fits right behind the ears. Some English money is called *crowns*, while a similar name in other countries is *krona, kroner,* and *krone.* Even more metaphorically, a woman's children might be called *jewels in her crown.* The first bottle caps for carbonated soda were patented under the name *Crown Caps* because their crimped edges made them look like miniature crowns.
corona (Latin *crown*)	corolla corollary corona coronary coronation coroner coronet	A *coroner* is the *crown's* (the government's) officer assigned to examine dead bodies and rule on the causes of death. In the southwestern United States, *Corona del Sol* (Spanish for *crown of the sun*) is a popular place name. The *Corona Borealis* constellation is also called the *Northern Crown.* The official *crowning* of royalty takes place at a *coronation.* *Corona cigars* have bluntly cut ends that look like little crowns, as contrasted to *panatella cigars,* which are tapered at the ends to look like miniature loaves of bread. The *coronary arteries* of the heart branch out from the aorta and circle around like a crown to provide blood to the heart itself.
veil	velum	A *veil* is a kind of covering, as a bridal *veil.* Metaphorically, if something is *veiled* it is kept secret or semisecret. The *velum* hangs down in the back of people's mouths to help block off air for speaking.

The term *corolla* is also used for the petals or inner leaves of flowers, but long ago it referred to a small garland or *crown* of flowers given to people who had done an especially good job. Eventually, employers began giving good workers the money that the *corolla* would have cost and so the word took on the meaning of "something extra." It was a tip or a present that went along with good behavior. Today, mathematicians talk about a *corollary* as a statement accepted without proof because it is so closely based on a proven principle. Outside of math, people think about a *corollary* as being a natural consequence or a direct result of something as shown in this sentence: "While his main argument was that if the school year were longer, students would learn more, his *corollary* argument was that keeping kids busy would cut down on delinquency."

Choose the appropriate words and phrases and write them in the blank spaces of these sentences. Talk about the features that are being emphasized.

A. corollary   coronation   coronet braids   kroners

1. _____ are worn on the tops of people's heads to look like the small crowns worn by princes and princesses.

2. Before adoption of the Eurodollar, tourists in Norway had to change their money into _____.

3. Queen Elizabeth's _____ was one of the first internationally televised events.

4. Psychologists have suggested that intellectual ability might be a _____ to being an only child.

B. coronas   coroners   crown   crown prince   crowning glory

1. In June 2001, news stories said that the _____ of Nepal shot his parents and himself, along with five other people.

2. The round chandeliers often hung in churches are called _____ because they look like crowns.

3. Today's _____ have technological advantages that Sherlock Holmes never dreamed of in his detective work.

4. The British coin called a _____ originally had a picture of a crown stamped on one side.

5. Women's hair is sometimes referred to as their _____.

C. cap   Hood   hoodwink   veiling

1. The capitals on the tops of columns are like a _____ sitting on the head of a tall person.

2. Teenagers are fairly good at _____ their true feelings.

3. We know something about how people used to dress from such stories as "Robin _____" and "Little Red Riding Hood."

4. To _____ someone is to keep them from knowing that you are pulling a trick.

D. cape   hat   helmet   milliners

1. People need to remember that a _____ is only a "little" protection.

2. Because of what happened to _____, scientists uncovered the damage done by mercury poisoning.

3. When a candidate throws his _____ into the ring, he is officially declaring that he is running for office.

4. It is wet and windy on _____ Cod because of the way it sticks out into the Atlantic ocean.

FOOT COVERINGS

Probably because we are so conscious of our shoes and the comfort of our feet, we have several proverbs about shoes. Describing something as "where the shoe pinches," is a way to allude to a problem. "If the shoe fits, wear it," is telling people to make up their own minds about the applicability of something, while "those are big shoes to fill" refers to the difficulty of finding a replacement for someone who is retiring from a position of heavy responsibility. "The shoe is on the other foot now" refers to a turn-about in circumstances, while "waiting for the other shoe to fall" is based on the image of a person in a first floor apartment who has just heard the upstairs tenant drop something on the floor. From past experience, the downstairs person assumes the upstairs person is getting undressed for bed and so can't get to sleep because she is preparing herself for the next "big bang." The expression is used to warn people against the futility of being apprehensive about trivial things that may never happen.

E.   **bet your boots**   **Boothill**   **bootlicker**   **boots on**

1. The expression _____ means to bet something you really value.

2. A _____ is overly servile or fawning.

3. To die with your _____ means that you were active until the very end.

4. The image relates to _____ Cemetery in Tombstone, Arizona, where tough westerners gunned each other down at the OK Corral.

F.   **boot camp**   **booted out**   **boots**   **high top**

1. In England, the trunks of cars are called _____.

2. British speakers sometimes refer to shoes as *boots,* while Americans reserve the term for _____ foot coverings that come up past the ankle as with *hiking boots, fashion boots,* and thigh-high *fishing boots.*

3. Soldiers receive their initial training at _____, which is where they first put on their *army* or *combat boots.*

4. However, some soldiers might think *boot camp* is where they get *kicked around* or are in danger of getting _____.

Anyone who has gotten blisters from wearing new shoes without stockings has learned to appreciate the cushioning provided by *stockings, socks,* or *hosiery,* all words used for footwear made to be worn inside shoes. Before the invention of a circular loom in the mid 1500s, these items of clothing had to be knitted by hand, which explains why people were so careful to darn or repair holes that developed from the rubbing of toes and heels against the insides of shoes and boots.

Early Greek and Roman women wore a kind of soft leather sandal that wrapped around their toes and heels and later went up their legs. These were called *soccus,* from which English took the word *sock.* In an early example of sexism, this dainty footwear was considered inappropriate for men and so male actors playing the roles of clowns and buffoons wore *soccus* as a way to get easy laughs. For centuries, *soccus* were as important to European and British clowns as baggy pants have been to American clowns.

Scholars are unsure of the origin of *sock* with the meaning of hitting or punching, but the long-time association between *socks* and buffoonery probably helped to cement the meaning, just as the *Punch and Judy* shows increased people's awareness of the pugilistic meaning of *punch*. More clear-cut lexical extensions based on the names of footwear are shown in the chart below.

Foot Covering	Lexical Extensions	Sample Sentences
shoe	horseshoe shoe horn shoe shop shoe tree shoemaker shoestring	Our mechanic recommends replacing a car's *brake shoes* every 30,000 miles. Architects and engineers talk about the placement of *shoes* as a base for the steel supports of bridges and buildings. *Shoestring potatoes* are miniature French fries. Both a *shoestring tackle* in football and a *shoestring catch* in baseball are near-misses that happen low to the ground.
socks	stocking to sock sox	*Socks* (both the word and the item) are shorter than *stockings*. A *silk stocking* event is one for rich people based on how luxurious silk stockings were before the invention of nylon in 1938. The *Boston Red Sox* are a "classic" baseball team. Children want their *Christmas stockings* to be big enough to hold lots of goodies.
hose	fire hose hosiery pantyhose to hose	*Hose* is cognate with *house* and *hoard*, which mean to cover and protect. The first *hose* covered people's legs but not their feet, so it's easy to see why the name was given to long, flexible tubes made from canvas and designed to carry water. To *hose down* a stable or to *hose off* a driveway is to wash away debris with a powerful stream of water. This may relate to describing a failed computer or a failed attempt at something as *hosed*, meaning it's totally gone. While men don't refer to their *socks* as *hosiery*, they nevertheless buy them in the *hosiery department* of a store.
spurs	larkspur spur gear spur ridge	*Spurs* were named from a Middle English word that meant to kick or push away as in *spurn*. Roosters have a natural *spur* on the back of their feet, which may have inspired the design of this piece of equipment that cowboys wear on their boots. A *spur gear* is a wheel with feet or sprockets sticking straight out from the rounded part. *Spur* railroad lines extend out from a main line. A *spur ridge* of mountains is a range extending laterally from a larger and higher mountain range. Teachers and coaches *spur* their students on, but we hope not through kicking them in the sides.

Choose the most appropriate word to write in each of the blank spaces below.

G.   horseshoes   shoestring   socking   stocking

1. Someone on a _____ budget has very little money.

2. _____ caps are a good invention because they can keep both your head and your neck warm.

3. Today if you are _____ away money, your are probably putting it in a bank rather than in an old sock.

4. _____ are a symbol of good luck.

H.   garden hoses   larkspur   spurs   spur of the moment

1. When people do things on the _____, they act as if they have been suddenly jolted.

2. Today's _____ are made from rubber or plastic.

3. Some flowers such as the _____ have spurs that extend from one or more petals.

4. The _____ on the back of rooster's feet probably inspired the design of cowboy spurs.

Accessories

Name: _____ **Period:** _____ **Date:** _____

Accessories are items of clothing or jewelry that are nonessential, but, like a person who is an *accessory to a crime*, they nevertheless influence the final outcome. With clothing, this outcome might relate to appearance—as when a businesswoman *accessorizes* her outfit with a beautiful silk scarf—or to usefulness—as when a horseman puts on a pair of spurs.

Because people are familiar with accessories, their names have naturally been extended to related concepts. An example is the word *apron*, which English speakers took from the French *napron*, meaning napkin. The *n* was dropped at the beginning of the word because English speakers thought the French were saying two words: *an apron*. Now that doing the laundry is so much easier than it used to be, women do not bother wearing aprons as much as they used to. Nevertheless, most speakers are well enough acquainted with aprons that when they hear about such things as the *apron* of a stage, the *apron* along a waterfront area, or the *apron* of an airport terminal, they envision a flat, fan-shaped area extending in front of the main part. The vertical coverings put in front of sinks and washbasins are also called *aprons*, as are concrete slabs poured to prevent the erosion of soil caused by running water. More abstractly, speakers talk about someone, usually a man, being *tied to his mother's apron strings*. The implication is that the man is emotionally dependent on his mother long after he is at the age when he should be able to stand on his own.

Accessories illustrate a middle category of words in that they have been both the sources and the targets of metaphorical processes. For example, when looking for ways to name new technological developments, speakers often dig into the past and give new life to old words. The small *lavalier microphones* that are hung around speakers' necks, and more recently pinned to clothing, got their name from a very old accessory. In 1667, King Louis XIV honored his first mistress by making her Madame la Duchesse de La Valliére. This new duchess was known throughout France for her great beauty and her fondness for pendant necklaces. Such hanging necklaces became known as *lavallieres*. In the 1960s, when smaller, inconspicuous microphones were developed for people speaking on television, the name was brought out of relative obscurity, the spelling was streamlined a bit, and the word given a whole new life. By now it has even lost the idea of hanging since most *lavalier mikes* are clipped on instead of being hung around someone's neck.

Some accessory names illustrate the linguistic principle of analogy in which speakers working within a semantic area create names that are in some way similar. For example, the words *cuff*, *muff*, and *ruff* rhyme, and these are all items that wrap around parts of the body. Another example is words that have been downsized so that they are analogous, for example, *bracelets, anklets, corsets,* and *helmets*. A *bracelet* is a small brace for the arm and, once this word became well established, then the similar term, *anklet,* could be created for a small leg decoration worn on the ankle. *Corsets (little bodies)* are undergarments that were popular in the 1800s. They lace up the back and are designed to make women look like they have small waistlines because they force body fat either down to the hips or up to the bust line.

Extensions from several other accessories are shown in the following chart. Use what you learn from reading the material in the chart and talking about it to do the exercises that follow.

Item	Lexical Extensions	Sample Sentences
broach	brooch	*Broaches* are tapered tools or instruments used to enlarge holes or open such things as casks of wine. The kind of *broach* (also spelled *brooch*) that is an accessory is a large decorative pin that women used to use to fasten shawls or lace collars. Because these pins are so heavy, they have to have a large pin that pokes through or "opens" the cloth. Metaphorically, to *broach* a topic in a conversation is to carefully insert it, as when employees *broach* the subject of a raise with their boss.
button	belly button buttonhole campaign buttons pushbutton	My niece is darling with her *button nose*. If I tell you this, you've got to promise to *button your lips*. The dress code says *belly buttons* have to be covered. I avoid making eye contact with him for fear he will *buttonhole* me to help with some "worthy" cause. *Campaign buttons* are fun to collect. Today we take *pushbutton* tools and implements for granted. There's a real danger in thinking that we can have a *pushbutton* war. My brother really knows how to *push my buttons*. Even after all these years, abortion is still a *hot-button* issue.
cuff	cufflinks handcuffs	*Cuffs* are the turned up or sewed on parts that finish off sleeves, but they can also be the turned-up bottoms of pants. *Cufflinks* are not likely to be worn by the same people who wear *handcuffs*. Someone who is hit or slapped with an open hand can be described as having been *cuffed*. Speaking *off the cuff* is speaking extemporaneously, as if from only a few notes written on a shirt cuff.
ruff	ruffle to ruffle	*Ruffs* are those great frilled collars worn by European aristocrats during the sixteenth and seventeenth centuries. Some animals and birds have natural *ruffs*. The male sandpiper is called a *ruff* because of the band of bouffant feathers that grow around his neck during the courting season. *Ruffles* are smaller than *ruffs* and might appear on almost any part of women's clothing. The wind might *ruffle* your hair, pages in a book, or the water of a calm lake. Unlike pleats, which lie flat, *ruffles* stand out in irregular bunches; hence, the metaphorical meaning of upsetting something or someone. She gets her *feathers ruffled* whenever anyone mentions her former husband.

muff	earmuff muffle muffler to muff	*Muffs* are pieces of fur sewn into a tubular shape so that people can slip both hands into them for warmth. Today only little girls dressed to look old-fashioned wear *muffs*, but lots of people wear *earmuffs*. Other people *muffle up* by wrapping their heads and necks in wool scarves. Some people call such wool scarves *mufflers*. Just as such scarves *muffle sounds*, a *muffler* on a car deadens the sound of the exhaust system. If a baseball player *muffs* a catch, it is as if his hands were in a *muff* instead of a baseball glove. This same kind of awkwardness is implied when an actress *muffs* a line or a hostess *muffs* an introduction.
gloves	glove compartment baseball glove foxglove	*Boxing gloves, baseball gloves,* and *driving gloves* are all made from leather. Finely made leather gloves were found in King Tutankhamen's tomb dating from 1500 B.C. The *glove compartments* in cars show how important gloves were to driving, especially before cars had heaters. He's always been handled with *kid gloves*. The detention officer works *hand in glove* with the local police. The leaves of the *foxglove* plant resemble little fingers.
lace	laced lacerated necklace shoelaces	The original meaning of *lace* was to snare or fasten something as with the lacings on ships. The decorative *lace* used on collars and cuffs and other fancy clothing or furnishings was made in imitation of such practical lacings. Tying their own *shoelaces* is a big deal for 6-year-olds. When Nicole Kidman starred in the 2001 film, *Moulin Rouge,* her corset was *laced* so tightly that one of her ribs was broken. *Necklace*s serve the same kind of ornamental purposes as lace, but they are made from beads *laced* together. *Lacewing flies* have see-through wings. New Orleans is famous for its wrought iron *lacework*. *Lacing* a drink with liquor or poison can be a criminal offence. The phrase *lace-curtain respectability* is sometimes used sarcastically to describe middle class values. Something that has been *lacerated* has been filled with holes.
belt	beltway fanbelt to belt	The first *belts* were probably just strips of hide tied around people's waists to keep animal skins in place. A *fanbelt* in a car connects the engine to the cooling system. A *beltline* on a trolley or a railroad circles back around to the beginning The *Corn Belt* is the agricultural area of the central plains and the Midwest. The *Sunbelt* stretches across the South from Florida to Arizona. In a kind of joking analogy, people talk about Northeastern industrial states as the *Rust Belt*. Religiously conservative states in the south are called the *Bible Belt*.

		To belt someone is to hit the person, but it doesn't have to be with a *belt*. The quick action and vigor that goes along with hitting is being stressed when someone *belts out* a song or *belts down* a drink. *Hitting below the belt* is a euphemism for doing something unethical as when a boxer hits an opponent in the groin.
collar	to collar	*Blue-collar* workers mostly work with their hands while *white-collar* workers are in office jobs. By analogy, *pink-collar* jobs are service jobs traditionally held by women. The Marines are called *leathernecks* because they once wore leather collars. Ministers sometimes joke about wearing *dog collars*. When the police *collar* someone, they probably don't really grab their collars. *White-collar* criminals are businessmen who have embezzled company funds.

PART I The following lists of terms based on accessories (including footwear) are in alphabetical order. Number the lists, putting *1.* by the clothing item and *3.* by the most metaphorical of the terms. Briefly explain the feature(s) that the more metaphorical usages are stressing. Notice how it takes more words to explain the meaning of the most metaphorical.

> **Example:** If the words are *baseball cap, capstone experience,* and *snowcapped mountain*, your numbering should be:
>
> **1.** baseball cap—Clothing item.
>
> **2.** snowcapped mountain—The mountain looks like it is wearing a white cap.
>
> **3.** a capstone experience—The person feels as if she has completed a big building project and is placing the last stone on top.

A. _____ muff for your hands

_____ muffler on a car

_____ to muff your lines in a play

B. _____ leather belt

_____ the Washington beltway

_____ to belt out a song

C. _____ pair of socks

_____ "Sock it to me!"

_____ stocking cap

D. _____ belly button

_____ hot-button issue

_____ shirt button

E. _____ glove compartment in a car

_____ leather glove

_____ to work hand in glove

F. _____ brake shoes

_____ living on a shoestring budget

_____ pair of shoes

G. _____ blue-collar worker

_____ lace collar

_____ to be collared by the police

H. _____ cuff on a shirt sleeve

_____ handcuffs

_____ to speak off the cuff

PART II Figure out the accessory (including footwear) that is the basis for each of the italicized terms in the following sentences. Write the name of the accessory in the blank space and then explain the feature that the accessory has in common with the extended use in the sentence.

_____ **1.** She has a collection of presidential *campaign buttons* dating back to Eisenhower.

_____ **2.** I don't like the way Tex-Mex restaurants *lace* their food with smoke flavoring.

_____ **3.** The new coach resigned when a reporter found out that he had been *booted off* his college team for betting.

_____ **4.** It makes me furious when my sister tells me not to get my feathers *ruffled*.

_____ **5.** He is always *buttonholing* people to get them to sign a petition for his latest cause.

_____ **6.** Terrorist attacks make all of us more aware of the possibilities for *sabotage*.

_____ **7.** I'm afraid to *broach the subject* of borrowing more money.

_____ **8.** I would have given up if Jeremy hadn't been there to *spur* me on.

PART III Talk about the meanings of the following clothing-related metaphors. On the space following each sentence write either ACTION or SHAPE. The idea is to figure out whether the metaphor alludes to the basic shape of an item or to some action that people connect with the item. For example, with *belt,* you would write SHAPE by the first sentence because belts are considered to circle around people in a similar way to how circumferential highways circle around cities. You would write ACTION by the second sentence, because *belting* someone or something is hitting the person or the thing hard as if with a belt. This same kind of decisive and strong action is alluded to when a singer *belts out* a song or a person at a bar *belts down* a drink.

Belt: _____ **1.** The *Washington Beltway* is a freeway that circles around the nation's capital.

_____ **2.** Elvis Presley really knew how to *belt* out a song.

Button: _____ **1.** She's a darling little girl with her *button nose* and her naturally curly hair.

_____ **2.** Michael is a master at *pushing his parents' buttons.*

Apron: _____ **1.** Young Italian men are not as worried about being tied to *their mother's apron strings* as are young Americans, so they live at home much longer.

_____ **2.** Stages, airports, and waterfront areas all have *aprons.* These are rounded areas that fan out from the central part as with the rounded front of a stage.

Pocket: _____ **1.** Uncle Dan resents it when people are nice to him in hopes he will dip into his *deep pockets.*

_____ **2.** We served *pita pocket* sandwiches at the children's picnic.

Sleeve: _____ **1.** The photo shop is good about putting the negatives in *sleeves.*

_____ **2.** You better not relax around Antonio; he always has something *up his sleeve.*

Skirt: _____ **1.** If you want to *skirt* the after-game traffic, go on the Hohokam Freeway.

_____ **2.** It is easier to find good restaurants in the *outskirts* of the city.

The Making of Clothes

Name: _____ **Period:** _____ **Date:** _____

Whenever prehistoric remains are found, anthropologists are always interested in examining whatever bits of clothing are found. In the Biblical story of Adam and Eve being turned out of the Garden of Eden, one of the first things they do is to "sew fig leaves together" to cover their nakedness (Genesis 3:7). Later in the Old Testament, readers see how far the making of clothing has developed when Joseph, as the favorite son of Jacob, is given a beautiful *coat of many colors*. His brothers are so jealous that they sell Joseph to slave traders who are passing through on their way to Egypt. The brothers stain Joseph's coat with the blood of a slaughtered lamb and take it to their sorrowing father telling him that Joseph must have been eaten by a lion. The story is so well known that over 2,000 years later multicolored coats are called *Joseph coats* and Donnie Osmond continues to star in a long-running musical, *Joseph and the Amazing Technicolor Dream Coat*.

Because clothing has such a long history of being important to people, it is not surprising that many English words are taken from clothing and from the processes of making clothes. In the Middle Ages, the making of cloth was a leading cottage industry. This was the time period (600 to 800 years ago) when the custom of having family names passed from one generation to the other was developing. Occupations were commonly used as the base for family names, and many common English names relate to the making of cloth and the sewing of clothes. Popular surnames include *Taylor* (an old spelling of *tailor*) and *Snyder* and *Schneider* (German for *tailor*); *Walker, Fuller,* and *Tucker* (people who cleaned and thickened cloth); and *Weaver, Web, Weber,* and *Webster* (people who wove cloth).

The people with these names made yarn or thread from such animal substances as silk and wool, from such plants as cotton and flax (from which linen is made), or today from such human-made synthetics as nylon, rayon, Spandex, and various polyesters. When spinning was done in the home rather than in factories, it was mainly the job of women, as shown by the modern word *distaff* to refer to any of the following: "women's work," the female side of a company, or the maternal side of a family. The word comes from *distaff*, a smooth stick also called a *spindle*, which would support a loose bunch of flax or whatever material was to be spun into thread. The spinner would hold it in one hand and with the other hand would pull out strands of the substance to twist into thread or yarn. This image of spinning a pile of fluffy stuff into a connected and continuous substance is the basis for talking about the making up of stories as *spinning yarns*.

Spindles were such basic household items that besides their many uses related to the making of thread, the word *spindle* is used for the thin round rods in a *spindle-backed* chair and for the thin posts that are part of some stairway banisters or porch railings. On a sewing machine, a spool of thread sits on a *spindle*, much like a record sits on the *spindle* of a phonograph. People with Abraham Lincoln's build have been teasingly described as *spindle shanks*. *Spindle files* are sharply pointed pins braced to stand upright so that papers can be pierced and kept in a loose kind of chronological order.

A *spinster* was originally anyone who spun, but then the word developed the specialized meaning of an unmarried woman, probably because this was the main job open to single women from respectable families. Today, *spinster*, along with *spinster-hood* and *spinterish*, are falling out of use because of new social attitudes toward both male and female *singles*.

The *spinning* action associated with *spindles* has been the source of such words as *spinning wheels, spinning jennys* (or *janes*), and more recently *spinning frames*, all of which ease the labor involved in spinning. In the early 1800s, scientists agreed on the word *spinneret* to name the part of the body of caterpillars and spiders from which they secrete their own kinds of threads, while in factories *spinnerette* names the manufactured plate or opening through which chemical solutions are forced to spin human-made filaments for such fabrics as rayon and nylon.

Moving away from the making of threads, speakers talk about *spinning reels* on fishing rods and other pieces of equipment. *Going for a spin* in a car alludes either to the spinning of a car's tires or to the idea that people are going out just for the fun of a ride. Instead of traveling to a predetermined goal, they will go in a circle and return home. *Spinning out* refers to a rotational skid, which might also be called a *tailspin*. An airplane in a *tailspin* is heading downward with the tail making larger arcs than the nose because the tail weighs less and so can be buffeted by the wind. It is most likely going to crash, which is the root of the metaphor about people going into *emotional tailspins*.

More recently and more metaphorically, speakers talk about *spin-off* companies as those that break away from parent companies and about *spin-off* television shows where a supporting character from one show becomes the leading character in a new but related show. The metaphor is based on the concept of centrifugal force, which is what makes the mud fly off a spinning tire or the fluffy *spun sugar* go to the outer edge of the equipment used for making cotton candy.

A more recent and more metaphorical use is shown in the name of the television program "*Spin City*," in allusions to *spin rooms* at newspaper and television stations, and to *spin doctors*, who serve as public relations agents for individuals as well as for political parties, companies, and institutions. The idea is that by putting a particular *spin* or slant on something, *spin doctors* can shape public opinion.

Users probably connect this metaphor as much to the spinning of records as to the spinning of thread, but the idea that people can spin the same basic material into very different things goes back a long way as shown by the old folktale about Rumplestil-skin. In this story, the father of a talented young woman brags that she can spin straw into gold. When word gets out, the girl is brought to the king's palace and locked in a room with a spinning wheel and a stack of straw. Of course she cannot obey the king's command, so instead of marrying the king's son, she will lose her life. But then she gets magical help from an elf named Rumplestilskin, who, in fact, can spin straw into gold, but at tremendous cost.

Examples given in the chart below demonstrate how speakers have extended both the literal and the metaphorical meanings of several other terms related to spinning.

Item	Lexical Extensions	Sample Sentences
cotton	cottonmouth cottonseed	More clothing is made from *cotton* or from cotton blended with polyesters than from any other fiber. *Cotton* plants produce fluffy balls, called *bolls*, of white fiber attached to seeds. From the seeds come such byproducts as *cottonseed meal* and *cottonseed oil*. The *cotton gin*, which was invented in 1796, separates the fiber from the seeds. Because picking cotton by hand is such a disagreeable task, the phrase *cotton-picking* has been generalized so that speakers now refer to any disagreeable task as a *cotton-picking job*. The *cottonmouth snake* (also called the *water moccasin*) was named for the white color of its mouth. *Cotton candy*, like the tail of Beatrix Potter's famous little rabbit named *Peter Cottontail*, physically resembles a fluffy ball of cotton.
flax	flaxen	*Flax*, which is woven into linen, is one of the oldest plants to be cultivated for its fiber. Figuratively, *flaxen* describes something pale and soft, as with *flaxen hair*.
linen	linens	Today most tablecloths, napkins, sheets, pillowcases, and towels are made from cotton and polyester blends, but they are still referred to as *household linens*. High-quality paper might also be called *linen* if it contains some linen or has a finish made to resemble a *linen weave*.
homespun		*Homespun* came into the language in the 1600s to describe cloth made from coarse yarn. The idea is that yarn spun at home by any family members with spare time is likely to be coarser than that produced by specialists with better equipment. Figuratively, the term is used to describe anything homey or folksy, such as *homespun humor* or *homespun philosophy*.
silk	silken silkworm silky	Silk yarn is spun from the material that various insects, loosely called *silkworms*, produce for their cocoons. Marco Polo in the 1300s established the great *Silk Route*, which enabled wealthy Europeans to acquire silk cloth from China. The *Silky Terrier* has a coat that feels very different from that of the *Wirehaired Terrier*. So-called *silk stockings* and the *silk screens* that are used to put designs on T-shirts are also likely to be made from polyesters. A *silk-stocking district* or a *silk-stocking event* is connected to wealth and aristocracy. But sometimes when speakers use such terms as *silken compliment* or a *silken explanation*, they are saying that something is overdone or insincere. They might be accusing the speaker of being a *silken-tongued* orator.

string	string bean stringed stringent stringy to string	*String* is spun and twisted like thread but is heavier and so is used mostly for tying or binding things rather than for sewing or weaving. While jewelry makers literally *string beads* together, writers metaphorically *string words* together. *Stringed* instruments in an orchestra have specially designed strings as do tennis and badminton racquets. *String beans* have fibrous strings provided by nature as a closing to their pods. *Stringy* hair is wiry and lacking in softness and shine. Part-time reporters assigned to cover outlying areas for newspapers are called *stringers*, perhaps because, on a map, the little towns they cover look like beads on a string, or perhaps the idea is that they tie together a large area. Carpenters use *stringer* as the name for long timbers joining two sides of a building or holding up the steps of a stairway. *Stringent* is a cognate word that refers to something that is tightly bound or specified. Some religions have *stringent rules* about food and drink, while others have *stringent* rules about what activities are allowed on the sabbath.
thread	threadbare threading to Thread	*Thread* is finer than string and is used either in sewing cloth together or in weaving cloth on a loom. *Thread* comes from a word meaning "to twist or turn," which probably relates to how thread is made, but it also describes what people do with *thread*. You would use similar instincts as with *threading* a needle when *threading your way* through an underground set of caverns or caves. The *threading* on screws and bolts is fine like a thread and also twists and turns. If you are following the *thread of a story* or figuring out a *common thread* between two stories, you are following the twists and turns of an author's mind. A *threadbare* existence alludes to clothing so worn that individual threads are showing.
wool	woolen woolly	*Wool* is sheared from sheep and is washed, combed, or corded, and then spun into yarn. Based on the appearance and texture of a pile of wool, some hairy insects are called *woolly aphids*, while a large hairy moth is named the *woolly bear*, and a much larger (but extinct) mammal is named the *woolly mammoth*. British speakers use the phrase *cotton wool* for what Americans simply call *cotton*. *Woolgathering* refers to indulgent or idle daydreaming based on the boring task of walking through brush and along fences to pluck off any bits of wool that might have been snagged from passing sheep. When something is *dyed in the wool*, the color is likely to be stronger and more vibrant and durable than if the weaver waited and dyed it after it was cloth. When people have *dyed-in-the-wool* attitudes or opinions, they are not likely to change their minds.

Write the appropriate terms from these lists in the blank spaces of the following sentences.

> **A.**   flaxen   spinning yarns   spinsters   stringent

1. Most unmarried women resent being called old maids or _____.

2. The entrance requirements are way too _____.

3. It was the fashion in early Rome for people to wear _____-colored wigs made from the hair of German captives.

4. Frontier cowboys became good at _____ because they did not have anything else to do while sitting around their nighttime campfires.

> **B.**   homespun   silks   spindle   string   tailspin

1. It seems funny to see a brand new computer system sitting right next to a _____ file with papers stabbed through the middle.

2. Her parents are going to hire a _____ quartet for the wedding reception when what she wanted was a disc jockey.

3. Jockey's uniforms are called _____ even though today they are mostly made from polyesters.

4. The arrest of his father put him into an emotional _____.

5. Mark Twain created a distinctive kind of _____ humor.

> **C.**   dyed-in-the-wool   spin   stringer   threaded

1. A _____ discussion on a computer is when participants communicate one after the other instead of all writing at the same time.

2. Today even local politicians have _____ doctors.

3. My grandmother was a _____ for the *Provo City Herald* so we always got our names in the paper when we went for a visit.

4. As long as I can remember, my family has been _____ Republicans.

> **D.**   string beans   strings you along   the wool   threads

1. People who are called _____ are lean and sinewy so that their heads, shoulders, elbows, hips, and knees vaguely resemble the bumps made by beans in their pods.

2. The phrase *pulling* _____ *over someone's eyes* alludes to pulling men's wigs down to keep them from seeing something.

3. When people jokingly refer to their clothes as their _____, they are saying the clothes aren't even worthy to be called *rags*.

4. If someone _____, the comparison might be to the way fish are left dangling on a fishing line waiting to be pulled from the water.

Weaving Cloth

Name: _____ **Period:** _____ **Date:** _____

Cloth is material for clothing that has been woven, knitted, or pressed (as with *felt*) from natural or synthetic fibers. It is so integral to *clothing* that, long ago, the word *cloth* was used for both concepts. This archaic usage is still seen when a minister or a priest is referred to as a *man of the cloth*, meaning a man who wears special *clothing* as a sign of his calling.

As shown by two classic Greek stories, weaving has been a part of the world's culture for thousands of years. In the myth about Athena and Arachne, Arachne was such a skillful weaver that she challenged the Goddess Athena to a contest. When they ended with equally beautiful pieces of cloth on their looms, Arachne was so distraught that she hung herself. Out of respect for her worthy opponent, the Goddess Athena changed Arachne into a spider so that she and her descendants could go on using their unusual skill at weaving webs forever more. And indeed they have done exactly that, even inspiring the name, if not the substance itself, of today's *World Wide Web*.

When Ulysses went on his odyssey, he left his wife Penelope home in Ithaca. During his twenty-year absence, Penelope was courted by over a hundred powerful warriors, each one demanding her hand in marriage. She held them at bay by saying that first she must finish weaving a shroud (a long burial cloth). All day she would sit and weave; then at night she would sneak out and undo the work she had done in the day-time, thus saving herself for Odysseus.

PART I As you read the following paragraphs about weaving, try to figure out which word to write in the blank spaces that are left.

loom	shuttle	tela	textiles

A. Weaving is accomplished on a **1.** _____, which is a frame or machine set up to hold thread or yarn so that it can be woven into cloth. Threads are strung vertically (the *warp*) and held in a taut position. A **2.** _____ is used to send other threads across in a horizontal (the *weft*) position going in and out of the vertical (the *warp*) threads. *Loom* comes from an Anglo Saxon word *gelome*, which was a general term meaning *tool* or *utensil*. It is unclear whether the weaving *loom* is the precursor of the verb *to loom up* as when an appari-tion, a mountain, or something else fearsome *looms up* in the fog or in the darkness, but there could be a relation-ship because of the indistinct or foggy view seen through the taut threads. This idea of indistinctness is reinforced by the word *subtle*, which has been traced to weaving and to the making of **3.** _____. *Subtle* literally meant *under (sub)* the *tela* (a Latin word for cloth), so it was a reference to the underneath side of the cloth. Even though the *b* in *subtle* is not pronounced, it is there as a leftover from the original *sub-* **4.** _____. While today, speakers might still refer to a design or to the weaving of a piece of cloth as *subtle*, they are just as likely to use *subtle* in reference to someone's perfume, to a monochromatic color scheme, to an ambiguous invitation, or to an idea they aren't sure they understand.

> chintz   corduroy   text

B. *Texere,* Latin *to weave,* has come into English as *textile,* meaning *cloth,* but more importantly it is related to *technology* and has expanded into such English words as **1.** _____ and *texture.* Because the weaving of cloth is a visible act of creation, it makes a good metaphor for talking about kinds of creation that can't be seen. With cloth, one can see and feel different textures. **2.** _____ with its ribbed texture is different from velvet with its soft and smooth texture and from **3.** _____ with its shiny surface and from dotted Swiss with its see-through fineness except where the dots are. Virtually everyone, even infants with their stuffed toys, have experiences with different textures of fabric. This serves as readiness for such metaphors as the *texture of a poem,* the *texture of a Sunday sermon,* the *texture of a compromise offer,* and even the *texture of someone's life.*

> edges   ends meet   loose ends   warp

C. *Loose ends* are threads or strings hanging from a rope or from a piece of woven or knitted fabric. In the modern, commercial weaving of cloth, a *selvedge* or *selvage* is woven into the two vertical edges. These are literally *self* **1.** _____, meaning that they do not have to be hemmed to keep them from fraying or developing *loose ends.* Extra strong **2.** _____ threads are strung down the sides so that the weft threads can be wrapped around and tucked in. Weavers do not want to have loose ends hanging from their cloth any more than people want to be *at* **3.** _____, meaning they are adrift or outside of their normal patterns of behavior. People who weave or sew, are interested in literally *making* **4.** _____, while other speakers use the term figuratively to talk about having enough money to meet their expenses.

   Here in chart form are other examples of words that have been extended from their earlier meanings related to cloth.

Item	Lexical Extensions	Sample Sentences
shuttle	shuttlecock to shuttle	*Shuttle* comes from old English words related to *bolt* and *shoot.* Skilled weavers could send their *shuttles* with great speed from one side of the loom to the other. In the Old Testament (Job 7:6), Job, who is being tested by God, complains, "My days are swifter than a weaver's *shuttle,* and are spent without hope." By the mid-1500s, the quick back-and-forth movement was extended to *shuttlecocks,* the flying balls or birdies used in the game of badminton.

		Within a hundred years, *shuttle* had acquired metaphorical meanings related to tossing various things (including ideas) back and forth. Today, we think of *shuttle busses* quickly moving airplane passengers from one terminal to another. Space *shuttles* move people, supplies, and equipment to the space station. Jet-setters *shuttle* between New York and Los Angeles, or even between New York and Tokyo. In the 1970s, Secretary of State Henry Kissinger brought the term *shuttle diplomacy* into dictionaries because of the way he *shuttled* complaints and demands back and forth between disputants in the Middle East.
border	bordering to border	A *border* is an outer edge or boundary on a rug or a piece of fabric, usually with an ornamental design. A home owner might *border* a patio with flower boxes, while a landscape gardener might *border* an area with flagstone. The *borders* between cities, states, and countries are not always visibly marked. Metaphorical *borders* are even less clearly marked—e.g., those between ethical and unethical behavior and those between teasing and humiliating someone.
canvas	canvass	*Canvas* is an important cloth used for sails on ships and for making tents. It inspired the verb *to canvass* as when someone *canvasses a neighborhood* asking questions and gathering information. Some etymologists think the metaphor is based on the fact that *canvas* was used for sifting things. Others think it developed as a comparison to the way a tent covers or *canvasses* an area.
fabric	to fabricate fabrication	*Fabric* is another word for cloth. Seeing cloth develop out of a pile of fiber is so surprising that it has inspired the use of *fabricate* and *fabrication* to refer to lies—something a speaker just makes up. When speakers talk about the *fabric* of someone's life, they are referring to its character or to its basic structure.
fringe	fringed fringes	*Fringe* is an ornamental border or trim, that consists of twisted or cut fibers hanging from a band. Metaphorically, someone who is just "hanging on" can be described as living *on the fringes* of such things as poverty or alcoholism. Cities might be *fringed* with public parks or roadside businesses. *Fringe benefits* on a job are such extras as health insurance and paid vacation time.

PART II Use these lexical extensions and metaphors to fill in the blanks in the following sentences.

A. fringe shuttle subtle text weave

1. The _____ benefits are more important than the salary because she needs health care insurance.

2. They weren't satisfied with the _____ of traditional wedding ceremonies and so they wrote their own.

3. Country music is not what would be called _____.

4. Soccer moms _____ their children between school and practices.

5. Some authors of mysteries can really _____ tales.

B. borders corduroy fabrication loose ends weaving

1. In early America, _____ roads were made from logs laid straight across to make bumpy, but relatively dry passageways through forests and swamps.

2. People cross _____ to extend their horizons.

3. She's been at _____ since Mark and Sandy moved.

4. _____ from lane to lane on the freeway is really dangerous.

5. The story he told was untrue; it was a complete _____.

C. arachnids canvassing fringes loom web

1. Especially at twilight, the mountains _____ over the village.

2. She got a job doing political _____.

3. People without money are forced to live on the _____ of society.

4. In *Charlotte's Web*, the doctor uses a spider _____ as a metaphor for all the things in life that people cannot explain.

5. _____ are a genus of insects who can weave webs.

Sewing

Name: _____ **Period:** _____ **Date:** _____

In the history of the world, sewing has been viewed as both pleasant and terrible as shown by these two poems. The first is an old nursery rhyme, while the second is an excerpt from poet Thomas Hood's 1843 "The Song of the Shirt."

> Curlylocks, Curlylocks, Wilt thou be mine?
> Thou shalt not wash dishes, nor yet feed the swine,
> But sit on a cushion, And sew a fine seam,
> And feed upon strawberries, sugar, and cream.

> With fingers weary and worn, With eyelids heavy and red,
> A woman sat, in unwomanly rags, Plying her needle and thread—
> Stitch! Stitch! Stitch! In poverty, hunger, and dirt,
> And still with a voice of dolorous pitch, She sang the "Song of the Shirt."

Whichever picture is true, and probably they both were for different people at different times and in different circumstances, they reflect how requisite sewing was for most women. Today, only the very wealthy go to designers and have their clothes individually styled and sewed. The rest of us buy our clothes *off the rack*, meaning they were put together in a factory and marketed to the general public. This was much less common during the first half of the twentieth century when either local seamstresses or the women in a family sewed clothing for themselves and their children.

Then, it was a special treat to wear something *boughten* (or *botten*), while today it is a special treat to wear something *handmade*. Economic patterns have changed, so that now it generally costs more for people to sew their own clothes than to buy them *ready-made*. Even very poor families buy ready-made clothing at secondhand shops; nevertheless, most speakers still have enough experience with sewing to appreciate many of the sewing-related metaphors and proverbs that are in contemporary use. For example, someone who puts off fixing a hem that has started to come undone, and as a consequence must redo practically the whole hem, is in a position to appreciate the proverb, "A stitch in time saves nine." Similarly, someone who goes to the trouble of sewing something out of cheap cloth and is then disappointed can understand the old saying, "You can't make a silk purse out of a sow's ear."

The following paragraphs illustrate some of these old usages. As you read the paragraphs, choose the most appropriate word or phrase to write in the blank spaces. Then talk about the connection between the sewing meaning and the extended meanings.

all tied up   **in knots**   **knotty**   **needling**   **pins and needles**

A person sewing on a button and becoming frustrated when the thread gets tangled or *knotted up* is likely to have empathy for someone who says, "My stomach is **1.** _____" as well as for a City Council struggling with a **2.** _____ problem. People who do not want to do something for someone else can offer the metaphorical excuse of being **3.** _____ or having their *hands tied*. People who have accidentally poked themselves with a needle or a pin understand the apprehension being expressed by someone saying, "I'm sitting on **4.** _____ while waiting for the doctor's report." They can also understand what is meant when a frustrated person says to someone who has been harassing him, "Quit **5.** _____ me!"

B.   **needle**   **patched**   **pin money**   **seamy**

Today we view people who *pin* their clothes together as careless or slovenly, but a few hundred years ago most people wore loose fitting robes tied with sashes or belts. When fitted clothing became fashionable, the person with pins was the neat one, but in preindustrial societies, pins were so expensive that families had to save up their money to buy them. This means that **1.** _____ was not the small change that it is considered to be today. *Needles* were even more expensive, so then people might really have searched for a **2.** _____ in a haystack. Another way to be frugal was to use even the tiniest bits of cloth, which is how *patchwork* quilts were invented. Today if we talk about something being **3.** _____ together, we are implying that it is done carelessly or in an ad hoc fashion. If we describe something as *on the* **4.** _____ *side*, we are saying that it is inappropriate or is something that would be better kept hidden. When someone makes a *seamless* transition, we are saying that it is smooth.

C.   **patterns of behavior**   **seamstresses**   **tailored**   **tailors**

Tailoring is the sewing of clothes with trim, simple lines as with wool suits and trousers. It used to be that men were called **1.** _____ while women were called **2.** _____, but today women can also be called tailors if they are doing that kind of sewing. Metaphorically, *tailor-made* means that something has been individually designed and created as with a speech *tailor-made* for an audience of computer technicians or an examination **3.** _____ to a particular student. Both tailors and seamstresses use *patterns*, which are printed on tissue paper and sold in particular designs for a variety of clothing sizes. Because they are a relatively recent invention, they are not the source of such terms as *leaf patterns, test patterns, frost patterns,* and **4.** _____. Nevertheless, they may be the most concrete patterns that many people have worked with and so are what people think about when they hear the word.

D.	rendered	rending	ripping	tearing into

Tearing, rending, or *ripping* can be done with paper but the consequences are greater when done with cloth and so *tearing,* **1.** _____, or *ripping* cloth seems more dramatic as in this Biblical quote from Ecclesiastes 3:18: "To everything there is a season, and a time to every purpose under the heaven.... A time to rend, and a time to sew..." *Rend* has an archaic sound to it and is more often heard with metaphorical than literal meanings as when we talk about a *heart-rending* decision or a nation **2.** _____ into opposing factions. *Ripping* is usually accidental unless someone is *ripping out* seams that need to be replaced or **3.** _____ down a poster. *Ripping* implies more force and consequently carries more negative connotations than *tearing.* When people want long straight edges, they can *tear* rather than *cut* cloth because, once started, cloth will tear directly along the thread lines of either the *warp* or the *weft.* Metaphorically, speakers talk about construction workers *tearing down* (demolishing) a building, about a bullet **4.** _____ (wounding) someone's flesh, or about kids *tearing up* (messing up) a room or *tearing down* (running or racing down) a street. More abstractly, someone might say, "I could hardly *tear my thoughts away* from the disaster," or "My heart was *torn* by their troubles." Someone can *tear down* a person's reputation or *tear into* a person, but neither one is as powerful as *ripping* someone, which implies a strong insult or scolding.

E.	being biased	bind	binding	bound

Tailors often *bind* cloth together by folding a narrow strip of cloth and sewing it to cover both edges. When things are **1.** _____ like this, they are held more solidly than they would be with a regular seam. The strength of such a joining is seen when opponents in a disagreement agree to **2.** _____ arbitration or when criminals **3.** _____ and gag their victims. If a tailor needs binding that can be stretched to fit around curved edges, he will cut it on the *bias,* meaning that it crosses over both the lengthwise and crosswise threads and is therefore a looser weave. From this, comes the metaphor of **4.** _____, which means bending or fitting one's perceptions to preconceived ideas. Bowling balls that swerve in a particular direction are described as *biased.* In another example, teachers or researchers might systematically introduce something into a test or a questionnaire to *bias* the answers.

F.	amendment	encircled	hemmed	on the mend	unraveled

Hemming is the folding up and stitching of an edge of cloth so it will stay that way permanently. Someone who is feeling all **1.** _____ in is frustrated. Because hems are usually on the rounded bottoms of skirts and pants legs, a battalion that is *hemmed in* by enemy fire is **2.** _____. One of the main reasons for hemming clothes is to keep the cloth from unraveling or falling apart. Metaphorically, speakers use this term when they say something like, "The more the police questioned him, the more his story **3.** _____. When clothing starts falling apart, *mending* is needed. Metaphorically, politicians talk about *mending* their fences to keep from losing votes. Injured people can also be **4.** _____, and if a law needs fixing, legislators can create an **5.** _____ for it.

Workshop 6.2: A. 1. coronet braids, **2.** kroners, **3.** coronation, **4.** corollary. **B. 1.** crown prince, **2.** coronas, **3.** coroners, **4.** crown, **5.** crowning glory. **C. 1.** cap, **2.** veiling, **3.** hood, **4.** hoodwink. **D. 1.** helmet, **2.** milliners **3.** Hat, **4.** Cape. **E. 1.** bet your boots, **2.** bootlicker, **3.** boots on, **4.** Boothill. **F. 1.** boots, **2.** high top, **3.** boot camp, **4.** booted out. **G. 1.** shoestring, **2.** stocking, **3.** socking, **4.** horseshoes. **H. 1.** spur of the moment, **2.** hoses, **3.** larkspur, **4.** spurs.

Workshop 6.3: Part II: 1. button = shape, **2.** lace = action, **3.** boot = action, **4.** ruffle = action, **5.** buttonhole = action, **6.** sabot (shoe) = action, **7.** broach = action, **8.** spur = action. **Part III: Belt: 1.** Shape, **2.** Action. **Button: 1.** Shape, **2.** Action. **Apron: 1.** Action, **2.** Action. **Pocket: 1.** Action, **2.** Shape. **Sleeve: 1.** Shape, **2.** Action. **Skirt: 1.** Action, **2.** Shape.

Workshop 6.4: A. 1. spinsters, **2.** stringent, **3.** flaxen, **4.** spinning yarns. **B. 1.** spindle, **2.** string, **3.** silks, **4.** tailspin, **5.** homespun. **C.**

1. threaded, **2.** spin, **3.** stringer, **4.** dyed-in-the-wool. **D. 1.** string beans, **2.** the wool, **3.** threads, **4.** strings you along.

Workshop 6.5: Part I. A. loom, **2.** shuttle, **3.** textiles, **4.** tela. **B. 1.** text, **2.** corduroy, **3.** chintz. **C. 1.** edges, **2.** warp, **3.** loose ends, **4.** ends meet. **Part II. A. 1.** fringe, **2.** text, **3.** subtle, **4.** shuttle, **5.** weave. **B. 1.** corduroy, **2.** borders, **3.** loose ends, **4.** weaving, **5.** fabrication. **C. 1.** loom, **2.** canvassing, **3.** fringes, **4.** web, **5.** arachnids.

Workshop 6.6: A. 1. in knots, **2.** knotty, **3.** all tied up, **4.** pins and needles, **5.** needling. **B. 1.** pin money, **2.** needle, **3.** patched, **4.** seamy. **C. 1.** tailors, **2.** seamstresses, **3.** tailored, **4.** patterns of behavior. **D. 1.** rending, **2.** rendered, **3.** ripping, **4.** tearing into. **E. 1.** bound, **2.** binding, **3.** bind, **4.** being biased. **F. 1.** hemmed, **2.** encircled, **3.** unraveled, **4.** on the mend, **5.** amendment.

End-of-Chapter Activities

1. Here are pairs of clothing-related clichés. Try to figure out what they are saying. Each pair has something in common. However, with some of the pairs the overall meaning is similar, while with others the meaning is quite different. Talk about the meanings of the proverbs and decide whether they are communicating something similar or different.

Choose one of the sets to explain or illustrate either for your *Changing Words* book or for a presentation to the class.

☐ A whiskey bootlegger *versus* A gambler with cards up his sleeve

☐ To pull yourself up by the bootstraps *versus* To fly by the seat of your pants

☐ Going from rags to riches *versus* Being taken to the cleaners

☐ Clothes make the man *versus* It takes more than dancer's shoes to make a dancer

☐ Foot loose and fancy free *versus* Tied to his mother's apron strings.

☐ To lose your shirt *versus* To bet your boots

☐ To handle with kid gloves *versus* An iron fist in a velvet glove

2. Here are some other clothing-related proverbs or clichés that you could choose to illustrate either as a poster or as a page for your *Changing Words* book. When you show your illustration to the class, be ready to explain both the clothing-related meaning and its metaphorical extension.

☐ A feather in one's cap

☐ A wolf in sheep's clothing

☐ To tighten one's belt

☐ Don't criticize until you've walked a mile in my shoes

3. Do a study of different kinds of hats. Find several different names (*panama, mortarboard, derby, fedora,* stovepipe, *pillbox, stetson, ten-gallon, tricorn,* etc.) and trace how the hats got their names. Prepare a report in which you illustrate the naming processes and how they relate either to the designs of the hats or to something in the history of the hat. Maybe you can investigate the song "Yankee Doodle" and learn what was meant by "stuck a feather in his hat and called it macaroni."

4. The following literary quotes include allusions to the arts of weaving, knitting, or sewing. Talk about the meanings and why the writers used sewing-related metaphors to put their points across. You might choose one to use as inspiration for an essay of your own.

☐ The days may come, the days may go,
But still the hands of memory weave
The blissful dreams of long ago.
George Cooper, 1877

☐ O what a tangled web we weave,
When first we practice to deceive.
Sir Walter Scott, 1808

☐ Macbeth does murder sleep; the innocent sleep,
Sleep that knits up the ravelled sleave of care.
William Shakespeare, 1594

☐ May the warp be the white light of morning.
May the weft be the red light of evening.
May the fringes be the falling rain.
May the border be the standing rainbow,
Thus weave for us a garment of brightness.
"Song of the Sky Loom," Tewa Indian poem, n.d.

☐ I said "a line will take us hours maybe,
Yet if it does not seem a moment's thought
Our stitching and unstitching has been naught."
W. B. Yeats, 1904

CHAPTER SEVEN

Living and Dying

Teachers' Preface

Linguistic principles being illustrated in this chapter include:

1. New words come into languages faster than old words fall out of languages.

2. One of the reasons that English makes such heavy use of Latin- and Greek-related roots is that birth and death have religious implications, and Christian missionaries from Rome carried these root words to the world.

3. When metaphors become firmly established, speakers will use them as the basis for new metaphors—what we call second-generation metaphors.

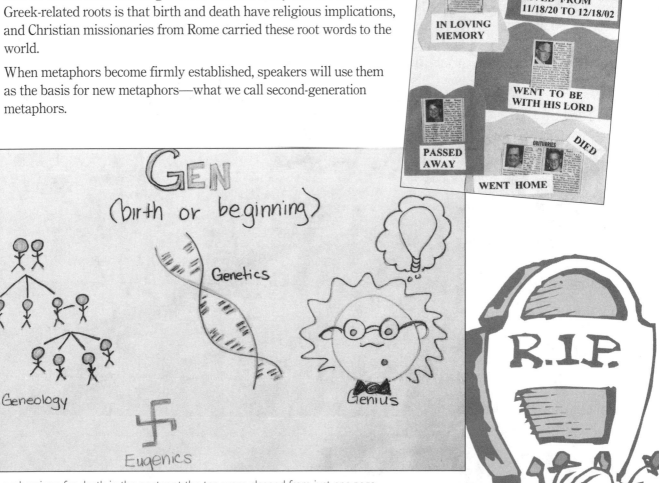

The euphemisms for death in the poster at the top were gleaned from just one page of newspaper obituary notices. At the bottom, students were surprised at how many words they knew based on the root *gen-*.

4. Because death is such an overwhelming concept, several words whose basic meanings are not related to death have become closely associated with death. Rather than being the source for metaphors, they are the goals.

5. Euphemisms for death and dying abound because people do not like to say the words.

This is a good chapter in which to teach the concept of *euphemisms*. If your local paper is like ours, family members of the deceased now write the obituaries and bring them to the newspaper. From one day's obituary pages, our students found the following ways of saying that someone has died:

Died peacefully…
In loving memory…
Left 125 family members…
Lived from 11/18/1920 to 12/18/2002…
Passed away…
Passed on…
Returned to his Lord…
Went home…
Went to be with the Lord…
Went to heaven…

One of our college students went to the Internet and found several sites that focused on euphemisms for death. In class we used them for a discussion on levels of formality and whether the term was trivializing death or making it more somber.

As a contrast to the somber subject of death, students enjoyed bringing in a baby picture or a page from their baby books. If they haven't already done it, students might also have fun researching what was happening in the world on the day they were born. Students enjoy making family trees, but you need to be flexible in such an assignment lest some students feel "different" because their family trees are not perfectly symmetrical.

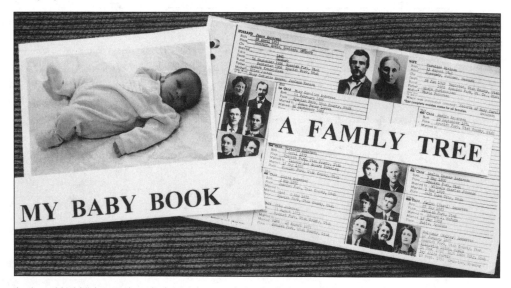

A plus with this chapter is to invite students to bring in their own baby pictures and family trees.

Being Born

Name: _____ Period: _____ Date: _____

Anything as important to us as life and death will, of course, be reflected in many parts of a language. In this chapter we will start with words for creation and birth, and then move on to words about death.

Conception, and the verb *to conceive*, refer to the joining of an egg and sperm so that an *embryo* is formed. All three of these terms are used metaphorically; for example, "The idea for a community fair was *conceived* as part of a bigger plan to attract tourists," and "It is hard to judge the proposal because it is still in such an *embryonic* state." If a person talks about the conception of an idea by saying something like, "The idea was *hatched* by the mayor's committee," then it sounds less important because the level of the allusion is lower. The idea is being compared to the birth of a bird, a fish, or some other animal that is hatched from an egg, rather than to the birth of something as important as a human.

Renaissance literally means rebirth, and so from the beginning it has been a metaphorical term because it does not refer to an actual biological birth. *The Renaissance* began in Italy in the fourteenth century and during the fifteenth and sixteenth centuries spread throughout Europe, which experienced a great revival of interest in art, literature, music, and learning of all kinds. The term is used as an adjective to describe architecture, fashions, paintings, and even ideas that date back to that period. Metaphorically, it is used as a name for any burst of creative new thinking, as in the *Harlem Renaissance*. During the 1990s in an amusing kind of lexical extension, the names of Italian renaissance painters were given to the Teenage Mutant Ninja Turtles: Michaelangelo, Donatello, Leonardo, and Raphael.

Puny is a term that sounds too slangy or disrespectful to use in relation to birth, but it is nevertheless related. It comes from French *puis* and *ne*, literally meaning "after born." With twins, the first-born is usually the bigger and the stronger, and so the one born second is more likely to be *puny*. While speakers might still use *puny* to talk about the size of a person, the term is more often used metaphorically to talk negatively about other things as with a *puny golf course*, a *puny defense*, a *puny excuse*, or a *puny attempt to solve the problem*.

Midwives are people who are "with women" at the time of childbirth. Today, at least in industrialized countries, most babies are delivered by doctors identified as *gynecologists* (*gyne* is cognate with *queen* as a name for women) or *obstetricians* (the Latin equivalent of *midwives*). These latter two terms are too specific to be used as metaphors, but *midwifery* is sometimes used to describe the act of coaching or helping someone achieve something as when a group of business leaders act as midwives to the *birthing of* or the *creation* of a business managed by teenagers.

Fetus is related to the word *fruitful*. It most commonly refers to an *embryo* old enough to have attained its basic structure. With humans this is at about three months, a period referred to as the *first trimester*, because it is one-third of the time that it takes for an embryo to develop into a baby. The adjective form of *fetal* is seen in such lexical extensions as *fetal research* to describe medical research connected to such ideas as using fetal tissue in transplants and *fetal position* to describe someone curled up as if still in the womb.

Abortion and the verb *to abort* often appear in news stories because of controversies over whether—and if so, what kinds of—abortions should be legal. In everyday language, *abortion* means a purposeful termination of a pregnancy. However, doctors might say that a woman is "trying to abort a child," meaning that her body is in some way rejecting the pregnancy rather than that she has made a decision to have an abortion. Metaphorically, *abort* is used to describe a situation in which great effort and planning have been involved and then for some reason a sudden and unwelcome decision has to be made in favor of cancellation. For example, bad weather may force military leaders to *abort* their plans for an invasion or a malfunction may force NASA to *abort* a space mission.

The most productive root word in this area is *gen,* from Greek *genos,* referring to the birth or to the beginning of a race or a group. This root appears in a title as old as the *book of Genesis* in the Bible and as new as recent headlines about scientists uncovering the human *genome* and mapping the approximately 30,000 *genes* that each of us inherits from our family's *gene pool.* In between the old and the new are such common usages as these shown in the chart below, along other related words.

Word	Lexical Extensions	Sample Sentences
gen (Greek *birth* or *beginning*)	congenital engender eugenics engine gene gender genealogy generic genetic genital genius genuine genus heterogeneous pregnant	*Genealogy* is the study of different *generations* of the same family. Your *progenitors* will be listed on your genealogy chart, and so will any offspring that you *engender.* *Genetics* is the study of *genes,* including the *genetic code* or *DNA (deoxyribonucleic acid),* which determines heredity. Related terms include *genetic engineering, genetic counseling, genetic disorders,* and *genetic fingerprinting.* In the 1940s, *eugenics* developed negative connotations because of the beliefs of Adolph Hitler and the Nazis who experimented in selective breeding of people. The *genital organs* are connected with reproduction as shown in such terms as *engender* and *gestation.* *Pregnant* literally means before (*pre*) birth (*gnant*). Both *geniuses* and *genial* people are born with special talents and abilities. Less fortunate babies are born with *congenital* defects. *Generate* often refers to creation by nonliving things such as *engines* and *generators.* *Genus* means *kind,* as when we talk about *genus* as a classification of various animals and *gender* as a description of sex differences. *Genuine* means something actually "born" as opposed to something artificial. *Generic* and *general* are in some ways the opposite of *specific.* Something *homogeneous* is of the same kind, while something *heterogeneous* is of different kinds.

beran (Old English *to carry*)	bear bairns born borne forebears to bear wheelbarrow	A pregnant woman is described as *carrying* a child. In Irish stories, young children are referred to as *bairns* or *wee bairns*. Your *forebears* are the ones who *bore* or gave *birth* to your parents. Seeds can be *borne* to islands on the wind or on ocean waves. Even such an inelegant word as *wheelbarrow* is related to this concept.
nascent (Latin *to be born*)	nationality native nativity natural nature neonatal	If you say that you are a *native born* American, you are being redundant because *native* and *born* mean the same thing. *Neonatal* is also repetitious in saying someone is *newly born*. It has developed a specialized association with premature babies (often called *preemies*), who will be cared for in a hospital's *Neonatal Unit*. People think that as long as medicine is *natural*, it can't hurt you.

PART I The following sentences demonstrate various uses of words related to birth. Try to figure out the appropriate word for each of the blank spaces. Sentences in the first group relate to the birth of a human or an animal; sentences in the second group are more metaphorical. They refer to the generation of something other than a living organism.

A. BASIC SENTENCES ABOUT THE BIRTH OF A HUMAN OR AN ANIMAL

> conceived   fetal   fetus   genome   gestation   native   neonatal   preemies

1. A common health problem for _____ is that their lungs are underdeveloped.

2. Human _____ takes nine months, while for elephants it is more like two years.

3. The _____ peoples of Australia and the United States have several things in common.

4. Scientists studying the human _____ found that people have about 30,000 genes.

5. Some people fear that _____ research will encourage abortions.

6. It is now common for a _____ to be checked through an ultrasound.

7. They named their daughter Paris because she was _____ while they were on their honeymoon in Europe.

8. A baby weighing less than three pounds was in the _____ unit.

B. MORE METAPHORICAL SENTENCES

> aborted   birth   embryonic   fetal   generative   natural   premature   puny

1. He is so depressed he lies on his bed all day in a _____ position.

2. In the 1700s, the idea of democracy was still in an _____ state.

3. A _____ grammar differs from traditional grammar in that it helps to create sentences as well as analyze them.

4. My _____ instinct tells me she is lying.

5. Plans for the new high school were _____ when the ground was found to be contaminated.

6. It is _____ to decide before hearing what he has to say.

7. The 1915 movie _____ *of a Nation* is considered to be the first feature film.

8. She was disappointed when her grandfather left her such a _____ inheritance.

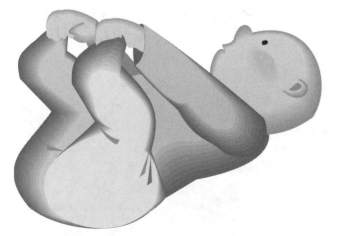

Words for Being Alive: *Quick, Bio,* and *Vivus*

Name: _____ **Period:** _____ **Date:** _____

The words in this workshop illustrate how much longer it takes for established words to disappear from a language as compared to how rapidly new words can be introduced into a language. This is because the creation and introduction of new words is an active process under conscious control, while in most cases, the words that are being replaced are left to "die a natural death." Even if an individual, or more likely a group, decides that a word is offensive and should be removed from a language, the process is extremely slow. The paragraphs below illustrate this process through discussing basic words that all relate to the concept of being alive. In the sentences that follow each explanation, choose the most appropriate terms to write in the blank spaces. Talk about the meanings and about which of the uses are basic and which are more metaphorical.

A. *Quick* in Middle English was the basic word for *alive*. We still see this usage when someone tears a fingernail down to the *quick*. It hurts because it has gotten to the part that is alive. Over time its meaning narrowed so that today *quick* is most commonly used to describe only one of the characteristics of being alive as when we say that someone "has a *quick* and *lively* mind," or when we ask someone to *quicken* her pace, meaning to *step lively*. But still, as English speakers moved toward using various forms of the Latin *vivus* and *vivere* to mean *alive*, remnants of the old Germanic use of *quick* remain in the language. When speakers talk about a baby being *stillborn*, they are using *still* as an antonym to *quick* or *alive,* as in the phrase *the quick and the dead*. A *stillborn* baby has been born dead. Metaphorically, the term can describe a situation that turns out to be less than expected as in, "His candidacy was *stillborn*."

mercurial	quicksand	quicksilver	to the quick

1. Metaphorically, people might say that someone's remark or the actions of a loved one cut them _____, meaning that it touched their heart and soul; it hurt them where they live.

2. _____ appears to be alive in the way it traps people and pulls them underground.

3. Mercury, which is called _____, also appears to be alive because of how it puddles and how shimmering drops will move around on flat, nonpermeable surfaces.

4. A crossover meaning is seen in the other name of *quicksilver*, which is *mercury*. Someone with a _____ personality undergoes *quick* changes of mood and temperament.

B. *Bio* is the Greek word for *life*, which we see in such common words as *biology* (the study of life), *biography* (the story or graph of someone's life), and *biophysics* (combining the study of physics with the study of biology). In fact, *bio* is such a useful prefix that it is continually being attached to other words as with *bioterror* to refer to the purposeful spreading of diseases such as anthrax or smallpox and *biopharmaceutical* to refer to drug companies that are trying to develop vaccines.

biomass	bionic	biopsy	biorhythms	biosatellite

1. A _____ is something that is growing, such as a tumor or a cancer.

2. When people get depressed and have emotional problems, their _____ are upset.

3. A _____ is similar to an autopsy, except it is performed on living tissue.

4. People worry that the fictional _____ characters that children see keep them from understanding what it really means to get a serious injury.

5. A _____ carries living organisms as it circles the earth.

C. *Vivere* is a Latin word for *live*. English speakers use the Latin root in several different ways. Zoologists describe animals whose babies are born alive, as opposed to developing in eggs, as *viviparous*. The movie title *Viva Zapata* translates into English as something like "Long Live Zapata!", which is similar to the European cry, "Long live the King!" People who go to a religious *revival* sometimes describe themselves as being *born again* or having a new *life,* while people who are applying for jobs put together *curriculum vitae* to document the "course of their lives."

bon vivant	viable	vivaciously	vivid	vivisection

1. A person who moves and talks _____ has a lively personality.

2. _____, which is the dissection of living animals, is very controversial.

3. If you have _____ memories of an accident, it means they are still alive in your mind.

4. English speakers borrowed the French phrase _____, which means "good living."

5. A _____ solution is one that is still alive.

Words Related to Death

Name: _____ **Period:** _____ **Date:** _____

For the concept of death, English speakers make ample use of the Latin word *mortalis*. The famous book compiled in 1634 by Sir Thomas Malory, *Le Morte d'Arthur*, is the story of King Arthur's life and death. The English word *murder* is related, and so are the terms *moribund*, which means "like death," and *postmortem exam*, which literally is the examination of a body after death but metaphorically is the examination of any enterprise that has failed.

In the first few hours or days after an infant is born, its life is so precarious that some insurance policies do not go into effect until the baby is three days old. The risks of early death are summarized in the term *infant mortality*. This term is likely to appear in news stories about countries at war or rural areas suffering from droughts or other misfortunes so that babies are not receiving adequate care. When owners *mortgage* their home, they are in a way killing their ownership of it. The *a-* in *amortize* means "without" or "not," and so when owners *amortize* a mortgage, they are arranging to pay it off and to remove the death threat from their ownership rights.

The terms listed below also come from the root *mort*. Talk about their meanings and then choose the most appropriate term to write in the sentences that follow the explanations.

> **A.**   morgue   mortality rates   mortally   rigor mortis

1. Insurance companies use _____ to set their prices.

2. When _____ sets in, a person's clothing has to be cut off because the body is too stiff to bend.

3. So many people were killed that the bodies had to be laid out in a temporary _____ .

4. Newspapers would rather describe someone as _____ wounded rather than to write that the person was shot to death.

> **B.**   infant mortality   mortal   mortified   mortuaries

1. Metaphorically, startup companies worry about being victims of _____ because in their first few years they are especially vulnerable to failure.

2. In Catholicism, _____ sins are those that are considered so serious that the sinners will lose their eternal souls.

3. Owners of _____ prefer the term *funeral homes*.

4. She was so _____ about calling her new husband the wrong name that she said she wanted to die.

Other Words Related to Death

Name: _____ **Period:** _____ **Date:** _____

Some words that are commonly used in relation to death have other more basic meanings. They are different from most of the words talked about in this chapter because they are the receivers or the targets of the metaphorical process. For example, the adjective *fatal* and the noun *fatality* come from the idea that humans are all subject to *fate*, meaning to conditions they cannot control. While there can be other fates besides death as shown in the phrase *a fate worse than death*, being dead is the most extreme thing people generally think of. This is why the word became closely connected to death.

To *execute someone* is to carry out a legal decision that a court has made declaring that the person deserves to die. *Execute* literally means "to follow." An *executioner* is following orders, just as the *executor* of a will is following the wishes of the deceased. People can also *execute* a tricky dance step, a U-turn, or a computer program.

The basic meaning of *dispatch* is to send or relegate something as when a *dispatch center* sorts out parcels for delivery or tells taxi drivers which passengers to pick up. Reporters send *dispatches* to their home newspaper while hungry people *dispatch* the food set on the table. Only metaphorically is the term used for killing someone. The implication is that the person is being sent to the afterlife with no more feeling than would accompany a package. This lack of feeling is why the term is often used in science fiction.

When Arnold Schwarzenegger starred in *The Terminator*, he was an android from the future sent to earth on a mission of *extermination*. Even though this was an exaggerated comic-book kind of adventure, it is still chilling to think of people being *exterminated*, because that is what we do to cockroaches. Nevertheless, speakers find it easier to say that someone has a *terminal illness* than to say that the person *is dying*. In Latin *terminus* means *boundary*, thus in reference to death it means the edge of one's life. This is similar to the way that a *bus terminal* or a *train terminal* is a stopping place or a divider. The *terms* in schools are time dividers, while the *terms* of a legal agreement set out the boundaries of what is acceptable.

The following terms differ from the ones just talked about in that their basic meaning relates to death. As you read these paragraphs, circle the examples that are metaphorical, then be ready to talk about the difference between the metaphorical and the literal meanings.

- *To kill* is a verb that requires an actor. Someone or something causes a death, with the implications being that the event happens suddenly, either intentionally or unintentionally. Speakers are using the term metaphorically when they exaggerate and say something like, "That joke was a killer," or "Our manager keeps us on a killer schedule." These metaphors reflect the same kind of exaggeration as when speakers complain about *cut-throat competition* or about someone *murdering* the English language.

- **To slay** and **to slaughter** are related and have the connotations of a killing being done without compassion or feeling. People convicted of *manslaughter* in courts will not be punished as heavily as if they were convicted of *murder*, which is an act of preplanned killing. *Slaughter* is most often used to talk about the killing of animals, so when it is used in reference to people—as "the slaughter of the ethnic Albanians..."—the idea already comes close to being metaphorical. One of the reasons the title of Kurt Vonnegut's World War II novel *Slaughterhouse V* is so memorable is that human prisoners were being held and were risking death in a place originally built for the slaughtering of pigs. The word *slay* is definitely metaphorical in such a statement as, "That comedian slays me!"

- **Martyrdom** comes from the Greek *martur*, meaning witness. *Martyrs* will die rather than give up their religious convictions. Many of the saints honored by the Catholic Church are martyrs. It is not clear whether the term is being used literally or figuratively when individuals are killed either in the line of duty or while engaging in some kind of a protest. After their deaths, their families and supporters set out to tell their stories in a way to make them heroes or martyrs. However, the term is definitely being used metaphorically when we joke about self-sacrificing mothers being martyrs to their families as in the riddle:

Q How many devoted mothers does it take to change a light bulb?

A None. She will just sit in the dark.

- **Thanatos** is a Greek word for death, hence *thanatology* is the study of death and people's psychological reactions to it. Knowing this, we would expect that in his famous essay, "Thanatopsis," Ralph Waldo Emerson would make some observations about death. Evelyn Waugh in his book about the funeral business, *The Loved One*, named his leading character *Aimee Thanatogenous*. We most often see the term in English as part of the word *euthanasia*, which literally means "good death," or what in plain English is described as *mercy killing*. The idea of euthanasia is that people who are terminally ill can choose to die through some kind of medical intervention rather than suffering while they wait for a natural death.

- **Lethal** means deadly, as when people condemned to death are given *lethal injections*. In Greek mythology, *Lethe* is the name of the river of forgetfulness or death. People who drank from it forgot their past, which is why people who are in a kind of stupor so that they do not attend to their work are described as *lethargic*.

- **To die** is a change-of-state verb that does not require a doer in the same way as does *kill*. Also, the process of *dying* is slower. Metaphorically, we might talk about how a controversy is *dying down*, how languages around the world are *dying out*, or how the plans for a new stadium *died on the vine*, meaning the project was abandoned before it was fully developed. When the Sears Company named its batteries *DieHard*, they created one of the most successful trademarks of our era because the term was already in the language to name a person who remains on task long after others have stopped working.

- *Deceased* is usually used in the past tense except in legal documents, which occasionally make statements about someone predeceasing someone else. It literally means "to go from," but once it became associated with death, speakers hesitated to use it in any other connection than talking about someone "going from life."

- An *assassin* murders someone, usually an official or a prominent person, through a surprise attack. The word is related to *hashish* (marijuana) and comes from a militant eleventh-century group of Islamic fighters (called Assassins) who believed it was their duty to harass and murder the enemies of their culture. They used hashish to increase their bravery as they risked their own lives. The term is being used metaphorically when blood-sucking insects are called *assassin bugs*. Another metaphor is to accuse someone who is spreading vicious rumors of *character assassination*.

- *Suicide, homicide,* and *genocide* all relate to killing. *Suicide* is the killing of one's self, *homicide* is the killing of a human, while *genocide* is the killing of a whole group of people. We also have the less common words of *matricide* (killing one's mother), *patricide* (killing one's father), *fratricide* (killing one's brother), and *sororicide* (killing one's sister). During the war in Afghanistan when three soldiers were accidentally killed by a U.S. bomb, some newscasters used the term *fraticide* to mean what is more commonly called *friendly fire*. People are usually exaggerating or speaking metaphorically when they talk about *genocide* (the destruction of a race of people) or when they say someone has committed *political* or *social suicide*. However, *suicide bombings* and *suicide missions* are literal descriptions of events such as the destruction of the Twin Towers on September 11th. During World War II, the term *hara-kiri* (often written *hari-kari)* came into English from Japanese where it literally meant "belly cutting" as practiced by Japanese warriors using Samurai swords in ritualistic suicides. During the war, Japanese pilots who volunteered for suicide bombing missions were said to be committing *hara-kiri*.

- *Dead* is an adjective and has such a sound of finality to it that many speakers and writers try to avoid saying the word in reference to humans. The noun form, *death*, does not seem quite as harsh, but insurance companies still prefer to call "death insurance" *life insurance*, and even obituary writers say that people *passed on* rather than that they *died*. Instead of referring to someone as *dead*, speakers talk about *the late...,* *the deceased...,* or *the (dearly) departed....* Real estate developers interested in selling suburban houses have found that the French term *cul de sac* ("bottom of the bag") is more appealing to buyers than the harsh-sounding *dead end*.

Metaphors Based on Death

Name: _____ **Period:** _____ **Date:** _____

In spite of our fears of death—or maybe because we are trying to get over these fears—we make frequent use of death-related terms in metaphors as illustrated in the following sentences. Try to figure out the basic meanings of the italicized parts of these sentences and write them in the appropriate part of the pie chart in Figure 7.1. The sentences most likely refer either to:

A. An actual death of a living organism.

B. Something that is the ultimate, the most that something can be, which is what death is.

C. A metaphor based on exaggeration.

D. A change from a previous state so that something is less "alive" than it used to be.

Category C will have the most terms in it because it is a miscellaneous catchall. Put the terms referring to something as "the ultimate or the most that something can be" in Category B, even though they are also exaggerations.

1. Interns in hospitals are put on *murderous schedules*.

2. The combination of drugs that he took proved to be *lethal*.

3. I could have *died from embarrassment*.

4. Even in a Sunday afternoon tennis game, she displays a *killer instinct*.

5. The light is *dying fast* so you should take the pictures now.

6. It was *political suicide* for him to change parties after he was nominated.

7. You cannot miss it if you *go dead ahead*.

8. The bank's pulling out was a *death blow* to the project.

9. On campus, support for fraternities and sororities *seems to be dying out*.

10. The case of the *killer dogs* in San Francisco has caused cities to make new leash rules.

11. *Assassin bugs* are various kinds of predators that suck blood from mammals.

12. That child is going to be *the death of me*!

13. The accident caused three *fatalities*.

14. Few plants grow in *the dead of winter*.

15. His girlfriend is always *dressed to kill*.

16. Company morale is low because an outside reviewer recommended clearing out *the deadwood* and employees are worried about their jobs.

17. One of his grandparents was in a WWII *death camp*.

18. Plans for the new stadium are *pretty much dead*.

Figure 7.1 Pie Chart Showing Different Meanings of Terms Related to Death

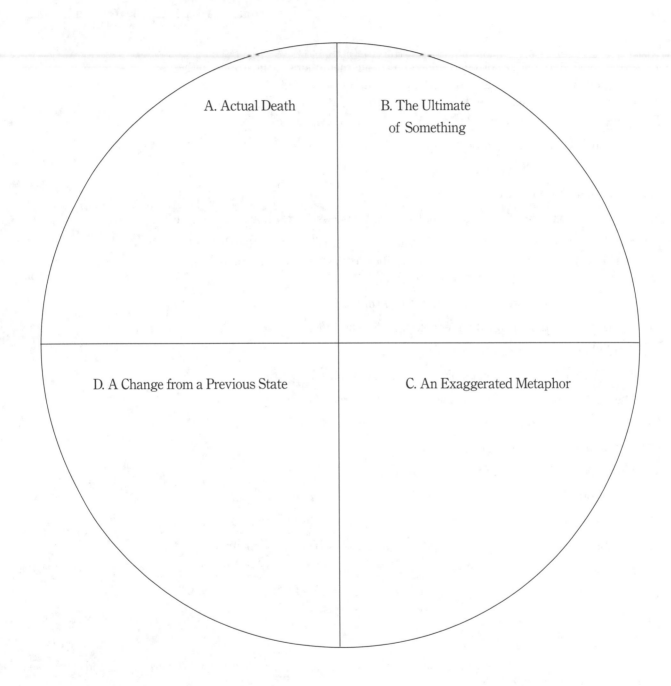

The Remains

Name: _____ **Period:** _____ **Date:** _____

While watching a detective show on television and hearing people talk about a *body*, listeners are left guessing, but as soon as they hear the word *corpse*, they know the victim is dead. *Corpus* is the Latin word for body, which in English evolved into *corpse* with the specialized meaning of a *dead* body, or what is euphemistically referred to as someone's *remains*. These remains, as illustrated in the chart below, are basically of two kinds: spiritual and physical.

Word	Lexical Extensions	Sample Sentences
spiritus (Latin *to blow* or *to breathe*)	aspire aspiration *esprit de corp* expiration expire inspiration inspire spirit spiritual	*Spiritual* experiences are religious experiences. Most churches teach that a Supreme Being endows the *human spirit* with the *breath of life*. In speech, *aspirated sounds* are those that include audible breath noises as with *p, t,* and *h*. Having *school spirit* means enjoying *esprit de corp*, French for having a strong feeling of enthusiasm for a group or a body (*corp*). To *breathe new life* into a project, you need someone who is *inspired* or who has strong *aspirations*. If you partake of *alcoholic spirits*, you may act as if there's a different *spirit* inside you. An alternate way to say someone has died is to say he or she has *expired*.
gast (Old English *breath* or *spirit*)	aghast ghost ghostly Zeitgeist	*Ghost* sometimes has religious connotations as when Christians talk about *The Father, The Son, and The Holy Ghost*. More often it is used with secular meanings as in *ghost stories* and *ghost towns*. To be *aghast* at something is to be shocked or frightened by it. The *ghost of a smile* and a *ghost of a chance* refer to things that are marginal or slight. A *ghost* on a computer, television, or radar screen is barely visible and is most likely a leftover image. A *ghost writer* does the writing that someone else takes credit for. *Zeitgeist* is borrowed from German and means *the ghost* or *the spirit of our time*.
spook	spookery spookily spooky	*Spook* is an old Germanic word for *ghost*. R. L. Stine specializes in *spookery* in his *Ghost Bumps* books. A horse might get *spooked* or frightened by a blowing paper. Someone who moves noiselessly and secretly, like a spy, is a *spook*. James Bond, as Agent 007, is the most famous *spook* in the movies.

bone	bonehead	*Bones* are the longest lasting, and therefore the most dramatic remains,
	boner	of either human or animal bodies.
	boneyard	A horribly emaciated person might be described as being *all skin and bones*.
	bonfire	Another way to describe a *skull session* is to say that students are meeting
	wishbone	to *bone up* for an exam.
		The allusion is to the bone (the skull) that protects peoples' brains, but if we
		call someone a *bonehead* or say the person *pulled a boner*, we are saying
		that all the person has in his head is the *bone*.
		Bone china is a white translucent kind of fine pottery that actually contains
		ash from burned bones.
		Bonfires were originally *bonefires*. The pronunciation was probably changed out
		of respect for the dead, just as we find it more acceptable to talk about
		graveyards rather than *boneyards*.
		If you have a *bone of contention* or a *bone to pick with someone*, you have
		something to discuss that may turn into a quarrel as when dogs fight
		over a bone.
		A *bare-bones existence* is one of poverty.
skeleton	skeletal	A *skeleton outline* is just the *bare bones* of something.
		A *family skeleton* or a *skeleton in the closet* is a secret that you don't want
		to share.
		A *skeleton key* is a basic key that will open various doors.
		Now that large buildings are framed with steel, it seems appropriate to talk
		about a building's *skeleton*.
		The *skeletal remains* of something are the bones.

The terms listed below are all metaphorical uses of words related to a deceased person's remains. Put them in the appropriate blank spaces. One word is used twice.

| bones | dispirited | expiration | ghost | spirited | sprite |

1. A _____ protest is one that has lots of life in it.

2. When you are _____, you are gloomy and discouraged; you are deflated.

3. Plastic fishing nets abandoned to float in oceans or lakes are called _____ nets.

4. The _____ date on your driver's license or on film or medicine tells you when the item is no longer breathing or alive.

5. While _____ used to name a disembodied spirit or a ghost or elf, today it is used as the commercial name for a bubbly drink as well as a way to refer to someone with elfish or lively qualities.

6. If you feel something in your _____, you feel it deeply.

7. A _____ key is so stripped down that it works on many low-quality locks.

8. _____ citations are made by cheaters, who on scholarly papers make up references to nonexistent publications hoping to fool the teacher.

A Crossword Puzzle
on Living and Dying

Name: _____   **Period:** _____   **Date:** _____

Use these clues to work the crossword puzzle.

ACROSS

3. A _____ can be either the beginning of an idea or of an organism.

5. You are _____ if you are shocked or frightened by something.

9. The scientific study of living things is _____.

11. A cognate of *inspire,* the English word _____ is a synonym for *soul.*

13. A _____ solution is one that is workable or still alive.

14. At-risk infants are cared for in the neo _____ unit of hospitals.

15. Someone or something _____ is small, literally "born afterwards."

DOWN

1. When a body is stiff from death, *rigor* _____ has set in.

2. Borrowed from German, _____ means the spirit or ghost of our time.

4. _____ is a name for mercury that stresses its "liveliness."

6. Your _____ makeup determines your physical characteristics.

7. Based on *vivus,* something____ is important to life.

8. Based on *nasci,* your country of birth determines your _____.

10. _____ *de corps* is a phrase English speakers borrowed from French.

12. _____ is such a traumatic event that it has inspired many metaphors.

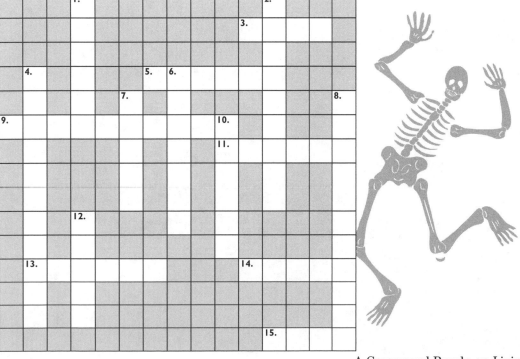

Workshop 7.1: A. 1. preemies, **2.** gestation, **3.** native, **4.** genome, **5.** fetal, **6.** fetus, **7.** conceived, **8.** neonatal. **B. 1.** fetal, **2.** embryonic, **3.** generative, **4.** natural, **5.** aborted, **6.** premature, **7.** birth, **8.** puny.

Workshop 7.2: A. 1. to the quick, **2.** quicksand, **3.** quicksilver, **4.** mercurial. **B. 1.** biomass, **2.** biorhythms, **3.** biopsy, **4.** bionic, **5.** biosatellite. **C. 1.** vivaciously, **2.** vivisection, **3.** vivid, **4.** bon vivant, **5.** viable.

Workshop 7.3: A. 1. mortality rates, **2.** rigor mortis, **3.** morgue, **4.** mortally. **B. 1.** infant mortality, **2.** mortal, **3.** mortuaries, **4.** mortified.

Workshop 7.4: Words and phrases to circle and discuss include the *killer* joke, a *killer* schedule, *cut-throat* competition, *murdering* the English language; comedians *slaying* people; self-*sacrificing* mothers being *martyrs*; *Thanatopsis*, Aimee *Thanatogenous*; *Lethe* (the river), *lethargic*; a controversy *dying down*, languages *dying out*, stadium plans *dying* on the vine, *DieHard* batteries; *assassin* bugs, character *assassination*; political/social *suicide*; a *dead end* street.

Workshop 7.5: A. Actual Death: lethal, killer dogs, three fatalities, death camp. **B. The Ultimate:** dead ahead, death blow, the dead of winter. **C. Exaggerated Metaphor:** died from embarrassment, murderous schedules, killer instinct, political suicide, assassin bugs, the death of me, dressed to kill, the deadwood. **D. A Change:** dying fast, dying out, pretty much dead.

Workshop 7.6: 1. spirited, **2.** dispirited, **3.** ghost, **4.** expiration, **5.** sprite, **6.** bones, **7.** skeleton, **8.** ghost.

Workshop 7.7: Across: 3. germ, **5.** aghast, **9.** bioscience, **11.** spirit, **13.** viable, **14.** natal, **15.** puny. **Down: 1.** mortis, **2.** zeitgeist, **4.** quicksilver, **6.** genetic, **7.** vital, **8.** nationality, **10.** esprit, **12.** death.

End-of-Chapter Activities

1. Here are some movie titles that include words related to birth and death. Without knowing what the movies are about, tell what the titles communicate to you. Which ones do you think are metaphorical and which ones are literal? Why do you think producers include birth and death allusions in their titles?

Born Yesterday	Death Takes a Holiday
Born on the Fourth of July	Dead Man Walking
Born Again	The Death Kiss
Born Free	Death Watch
Born to Be Bad	Dead Poets Society
Birth of a Nation	The Dead Zone
Birth of the Blues	The Dead Cannot Lie
The Birthday Party	Dead Men Don't Wear Plaid
	The Dead End Kids

2. Look on the Internet or in a book designed to help parents choose names for their babies. See what you can find about names related to birth. Vivian Herzog, former Israeli diplomat, has explained that his given name was *Chaim* (the same as the author Chaim Potok), but when he joined the British military, officials translated his Hebrew name to its English equivalent and henceforth he was known as *Vivian*. Apparently both words relate to *life*, similar to the way that in English *Eugene* means "good birth." Why is it more likely that in real life people will give their babies names related to life rather than to death?

3. Names related to death are more likely to appear as place names than as the names for people—for example, *Death Valley* in California and the country of *Mordar* in J. R. R. Tolkien's *The Lord of the Rings*. Look in an atlas to see if you can find similar place names. Do you think they would be given by people who plan to stay and settle a place or by people passing through and wanting to warn others away?

4. Do an exploration of *Gothic humor* showing how, even though it relates to death, it usually makes people smile. *Gothic* refers to a Germanic tribe of medieval times but has broadened to refer to anything associated with medieval ideas or customs. Grotesque gargoyles and other frightening figures decorate Gothic cathedrals. Their purpose was to make people live righteously in hopes of avoiding a bad afterlife, but they were so scary that people gradually changed them into objects of amusement. Relate this to Halloween, which started as *All Hallowed Even*, a prelude to All Saints Day, which falls on the first of November. Can you think of urban legends that in some way relate to death? Do you think that telling such stories and laughing about them help people talk about a subject that truly is scary? Good sources to look at for such stories are the folklore collections of Alvin Schwartz: *Scary Stories to Tell in the Dark* (Lippincott, 1981), *More Scary Stories to Tell in the Dark* (Lippincott, 1984), and *Scary Stories III: More Tales to Chill Your Bones* (HarperCollins, 1991). You might prepare one of these stories to tell to your classmates.

5. Make a collection of "scary" terms such as *coffin, crypt, cemetery, ghouls, ghosts, goosebumps, vampires, black cats, bats, tombstones, monsters, skeletons,* and *haunted houses.* Choose one or two to study. Trace their histories and find examples of modern usages. Which ones are being used metaphorically?

6. Check out a video of a humorous/horror film and do an analysis of the words in it that relate to death. Movies praised for stretching viewers' imaginations between the frightening and the ridiculous include *The Addams Family* (1991), *Addams Family Values* (1993), *Beetlejuice* (1988), *Ghostbusters* (1984), *The Witches of Eastwick* (1987), *Little Shop of Horrors* (1986), and *Batman* (1989), *Batman Returns* (1992), *Batman Forever* (1995), and *Batman and Robin* (1997).

CHAPTER EIGHT

Using Prefixes and Suffixes to Make Comparisons and Contrasts

Teachers' Preface

Linguistic principles being illustrated in this chapter include:

1. Prefixes and suffixes illustrate language efficiency and the skill with which speakers recycle bits and pieces of language.

2. Prefixes are good material to use in helping students understand assimilation, where sounds are influenced by those next to them—for example, when *in-* becomes *il-* if it is followed by an *l* as in *illegal* and *in-* becomes *im-* if it is followed by an *m* as in *immaterial.*

The *Maxi-* and *Macro-* group managed to work in a picture they found of *miniskirts* by explaining they were "the opposite." Among the words they illustrated were *maximum likelihood, Imax* theaters, *macroeconomics,* and *Maxwell Smart.* The making of these posters by students working in small groups gave them lots of practice with such *super-* words as *Superman, superscript, supercilious, superior,* and *supertanker;* and such *sub-* words as *submit, subdivision, subservient, subliminal, submarine sandwich,* and *submerge.*

3. Some words that are generally considered to be opposite really have many similarities. For example, some of the prefixes designed to indicate "opposites" differ in only one or two letters as with *hyper* (above) versus *hypo* (below), *sub* (below) versus *super* (above), and *inter* (within) versus *intra* (without).

4. Prefixes provide good illustrations of how popular spelling patterns "take over" so that speakers have to use what they know about the real world as well as what they know about the meanings of prefixes to understand words such as *antique*, which means something old or something that came before, even though it is spelled with the *anti* (against) spelling instead of with the *ante* (before) spelling.

At least the students who drew these posters for *ante-bellum* and *anti-war* are likely to remember the difference.

5. Words beginning with *ex-* provide good illustrations of how, over centuries, the meanings of words undergo both amelioration and pejoration. For example, to *execute* something meant to carry it out to completion, but today we think first of the most dramatic example of this — when a person is *executed* or killed. To *excuse* someone used to mean to remove pain from the person. While today it still has the meaning of making someone feel more comfortable, it usually refers to situations that are hardly worthy of being called painful.

It must be human nature to want to simplify complex matters by sorting things into two categories. Some historians think that Western cultures are more prone to this than are Eastern cultures because of the influence of the Greek philosopher, Aristotle. Three centuries B.C. he was teaching people how to make discrete judgments. One of his main teachings was that categories are distinct and mutually exclusive, an idea that, with such "squishy" subjects as language analysis, does not always work. Social critics also argue that in many other areas, such *dualistic* thinking oversimplifies matters. In line with this, they caution against dividing everything into opposites as in *yes* versus *no*, *right* versus *wrong*, *black* versus *white*, *boy* versus *girl*, *Democrat* versus *Republican*, *good guy* versus *bad guy*, and so on.

These critics also point out that many of the things speakers describe as opposites are really quite similar. Most speakers will include *man* and *woman* in a list of opposites, but a man and a woman are more alike than, for example, a man and a bear or a woman and a tree. Men and women are adult humans. They walk on two legs and have similar brains and similar speaking capacities. They are opposite only in the feature of gender. The question of their similarities versus their differences is at the root of the argument over whether *man* is a generic term so that women are included as referents in such words and phrases as *mankind*, *to man the barricades*, and *all men are created equal*.

A similar kind of confusion exists when speakers refer to *night* and *day*. In one sense these are opposites in that the earth is dark at night and light in the daytime, but when people talk about 24 hours in a *day*, or about *daily rates* for a hotel or a car rental, they are including *night* as part of *day*.

Even though speakers are sometimes confused over what is meant by *opposites*, in general the concept is tremendously useful. One bit of evidence supporting this is how speakers use prefixes that express "opposite" or contrasting meanings as with *maximum* versus *minimum*, *inductive* versus *deductive*, and *accelerate* versus *decelerate*. With many other prefixes, the "opposite" is not so clearly shown through matching pairs but instead through whole sets of words as illustrated in this chapter's workshops.

Pro and Con

Name: _____ **Period:** _____ **Date:** _____

When people talk about the *pros* and *cons* of something, they are talking about the positives and the negatives.

A. *Pro-* means *forward* as in *progress, project, proposal,* and *propeller.* Since moving forward is generally considered a good thing, *pro-* has become a prefix with positive connotations. This is why there are hundreds of registered trademarks beginning with *pro-* as in *Prozac, Provera,* and *Prolax.* People who create commercial names for new products, especially medicines, look for prefixes that will hint to potential buyers that the product will help them move forward to better health.

Other evidence of how speakers view *pro-* as having positive connotations are the efforts put forth by both sides of the argument about a woman's right to have an abortion. On one side are people who used to be called *anti-abortionists,* but who have worked hard to become known as *pro-life* advocates. On the other side are the people who used to be called *abortionists.* They have worked equally hard to become known as *pro-choice* advocates. Look at the following terms and write the most appropriate ones in the blank spaces in the sentences. Talk about the meanings of the root words and try to figure out how they relate to some kind of a forward movement.

> **I:** propelled proposes prospects protrudes provoke

1. When you figure out your _____, you are looking to the future.
2. If you _____ someone, you call forth an emotional response.
3. Something that _____ sticks out, in contrast to what happens when someone *intrudes* into your business or into your home.
4. When a man _____, he sets out what the future might hold.
5. A person who is _____ to fame is thrust into the public's awareness.

> **II:** prognosis programs promotion protest

1. If you _____ against something, you testify to your objections.
2. When someone gets a _____, the person moves ahead.
3. The _____ handed out at a recital are written records of what is to come.
4. A doctor's _____ consists of what she knows about the future of a patient's condition.

B. **Con-**, as a shortened form of *contra*, means *against*, and it is in this sense that it is used in the phrase *pros and cons*. Children first meet this notion in the nursery rhyme, "Mary, Mary, quite *contrary*…" Adults often see it in the related prefix of *counter-* in such words as *counterbalance, counterevidence,* and *counterculture*. Choose which of these words, with a meaning of *against*, best fits each of the blank spaces below.

> **I.** **contradiction** **contraindicated** **contravene** **controversy** **counteroffensive**

1. To _____ a policy is to violate it, that is, to act in a contrary way.

2. The troops launched a _____, but it was only a moderate success.

3. A _____ is a statement against what someone has said.

4. The doctor said that more exercise was _____ by the condition of his bones.

5. A _____ is made up of many arguments circling around.

The most confusing thing about *con-* is that it does not always come from *contra*. For example, if you read about someone who is a *con man*, the usage *con-* is a shortened form of *confidence*, a word that is based on *com* (with or together) and *fidelity* (trust or faith). When *com-* is used as a prefix meaning *with*, it is often changed to *con-* for easier pronunciation as in such words as *connect, conjugate, conserve,* and *convoy*. This means that when you meet words that begin with *con-,* you have to look carefully at the word and at the context to decide which meaning is intended. Read the following sentences and choose the word that fits best in each blank space. Draw a circle around the *con-* words that relate to coming together. Draw an arrow away from the *con-* words that relate to going against someone or something.

> **II:** **Congress** **contraband** **contractions** **contrasting** **convocation**

1. It makes sense for signal flags on ships to be in _____ colors.

2. The graduation _____ is a last opportunity for class members to speak together.

3. Merwyn got in trouble for having _____.

4. Several Presidents have found that it is not so easy to get _____ to come together.

5. Pregnant women are advised to go to the hospital when their _____ are twenty minutes apart.

| III: | confederates | conjurers | conspire | contractor's | Contras |

1. A _____ job is to pull everything together.

2. When people _____, they plot and scheme together.

3. In the 1980s, the Iran _____ were revolutionaries fighting in Nicaragua.

4. _____ band together to work for mutual goals.

5. Magicians used to be called _____ because of their sleight of hand tricks and the illusions they could bring to people's minds.

C. *Anti-* is another prefix that means *against*. It is often confused with the prefix *ante-*, which means *before*, because in speech the two prefixes sound alike. Some Italian restaurants mistakenly list *antipasto* as the appetizer to be eaten before the pasta. The correct term is *antepasto*. This happens because the *anti* prefix is seen the most often and so when in doubt, spellers tend to rely on it. Something similar happened to *antique*, which is based on *ante* (before or old), but is spelled with an *i*, and also the word *anticipate*, which means to have given advance thought to something. In spite of these exceptions, the usual meaning of *anti-* is *against*, but still you should check the context of your sentences so that you won't get tripped up by making the wrong assumptions about an *anti-war protestor* versus an *antebellum antique* from before the Civil War.

Anti- is such a productive prefix that standard desk dictionaries will list three or four columns of such words including, *anti-AIDS, antiapartheid, antibias, antidiscrimination,* and *antitechnology.* An *antiseptic* might also be called a *germicide* because it kills microorganisms, while an *antigen* is a substance that can stimulate an immune response as when you get a flu shot. Read these sentences and write in the most appropriate words in the blank spaces. Talk about their meanings and make up new sentences using other words with an *anti-* prefix.

| antibiotics | antioxidant | antipathy | antithetical | antitoxin |

1. Someone feeling _____ toward a project has little sympathy for it.

2. An _____ idea is opposite to whatever it is being compared to.

3. Doctors could not devise an effective _____ because the officials would not identify the gas they had used in the hostage situation.

4. In moist climates, you need to paint metals with an _____ to cut down on the rust.

5. Doctors worry that their patients rely too much on _____ for things that aren't really serious.

The Good and the Bad

Name: _____ **Period:** _____ **Date:** _____

The following prefixes "with attitude" express speakers' opinions of things as being either good or bad. They are the verbal equivalent of such body language as thumbs-up versus thumbs-down and a smile versus a frown. After you read the paragraphs, use what you know about the real world and about the other morphemes in the listed words to see if you can figure out which word is best to write in each of the blank spaces. So that you can get used to the way these morphemes are used, read the sentences aloud and talk about their meanings. Try making up other sentences and also finding other words that include these morphemes. At least for the prefixes, this will be easy because they will be in the same parts of your dictionary as are the listed words. However, you will need to be careful to read the etymological information and to think about the definitions because there are likely to be other words, that happen to start the same but are not based on the particular prefixes we are working with.

A. **Eu-** comes from Greek and means *well* or *good*. *Euphoria* is a feeling of satisfaction and happiness. In Christian religions, the *Eucharist* refers to the Holy Communion or to a Sacrament, which is a symbol of gratitude and rejoicing. *Euphemisms* are pleasant-sounding words used to soften harsh concepts. For example, because *death* is a word that frightens people, speakers use such *euphemisms* as *passed on, deceased,* and *gone to Heaven*. One of the earliest *euphemisms* is the word *Eumenides*, which literally means "good spirited." The ancient Greeks gave this name to *The Furies*, hoping to appease them.

    Eugenics is the study of how selective mating can improve the hereditary qualities of people or breeds of animals. The word was coined in the late 1800s by people who thought this was a good thing, but by the time Hitler and his fellow Nazis advocated *eugenics* in the 1930s and 1940s, most people were either skeptical of or hostile to the idea.

Eugene	eulogy	euphemisms	euphonious	euphoric

1. The person at a funeral who gives the _____ is of course expected to say kind words about the deceased.

2. The name _____ means something like "well born."

3. A performance by a middle school band is likely to be more cacophonous than _____.

4. After a long, cold winter, the first warm day of spring makes people feel _____.

5. Such words as *restroom, powder room, ladies' room,* and *washroom* are all _____ related to people's hesitation to talk about bodily functions.

B. *Mal-* has an almost opposite meaning to *eu-*. Someone who is *maladjusted* is poorly adjusted, while someone who is *malicious* is mean or full of *malice*. Today we know that mosquitoes spread *malaria*, but when the disease was first named in the 1700s, it was named for *bad air*, because people got the disease when they were in hot and swampy places where the air was *malodorous* (it smelled bad). If someone has a *malady*, the person has a disease or a diagnosed medical condition, while if someone suffers from *malaise* the person is uncomfortable or suffering from vague feelings of emotional or physical distress. Less common *mal-* words include *mal de mer* for seasickness, *malediction* for bad or *malicious* speech, *malapportioned* for an unfair division of voters, and *maladroit* for someone who is awkward.

Malapropisms are words that are inappropriate. The idea of something being *malapropos* has been in the language since the late 1600s, but in 1775, the playwright Richard Brinsley Sheridan made the idea famous by putting a humorous character named *Mrs. Malaprop* in his play, *The Rivals*. *Mrs. Malaprop* made so many mistakes with language that her name is now in the dictionary to define the kinds of mistakes that Archie Bunker made on "All in the Family." His mistakes included talking about America's *grossest national product*, the great explorer *Marco Polish*, the *Dunn and Broadstreet* investment company, and Mark Twain's book about *Blackberry Finn*.

malformed	malice	malignant	malnourished	malpractice

1. If you have a _____ tumor, you have cancer.

2. He holds so much _____ toward his parents that he says he will not attend their funerals.

3. Today you can look on the Internet to see which doctors in your area have been sued for

   _____.

4. People whose bodies have been badly burned or otherwise damaged might be described as

   _____.

5. _____ children often have protruding stomachs.

C. *Bene-* is often used to indicate the opposite of words that start with *mal-*. A *benign* tumor is one that is harmless as compared to a *malignant* tumor, which is cancerous. While *malediction* means *bad speech*, a *benediction* is *good speech* as in a prayer. Fifteen popes have chosen the name of *Benedict* because of its good connotations, as also seen in the name of the *Benedictine Order* of monks and nuns. A *benefaction* is "a good work" or a charitable donation. Someone who is *benevolent* wishes people well, while an insurance company or a health care group that puts *beneficial* in its name is trying to convince people that it has their best interests at heart.

benediction	benefactors	benefits	benevolence

1. There is a long history of artists and writers needing _____ to provide them with financial support.

2. When deciding on a job, people need to consider the fringe _____ as well as the salary.

3. She was asked to give the _____, which is the closing prayer at the evening service.

4. People in really poor countries often have mixed feelings about the _____ of wealthier countries.

D. *Orth-* means that something is *correct* or *right*. The meaning can refer to something concrete as with an *orthogon*, which is a figure with only *right angles*, or to something more abstract as with *orthodox* religious beliefs, which are considered to be the *right* beliefs by those who hold them. *Orthopedic* surgeons try to correct broken or misshapen bones, while *orthotics* is a branch of medicine that focuses on designing and prescribing supports or braces to help people straighten and strengthen weak joints or muscles. An *orthographic projection* is a straight-on picture of an item, while something described as *orthostatic* relates to people standing up straight.

orthodontics	Orthodox	orthoscopic

1. _____ Jews begin their Sabbath at sundown on Fridays.

2. As fluoride cuts down on cavities, a bigger percentage of dentists are specializing in _____, which is straightening teeth.

3. An _____ microscope presents images in their correct and normal proportion.

E. *Mis-* comes from an Old English verb *missan*, meaning much the same as it does today when speakers talk about *missing* a bus or *missing* out on an opportunity. Because when people *miss* something, it is usually a negative experience, the word gradually became a prefix communicating that something was bad as with *mistakes, misbehavior,* and *misperceptions*. A word that has fairly recently come into common use is *misspoke*, as a euphemism for *lying*. People working in public relations do not want to stand in front of television cameras and confess that whoever they work for told a lie, and so they apologize and "set the record straight" by explaining that their boss *misspoke*.

misaligned	miscarriages	misdiagnosed	misgivings

1. Most _____ occur during the first three months of pregnancy.

2. If your wheels are _____, your tires will wear out sooner.

3. Patients who seek out a second opinion are checking to be sure their condition has not been _____.

4 She had some real _____ about moving to a new town.

Directions: Near and Far

Name: _____ Period: _____ Date: _____

A. Com- means *with* or *together* as in such word as *combo, committee,* and *combine*. *Panis* is the Latin word for *bread* as seen in *companion*, which refers to people who share bread *with* each other. *Companies* are made up of many people who eat their bread together, while *combatants* are people who go with each other into battle. Sometimes the *m* is left off in such words as *cooperate, coordinate,* and *co-editor*. Other times, the *m* is changed to an *n* as in *configure, confide,* and *conduct*.

combined	comfort	compared	complete

1. People are usually relieved when they _____ their Christmas shopping.

2. Two candidates might be _____ with each other to see if they are equal (on *par*) to the task ahead.

3. In a battle, the soldiers who are able to _____ others are the ones who act with strength and fortitude.

4. The *bi* in *combine* means *two*, but today we talk about more than two things being _____.

B. Dis- means *apart* as with the word *distant*, which literally means *standing apart*. This prefix often has a negative connotation because it refers to a change in something that was considered to be the way it should be. If someone complains about being *dissed*, the person is using slang to complain about being moved away from a position of *respect*. A person who is *disconcerted* is acting strangely (not *in concert* with expectations), while something that is *discolored* has been damaged. Once money has been *disbursed* or *distributed*, it is gone. The words *discord* and *discourage* relate to *cor*, the Latin word for *heart*. They are similar in meaning to describing someone as *disheartened*. A person's *disposition* is the way the person moves emotionally from a central position toward either happiness and joy or toward depression and hostility. Occasionally, a *dis* word is viewed as a good thing as when someone *disinfects* a place suspected of being dirty or having germs or when someone *discovers* a treasure.

disagreement	disbands	discovered	distrust

1. When a group _____, it moves away from the bonds (probably metaphorical) that banded the members together.

2. Their basic _____ drove a wedge between Josie and her parents.

3. If you _____ someone, you have moved your trust away from the person.

4. If your secret has been _____ or *disclosed*, it has been moved from its *cover* or *closet*.

C. *De-* is a Middle English prefix meaning *down* or *away from* as when someone does the opposite of something. This meaning of opposition can be seen in such words as *deny, denigrate, destroy, deceive, descend,* and *de-empasize.* To *decline* an invitation is literally to turn it down. A teacher who teaches *inductively* uses supporting details to lead students into the main idea, while one who teaches *deductively* states the main idea and then expects students to take from that idea the smaller ones they need to know.

decentralized	decried	decriminalization	defaced	despise

1. The giant Buddha destroyed by the Taliban in Afghanistan had already been _____ centuries earlier.

2. If you _____ someone, you look down on him or her.

3. The _____ of marijuana is likely to remain a political issue.

4. If a company _____, it assigns leadership responsibilities to different people probably located in different parts of the country or the world.

5. The press _____ his claims of having never been influenced by campaign contributions.

D. *Trans-* means *across* as shown in the name of *Trans World Airlines* and the *transatlantic cable* that first allowed messages to be sent from Europe to America. *Translators* take a message from one language *across* to another, while someone *transcribing* proceedings in court *transfers* oral talk to a written record. When speakers talk about something *transpiring,* they are implying that whatever happened was as natural as *breathing.*

transact	transcend	Transcontinental	transfer	transmission

1. To _____ one's problems means to climb (or *ascend*) over them.

2. When pioneers heading west crossed the _____ Divide, they were undoubtedly happy to know that it would be downhill from there on.

3. The _____ in a car is crucial because it *transmits* the revolutions of the engine to the axle, which turns the wheels.

4. I hope my Advanced Placement credits will _____ to my college.

5. You need to know the language if you are going to _____ business in a foreign country.

E. **In-** has two quite different meanings. In one sense, it expresses negation in a work like *innocent,* which literally means "not to harm," but in the sense we will look at here, its meaning is directional as shown in such words as *inside, income,* and *infuse.* To *induct* an officer of an organization is to lead (from *ducere*) the person *into* new responsibilities, perhaps through an *induction* ceremony. A person who is an *incumbent* is already *in* the position. Being *inspired* to do something is as if you have *breathed in* a good feeling. If you get *involved* in something, you are *rolling* (from *volvere*) with it. When *in-* comes before words beginning with *p,* speakers have made the words easier to say by changing the prefix to *im-,* as shown by *impeach, impede, impelled, impending,* and *imprinted.*

| *in loco parentis* | indigenous | infringes | inoculated |

1. There is always a question about when someone's freedom _____ on the rights of another person.

2. When people get_____, they take something into their body as a protection.

3. _____ is a Latin phrase used to define the responsibilities of school and camp officials who are acting in the place of a child's parents.

4. A tree that is _____ to an area has been growing there as long as anyone can remember.

F. **Inter-** is related to *in,* but its meaning is in some ways opposite because it means *among* or *between* as when libraries cooperate to form an *interlibrary* loan system. When two people come together to *interface* on a possible solution to a problem, they are coming from different positions. The *Interstate Highway* system connects the continental United States, while an *interactive* video game allows the players to influence what will come on the screen.

| interacting | interception | interchange | international | to intermarry |

1. People can seldom find solutions to problems until they start _____ with those on the other side.

2. The Internet allows for a much quicker _____ of information across _____ boundaries.

3. Because today so many people from different races get married, the practice is no longer considered unusual and the term _____ is dropping out of English.

4. Many a football game has been won by a lucky _____.

G. *Intra-* is another related prefix, which comes much closer to the expected meaning of *inside*. *Intramural* sports are conducted with athletes from inside the walls (*murus* is Latin for *wall*) of their school. If the doctor gives you an *intramuscular* injection, you will probably feel it longer than if the injection is made just under your skin. An *intravascular* injection must go into a blood vessel.

| intrapersonal | intraplate | intraspecies | intravenously |

1. A person who has _____ problems has worries occurring within the person's own mind.

2. After surgery, people are usually fed _____ for at least a few hours.

3. Zoologists often find diseases that are _____, meaning they will not spread from one kind of animal to another.

4. An _____ earthquake occurs within the interior of a tectonic plate.

Ex- Marks the Spot

Name: _____ Period: _____ Date: _____

Ex- comes fairly close to being the opposite of the directional *in.* Common words that illustrate the meaning of *away from* include *exit, export, external,* and *exhaust.* It may be that the common use of *ex-* to mean *away from* or *beyond* influenced mathematicians and scientists to use *x* to stand for things that are unknown. *X-rays* were so named because their discoverers did not know what they were. In algebraic equations, people solve for *X* as the unknown, and when companies want to imply high-tech or scientific association they will put an *X* in their name, as with the *Xerox* company and with such car models as the *Mazda RX-7, the Nissan Maxima GXE* and *Pulsar NX,* and the *Honda Accord LX.* The *Ford Ranger XLT* has the extra advantage of looking like an abbreviation for *excellent.*

A. The beginnings of the following sentences are written with words showing the directional concept of *in-.* Read the sentences and complete them using a "matching" *ex-* term so as to illustrate how *in-* words and *ex-* words can serve as opposites.

1. An *inclusive* organization tries to make room for everyone who wants to join, while _____

_____ .

2. An *intramural* program is one that takes place within the walls (*mur*) of a school, while _____

_____ .

3. An *incision* (compare to *scissors*) is a cut into someone's body, while _____

_____ .

4. An *internal* memo is not to be shared beyond the office, while _____

_____ .

5. If you *impose* on someone, you insert yourself into their affairs, while if you _____

_____ .

B. When someone is described as an *ex-wife,* an *ex-convict,* or an *ex-president,* the speaker is talking about someone who has moved away from the position. An *ex-officio* member of a committee is coming, almost as a guest, from another office as when a past president is an *ex-officio* member of a board of directors. *Expatriates* are people who no longer live in their home countries or *fatherlands.* Here are some other words that include *ex-.* Study the sentences and try to fit the most appropriate words in the blank spaces. Talk about the meanings and see if you can make up other sentences using these or related words.

| I: | expired | extradited | extraordinary | extremities | *The Exorcist* |

1. One of the most gruesome movies of all time was _____, in which a young girl was possessed by the devil.

2. People with diabetes have to watch for signs of poor circulation in their _____.

3. Accused criminals are often _____ from other countries, meaning the country where they are living or hiding agrees to *expel* them and send them back to the country where they are wanted.

4. A euphemism for death is to say that a person has _____, which means that the air has gone out of the individual.

5. Something that is _____ is far from the usual.

| II: | ex cathedra | expedition | expelled | expurgate |

1. If you are _____ from school, you are *propelled outward*.

2. An excursion that includes walking or marching is best described as an _____, because this word makes use of the Latin morpheme for *foot*.

3. When a person is speaking from a position of authority, it might be described as _____, in a comparison to how bishops spoke from their cathedrals.

4. Censors often want to _____ or purge words or sentences from books before they are printed as school textbooks.

C. In some instances, fashions and customs have changed so that the original meanings of words are unknown to ordinary speakers. The result is that what used to be a metaphorical meaning is now viewed as a basic meaning. For example, *explode* (from *plaudere=clap)* is related to the word *applaud*. Around 1600, it was used to describe situations in which audiences clapped bad performers off the stage. Perhaps this is why stage productions that fail are called *bombs*, but the main point in relation to this lesson is that, because of technological developments, today's speakers are more likely to think of gunpowder and bombs than of people clapping when they hear the words *explode* and *explosion*.

   The following sentences use *ex-* words in ways that in earlier times were considered basic or literal, but like *explode*, they have developed other meanings that today seem more basic. See if you can devise sentences that use the words as they are most likely to be used today and talk about the relationship to the older meanings in these sentences and the newer meanings that you think of.

1. In the days before antibiotics, it was common for nurses to have to push on wounds to *express* the pus.

2. An *exodus* is a road leading out of someplace.

3. To *execute* something is to carry it out to completion.

4. To *extort* something is to get it by twisting as when you unscrew something.

5. To *exonerate* someone is to remove a load (an *onerous* burden) from the person.

6. To *excuse* someone is to remove pain.

Just Say No

Name: _____ **Period:** _____ **Date:** _____

Un- is one of most common prefixes to show that a word is negative. One of the dictionaries we looked in listed more than ten columns of *un-* words; for example, *unpredictable, unresponsive, unsolvable, unsinkable,* and *unforgiving.* The *un-* prefix is an alternate way of pronouncing *in-*, as with such words as *insecure, inactive, inconsiderate, incurable,* and *incompatible.*

In the last century, two negative prefixes (*in* and *non*) were at the root of an argument over what should be painted on the sides of tanker trucks or railroad cars that carried gasoline, fertilizer, or other substances that could burn. Such tankers used to be identified with *inflammable* (cognate with *to enflame*), where the intended meaning was that the tank's cargo could burst *into* flames. Some speakers were confused and thought the message meant *NOT flammable*. The drivers of trucks carrying milk did not want to be viewed as dangerous and so they had *noninflammable* painted on their trucks, but this just added to the confusion, especially since such a long word could not be immediately read and interpreted. Finally, someone pointed out that *flammable* said something would burn, while *not flammable* was easier to understand than *noninflammable*.

Today when so many different kinds of chemicals are transported, a simple two-way distinction between *flammable* and *nonflammable* does not provide enough information. Enclosed trucks, as well as boxcars and tankers are equipped with diamond-shaped sign holders where information can be slipped in for each different cargo. The signs provide firefighters and safety inspectors with coded messages about the possible dangers of both air and ground pollution as well as the likelihood of fire.

A. Read these sentences and talk about their meanings. Put LOC over the italicized words whose meanings are locational. Put an X through the italicized words in which *in-* is expressing negation.

1. *Insider trading* is one of the things that contributed to the economic troubles of the early twenty-first century.

2. Something that is *incredible* is hard to believe.

3. Americans celebrate July 4th as *Independence Day*.

4. In elections, *incumbents* usually have an advantage over their opponents because the voters already know them.

5. *Insubordination* will not be tolerated in an Army unit.

6. Babies who are conceived through *in vitro* (*vitro=glass*) fertilization can still be genetically related to both parents.

7. The *indignities* suffered by prisoners of war are almost as bad as the physical punishments.

8. Someone who is *incognito* will probably not be recognized.

B. Now use what you know about the real world and about the morphemes in the following words to figure out which of these negative *in-* words to write in each of the blank spaces.

inanimate	incomparable	indecency	indifferent	infirmaries

1. People can be arrested for public _____ based on a number of different actions.

2. She was _____ to her parents' wishes.

3. *It* is the appropriate pronoun to use for _____ objects.

4. Colleges and boarding schools have _____ for students who are not sick enough to go to a hospital but are too sick to stay alone in a dormitory.

5. There is nothing that is *on par* or equal to an _____ experience.

   Several other prefixes (*il-, ir-,* and *im-*) also make words negative. These are alternative forms of *in-*, which have been assimilated; that is, their pronunciation has been changed by the sounds that follow them. When complete assimilation occurs, the *n* sound becomes the same as the sound that follows. When partial assimilation occurs, the *n* changes to something that will get the speaker's mouth in a better position to say the sound that follows.

C. *Il-* has been created through assimilation in such words as *illicit* and *illusory*. To see why the *n* has been replaced by an *l*, pronounce *inlegal* and *illegal* and notice how *illegal* is easier to say. You might do the same experiment with the following words as you decide which one to write in each of the blank spaces.

illegible	illegitimate	illiterate	illogical

1. A person who is _____ does not know how to read or write.

2. Even though most people's signatures are _____, they still work well for identification.

3. People who can spot _____ thinking in their friends often cannot see it in themselves.

4. _____ insurance claims cause premiums to go up for everyone.

D. *Im-* is used as a negative prefix for *in-* probably more often than it is used as a directional prefix. Examples include such words as *improbable, immoderate, impropriety, impersonal,* and *impure.* As you figure out which word to write in the following sentences, again notice how it would be harder for you to say these words if they started with *in-*.

immaterial	immortal	impassable	imperfection	imprudent

1. Some artists purposely leave a little _____ in their work as a mark of their own humility.

2. The roads over the mountain range are _____ from late December to late February.

3. She said the pay was _____, but I find that hard to believe.

4. The gods in Greek and Roman myths are _____, meaning they cannot die.

5. I think that sneaking out after the teacher has taken the roll would be _____.

E. *Ir-* prefixes are fully assimilated in such words as *irrational* and *irregular*. Probably because they are thinking of *irrespective* and *regardless*, some speakers add the *ir-* prefix to *regardless* to create *irregardless*. This is considered nonstandard English because *regardless* is already negative. As you figure out which of these words to write in the blank spaces, notice how they would be harder to say if they started with *in-*.

> **irradicable**   **irreconcilable**   **irreproducible**   **irrespective**   **irretrievable**

1. An _____ condition is one that cannot be erased.

2. _____ differences are often given as the reason for a divorce.

3. The judge asked for documents that the attorneys say are _____.

4. Scientists are unimpressed with research studies that are _____.

5. Class rankings are made _____ of ethnic identification.

F. *A-* is a negative prefix assimilated from the Latin and Greek *un-*. The most confusing thing about it is that there also exists an Old English prefix *a-* that indicates location when used in such expressions as *abed, afloat,* and *afire.* When you run across words beginning with *a-,* you will have to use what you know about the world and the other words in the sentence to figure out if the meaning is negative, as it is in the following sentences.

> **amoral**   **anonymous**   **apolitical**   **atrophy**   **atypical**

1. Promising something he had no intention of giving was _____.

2. Even though her uncle is governor, she claims to be totally _____.

3. An _____ article is one without an author listed.

4. An _____ approach is one that is out of the ordinary.

5. If a muscle does not get exercise and nourishment, it is likely to _____.

Above and Below

Name: _____ **Period:** _____ **Date:** _____

A. *Sub-* means *under* both in a literal and a metaphorical sense. In the literal sense, a *submarine* goes underwater, while a *subway* is a train that runs underneath a roadway. Anything that is *subpar* (from *parity*, meaning equal) is below what is expected. To do something *sub rosa* is to do it secretly or in private. The term alludes to the ancient secret Society of the Rose. To *sublimate* one's interest in sex or some other basic instinct is to push it down below the threshold of consciousness. People do this by diverting their impulses to actions that are considered socially acceptable. Use what you know about the real world and about the following morphemes to figure out which word to write in each of the blank spaces.

> **I:** submerge submits subscribe subservience subzero

1. When a writer _____ an article to be considered by an editor, the writer is showing _____.

2. To *merge* is to plunge or blend together, so to _____ something usually refers to putting it under water.

3. Considering the wind chill factor, school children in the Midwest often play outside in _____ temperatures.

4. When you _____ to a magazine, you, in effect, sign your name on the bottom line of an agreement.

> **II:** subdivide subjects subjugating sublease subtitles

1. The _____ in movies are the translations that run across the bottom of the screen.

2. As soon as land developers come in and _____ large plots of land, the taxes are likely to be raised.

3. In medieval days, landowners had to walk a fine line between supporting and _____ the peasants who worked for them.

4. The king's _____ were the people under his control.

5. People who have the benefit of controlled prices on their New York apartments are not supposed to _____ them.

B. *Super-* means above, sometimes in a literal sense as with a *superscript* (a raised number or letter) in typing and with *supercilious*, which describes someone who is haughty. This latter idea is a metaphor, based on the image of someone who goes around with raised eyebrows (from Latin *supercilium*). More commonly, *super-* means *above* in the metaphorical sense of something that is *superior* or *super*. This is why kids talk about things being *super duper* and why a soup-and-salad restaurant makes a pun in its name of *Souper Salad*®. If someone loses a case in *Superior* Court, there is still the chance of appealing to the *Supreme* Court. A *superordinate* is a person who is *superior* in rank, while a *subordinate* is the opposite. A law that *supercedes* another one sits above it, while a *superstructure* is built atop or based on a lower structure. A *supertanker* can carry more than a regular tanker, just as a *supermarket* sells more things than does a convenience store. Use what you know about the real word and about these words to figure out the best word to write in each of the following blank spaces.

> | Super Bowl | superlatives | *Superman* | supersonic | "The Super" |

1. A person who speaks in ———————————————— exaggerates or goes overboard.

2. ———————————————— was one of the most successful comic books of the 1940s.

3. The windows in our house rattle whenever a ———————————————— plane goes over.

4. The ———————————————— draws a bigger worldwide television audience than any other event.

5. In the movies, people who live in big apartment houses are always calling for ———————————————— to fix things that are broken.

C. *Hyper-* means much the same as *super-* in the metaphorical sense of something being above or beyond, but it is more likely to be used in a negative sense. A *hyperactive* child may be suffering from ADHD (Attention Deficit Hyperactivity Disorder), while someone who is *hyperbolic* tends to exaggerate or overstate things. When speakers complain about all the *hype* for an upcoming event, they are implying that someone is overdoing the publicity. A *hyperparasite* is a parasite that lives on another parasite. Someone with a condition of *hyperthyroidism* has an overactive thyroid, while someone who is *hypercorrect* is too concerned about trivial matters of etiquette or speech. Based on this information, see if you can fit the most appropriate word in each of the blank spaces below.

| hyperbole | hypercritical | hyperglycemia | hyperirritability | hyperventilate |

1. It is hard for an athlete to stay enthused if the coach is _____ .

2. People who _____ breathe so fast and so shallowly that they are in danger of fainting.

3. What some people view as lying, others view as playful _____ .

4. Various medical conditions can cause _____ .

5. A diabetic with _____ is suffering from an excess of glucose, or sugar, in the blood and needs to have insulin.

D. *Hypo-* means *under* or *lower than*. A person with *hypoglycemia* has low blood sugar and needs to periodically eat something with glucose or sugar in it. This is the opposite of a person with *hyperglycemia*. In research, the *hypothesis* is the idea that scientists are using as the foundation for their experiments. A *hypodermic* syringe is one that should be injected under the skin. A *hypochondriac* is a person who is unduly worried about being sick. The word literally refers to the top of the abdomen that is under the cartilage of a person's breastbone. This is the part of the body that ancient people thought to be the source of worries. Use this information, along with what you have learned about other words, to help you figure out which of these words fit best in the blank spaces of the following sentences.

| hypocenter | hypogastric | hypotension | hypoxemia |

1. _____ is deficient oxygenation of the blood.

2. _____ is low blood pressure, as opposed to *hypertension,* which is high blood pressure.

3. The _____ is the point directly under a nuclear blast.

4. _____ pains are in the lower abdomen.

Time Out

Name: _____ Period: _____ Date: _____

Although some words related to time are viewed as "opposites," as with *day* and *night* and *sunrise* and *sunset*, most time words show relationships or comparisons. Because we refer to concepts about time so frequently, this is an obvious semantic area to make use of prefixes. Some prefixes already discussed have specialized meanings in relation to time. For example, *inter-* as in *intermission* is a period set aside for performers and audience members to have a little rest between parts of a performance. In medieval times, so much food was served at the great banquets that performers were brought in to entertain at *interludes* between courses so that people's food could digest. Some colleges offer *intersession* courses between semesters. Since the classes have to meet for several hours each day, students might complain that they seem *interminable*, meaning *never ending*. After reading these basic definitions of other words related to time, see if you can choose the correct word to write in the sentence blanks.

A. *Anno-* relates to year, as in *annual*.

> anniversaries   Anno Domini   annuals   annuity   biennial

1. A _____ report comes out every two years.

2. The A.D. in dates stands for _____, which means *The Year of Our Lord*.

3. Married couples celebrate their golden _____ when they have been married for fifty years.

4. Plants that are _____ complete their growing cycle in only one year.

5. An _____ is a fixed sum of money that is paid every year.

B. *Ante-* means *before,* as when people talk about the time before the U.S. Civil War as *antebellum* (*bellum=war*). When poker players say "Ante up!", they are telling all the players to put their money (or their chips) on the table so the players will know how big the stakes are. In political negotiations, it is common to hear allusions to one side or the other *raising the ante*, meaning they are asking for more concessions from the other side. The most confusing thing about this prefix is that in speech it sounds like *anti*, which means *against*.

> antecedent   antediluvian   ante meridian   antepasto

1. At an Italian restaurant the _____ salads are to be eaten before the pasta.

2. Something _____ is older than Noah because the term means before the flood or deluge.

3. In grammar, the _____ to a pronoun is the noun that comes before it in the sentence or the paragraph.

4. When we tell someone to be someplace at 10:00 A.M., we are using an abbreviation for _____, meaning before the middle of the day.

C. *Post-* means *after,* so if we tell someone to come at 10:00 P.M., we are using an abbreviation for *post meridian*, meaning after the middle of the day. In the history of the United States, the *postcolonial period* starts after the Revolutionary War, while in the arts, the *postmodern* period started in the 1950s as a reaction against what was then called *modern* art. College students who go on to do *postgraduate* work are usually rewarded with better jobs because they have studied longer and have learned more. New mothers who suffer from *postpartum blues* should probably seek psychological help for their feelings of depression after the birth of a baby. Patients who have had surgery need to pay careful attention to their doctor's instructions about *postoperative care.*

post hoc	postlude	postmortem	postpone	P.S.

1. The _____ at a religious service is the music played at the end while people leave the chapel.

2. If you _____ something, you *position* it to a later time.

3. _____ evidence is sort of like Monday-morning football in which people use what happened to argue for what should have been done differently.

4. A _____ is literally an examination of a body after death, but it might also be a meeting by a campaign team that has come together after their candidate lost an election to talk about what they could do better next time.

5. If you add a _____ to a letter, you are adding a *post script*, meaning something after your *manuscript* was finished.

D. *Pre-* means *before,* as in *prewar* as opposed to *postwar* and *pretest* as opposed to *posttest*. People who believe in *predestination* believe that their lives were planned before they were born. Someone with *prescience* has foreknowledge of the future, perhaps through divine help. When people talk about *pre-Columbian* America, they are talking about anytime prior to 1492. A baby born before nine months is *premature*. If something is *preempted*, it is taken over, as when a television program is *preempted* by a sports event.

I:	prefabricated	preface	preflight	premonition	preparing

1. When the soldier's wife saw two officers arriving in a taxi, she had a _____ of the dreadful news that was to come.

2. The invention of _____ houses did a lot to solve the housing shortage after World War II.

3. Now that people are more worried about safety, _____ preparations are more complicated.

4. When going camping, you can cut down on the confusion by _____ well.

5. If you read the _____ to a book, you may understand it better.

II:	prefixes	prelude	prep(are)	preposition	prequel

1. Emergency rooms often do not have the time to properly _____ patients before they go in for surgery.

2. Authors who have a popular book sometimes write a _____, in which they tell what was happening to the characters before the first book.

3. The _____ music at church helps to get the congregation settled in their seats before the service starts.

4. In English grammar, a _____ comes at the beginning of a phrase telling the position of something.

5. As shown in this chapter, _____ are morphemes that come at the first of words.

E. *Fore-* is a shortened way of saying *before,* and it can be used both in relation to time and to space. With space it means something that is in front as with someone's *forehead* or *forearm* or the *forerunner* (*frontrunner*) in an election. With time it means something that has come first as in such words as *foretell* and *foreshadow.*

foreboding	forecasting	forecloses	foreshadowing	foreword

1. The _____ in a book is a few *words* placed *before* the main part of the book.

2. My grandmother says that her arthritic knee does a better job of _____ the weather than does the TV weather person.

3. J. K. Rowling was good at _____ who would be Harry's friends and who would be his enemies.

4. The D. C. sniper filled many people with _____.

5. When a bank _____ on a mortgage, it takes the mortgaged property before the end of the specified time, probably because the owners were unable to keep up their payments.

F. *Neo-* means *new* as exemplified by premature babies being sent to the *neonatal* unit in a hospital to get special care. *Neo-Nazis* are a new generation who are reviving the beliefs of Hitler and the Nazis.

| neolithic | neologism | neon | neophyte | Neosporin® |

1. A _____ is a new word.

2. A _____ is a novice or a new convert to something.

3. _____ is an ointment, whose name was chosen by manufacturers to hint that it will help grow new spores or skin.

4. The _____ age is the latest period of the Stone Age when people had weapons made of polished stone.

5. The name of _____ lights, which date only to 1898, tells that the gas that makes them glow is a newly discovered substance.

G. Re- has the basic meaning of *again* as in *repeat*, *reconsider*, and *record*. A *recursive* function in a computer is one that keeps repeating itself. When this accidentally happens, some programmers say their computer has gone into *Sorcerer's Apprentice mode*, alluding to a scene in Walt Disney's *Fantasia* when, as the sorcerer, Mickey Mouse does not know how to stop the brooms that he has ordered to do the sweeping. If someone *reneges* on an agreement, the person is *renouncing* or going back on what was previously *negotiated*. When people *refinance* their homes, they turn in their old mortgages and repeat the process of getting new ones, probably in hopes of reducing their interest rates. When someone sends you a phone or electricity bill and asks you to *remit* the money, they are asking you to send the payment back. If you are *reminded* about something, it is brought *again* to your mind. When things are *recapitulated*, the terms of an agreement are being repeated or summarized.

| reconcile | recreation | recurrent | reflect | renewal |

1. We are hoping that the family members can come together and _____ their disagreements.

2. Complaining about growing up in a bad neighborhood is a _____ theme with my uncle.

3. _____ is literally supposed to restore people, that is, to make them as good as new.

4. Urban _____ has both its supporters and its detractors.

5. To _____ on something is to bend one's thoughts to it.

Actor or Agent Suffixes

Name: _____   **Period:** _____   **Date:** _____

Here are brief definitions of some suffixes that are commonly used to identify actors—most often people who are responsible for bringing about specified actions. Read about their basic meanings and then, using what you know about the root words and the clues that are given in the sample sentences, see if you can figure out which of the listed words to write in each of the blank spaces.

A. *-or* and *-er* are used to identify people who do something as with a *singer* who sings or an *instructor* who instructs. Because *-or* and *-er* sound alike, some agentive nouns are spelled with either an *-or* or an *-er* as when people write about either *the convenor* or *the convener* of a meeting or about either a *conveyor belt* or a *conveyer belt*. If you are in doubt about whether a *doer* word ends with *-er* or *-or*, you will need to look it up in a dictionary so as to keep from confusing a *minor* (a young person) with a *miner* (someone who mines). A general rule is that more common words likely to be spelled with an *-er*; for example, *teacher, dancer,* and *shopper*.

counselors	dictators	donors	tractor	transformers

1. Blood _____ are people who give or donate their blood to an organization such as the Red Cross.

2. At Hoover Dam on the Arizona/Nevada border, giant_____ are at work changing water power into usable electricity.

3. _____ are powerful rulers who tell (*dictate to*) people what to do, as opposed to letting the people vote.

4. We get the word for _____ from Latin *tractus*, meaning to pull.

5. One way to judge a school is by how many _____ it has in comparison to how many students.

B. *-ee* indicates that someone has received or benefited from a specific action as have *appointees, trustees, grantees,* and *addressees*. Police officers refer to *detainees* (people who are being *detained*) as well as to *escapees* (those who have escaped). Traffic schools send lists of *enrollees* to the Motor Vehicle Division to document that they should be excused from paying their fines. In most instances these people are the receivers of some kind of action. An *amputee* has had a body part cut off, while a *nominee* has been nominated for an office.

absentee	attendees	devotee	employees	trainee

1. As a _____, she did not dare to question company policies.

2. All company _____ are expected to contribute to the holiday toy drive.

3. Election results were delayed because 240,000 _____ ballots that had been dropped off at the polls had to be counted.

4. As a _____ of Sigmund Freud, she thought people's dreams revealed their inner feelings.

5. The _____ at the conference were asked to go to their doctors for a checkup because the hotel's air conditioning system was found to be contaminated.

C. *-ion* is a suffix that allows speakers to change words from verb forms into noun forms as when people who *reflect* on something want to share their *reflections* or when a farmer who *irrigates* his fields wants to talk about the whole process of *irrigation*. A vowel and a *t* are often put in as a kind of glue to connect the root word with the suffix, as when *add* becomes *addition* and *multiply* becomes *multiplication*.

elongation	extermination	illumination	situation

1. If a school has rooms in the basement, it is especially important to provide good _____.

2. In Army talk SNAFU stands for _____ *Normal, All Fouled Up.*

3. *Pest* _____ sounds more formal than *killing bugs*.

4. The _____ of race track made it so that more spectators could watch the racers during more of the race.

D. *-fy* is a suffix used to show that someone or something has caused a particular condition as in such words as *mortify* and *clarify*. If a sentence is changed so that the word is to be used as a noun or an adjective, usually an *–ation* suffix (or at least an *–ion*) will be appended, as in "A *clarification* is needed." Look at the following sentences and decide which of the forms to write in the blank spaces.

beautify	beautification

1. The _____ project had to be put on hold because of a lack of money.

2. It is harder to _____ areas where there is not enough natural rainfall to make plants grow easily.

putrify	putrification

3. The _____ of garbage causes bad smells.

4. The summer heat causes food scraps to _____ more quickly.

clarify	clarification

5. The City Council will _____ its ruling by September 1ˢᵗ.

6. She is seeking_____ on how firm the boundaries are.

modify	modification

7. The _____ of the guard rails between divided highways is going to cost more than people thought.

8. The plan is to _____the guard rails no matter how much it costs.

crucify	crucifixion

9. To _____ someone is to affix a person's body onto a cross.

10. At least in Christian countries, most people think of the_____in relation to Jesus.

mortify	mortification

11. She did not want to come back after suffering such _____.

12. It was cruel of the committee to _____ her like that.

More or Less

Name: _____ Period: _____ Date: _____

English has both suffixes and prefixes that serve to augment or extend the main idea of the words they are attached to. New speakers of English might describe something as "*more big*" or "*most biggest*," but these speakers soon realize that the terms *bigger* and *biggest* are more efficient as well as more euphonious. Common examples of comparative words making use of the *–er* suffix include *hotter, colder, meaner, nicer, cooler, sweeter, spicier, higher,* and *brighter*. If a word is three syllables or more, or is not very common, *more* and *most* are preferred, but *–er* is such a productive suffix that speakers will be understood even if they attach it to adjectives in nonstandard ways.

For example, when commenting on a cold and clammy room, someone might say, "It is *clammier* in here than I thought it would be."

The *–est* suffix identifies something as *the most*. Common examples are *dumbest, smartest, wisest, softest, sweetest, oldest, sickest, brightest,* and *coldest*. These prefixes and suffixes are called *superlatives* (the most) or *augmentatives* (more). They can be as English sounding as *mini-* and *maxi-,* or as foreign sounding as the Italian *–issimo*. Because Italy is the home of classical music, musicians are familiar with Italian suffixes. If the notation reads *fortissimo*, musicians know they are to play extra loudly, while if it reads *pianissimo*, they are to play extra softly. *Generalissimo* for a high military official is an adaptation of this suffix, and so is the ending on the Spanish word *machismo* to refer to an exaggerated sense of masculinity. *Accelerando* tells musicians to speed up, while *crescendo* tells them to get louder.

Augmentatives are in one way similar to, and in one way different from, a thermos bottle. They are similar in that they do not change the substance of whatever is put in, but they differ in that, while thermos bottles cannot make things colder or hotter (they keep the temperature the same), augmentatives increase the strength or the power of the word.

Some fairly common augmentative suffixes are explained below. Use what you have learned about root words and what you are learning about suffixes to choose the most appropriate word to write in the blank spaces of the sentences. Talk about the words and use them in other sentences so that you will begin to feel comfortable with them.

A. *-ence* (sometimes *-ense*) is a suffix that tells readers the word is being used to name a quality or a state of being as when *prevalence* is used to talk about how strong (compare to *prevail* and *prevalent*) something is. For example, "The *prevalence* of AIDS in many African countries is a terrible problem." One reason this is a kind of augmentation is that it implies a durative quality. The condition is considered permanent or semipermanent.

circumference	preferences	pretense	quintessence	reticence

1. We need to know the _____ of the table before we buy the cloth to make a skirt.

2. The _____ of something is the fifth essence, meaning that it is above and beyond the regular essences that ancient people believed in.

3. The candidate's _____ to answer questions is going to damage his career.

4. Her interest in politics was nothing but a _____.

5. Reading classes are more fun when students are allowed to pick books according to their _____.

B. *-ious* means full of and is even stronger in providing a sense of duration or continuance. It is used on several "zenith" words—those words that imply something is the most, the least, the best, or the worst and is likely to stay that way. Perhaps you remember the joke from *The Sound of Music* about the longest word in the dictionary being *supercalifragulisticexpealidocious*. This is not really the longest word in the dictionary; in fact, it isn't even in most dictionaries. Nevertheless, notice how it ends with *-ious*, which is an appropriate ending for a big, pretentious word.

Mendacious describes a person who is given to lying and presenting false information. It seems longer lasting than if someone is accused of *mendacity*, which might be just one instance of dishonesty. Similarly, a student might have done something *of merit*, but if the person is described as *meritorious*, the implication is that the student consistently deserves praise or reward. A *pugilist* is a fighter—a boxer—but when speakers describe someone as *pugnacious*, they are saying that the person is habitually hostile and belligerent. His nose might resemble that of a *pug* dog because it has been hit so often. A *specious* argument is one that is deceptively plausible or attractive because it fits in as if it belongs to a *species*, but it is actually false or misleading. A *fractious* person is one who brings about discord, who *fractures* or breaks things, while a *loquacious* person is one who likes to talk, based on the Latin word *loqui* meaning to speak.

I:	egregious	expeditious	obsequious	penurious	scrumptious

1. If you want your work expedited (done quickly), you better find a company with a reputation for _____ work habits.

2. If you go to a sumptuous banquet, you might describe the food as _____.

3. An _____ person follows others and gains the reputation of being excessively compliant or deferential.

4. Someone who is _____ is stingy and overly frugal.

5. Gregarious people, those who love to be the life of a party, are more likely to make _____ social blunders than are shy people who sit quietly on the sidelines.

II:	capricious	fortuitous	lugubrious	obnoxious	salacious

1. The _____ details printed in tabloid newspapers can also be described as *lascivious* or *lecherous*.

2. _____ used to mean that someone was exposed to harm or poison as with *noxious* gases, but today it describes a person who is highly offensive or disgusting.

3. *Lugere* is a Latin word for *mournful,* so someone who is _____ is exaggeratedly mournful.

4. Something _____ is fortunate.

5. A _____ person is governed by impulsiveness and caprice.

C. *Mini-* comes from the Latin word *minimus* and is cognate with such words as *minimal, minor, minority,* and *minus.* It is generally used as a comparison to show that something is smaller or lesser than something else. In school, the dress code might forbid *miniskirts;* a *minilesson* on a grammatical point might take only five or ten minutes, while a *minibus* might take athletes to events at other schools.

miniseries	minimalist	miniscule	minivans

1. She made only _____ changes when she was asked to revise thoroughly.

2. A television _____ is usually shown within one week or at least within the same month.

3. _____ artists like to hint at things through basic lines uncluttered with details.

4. As cars have gotten smaller, more and more families are buying _____.

D. *Micro-* comes from a Greek word for small or short and is used in such words as *microbe, microorganism, microphone,* and *microscope.* The *Microsoft* computer company specializes in making software for small computers as compared to the large mainframe computers that were first invented. A *microchip* is a compact electronic circuit. Some airplane crashes have been blamed on *microbursts,* which are sudden downdrafts that cause wind shears in localized areas.

microbus	microcosm	microfilms	micrometer	Micronesia

1. A _____ is a station wagon shaped like a bus.

2. Large libraries used to keep _____ of the major newspapers, but today they are more likely to rely on computerized accounts.

3. Some people laughingly say that high school is a _____ of U.S. culture.

4. _____ is a country made up of small islands in the South Pacific.

5. A _____ is used with a telescope to measure minute distances.

E. *Maxi-* from *maximum* is often used as a contrast to *mini-* and *micro-*. It is a shortened form of the Latin word *maximus*, meaning greatest, either in size or quality. In statistics the *maximum likelihood* is a method for estimating the applicability of a study taken from a sample population, while in social planning, bringing about the *maximum good with minimal damage* is a principle that people try to follow as they make decisions about such matters as condemning property for urban renewal and about when child protective services should get involved.

maxed	maxi	maxim	maximum	Maxwell

1. I think I've _____ out on pistachios.

2. _____ skirts are great for winter.

3. A _____ is a small statement with a big meaning.

4. On the old television show, "Get Smart," the chief detective's name of _____ Smart was a joke because he was neither smart nor maximally efficient.

5. _____ security prisons are expensive to run.

F. *Mega-* and *macro-* come from Greek words meaning *large* or *much*. *Mega-* has long been a part of scientific language as when engineers talk about a *megabar* being a measure of pressure equal to that of one million bars. Since the 1890s, psychiatrists have diagnosed people with delusions of personal grandeur as *megalomaniacs*, while doctors have talked about a condition of pernicious anemia as a *megaloblast*. In recent years, the term has come into popular use to talk about such things as *megabucks* (a million or more dollars), *megacorporations* created through *megadeals,* and *megastars* (both in the sky and in Hollywood). *Macro-* has come into English more recently to describe such things as *macroeconomics, macroevolution, macrofossil,* and *macronutrient*. And since 1851, the mark placed over vowels to show that they are to be pronounced in their long form has been called a *makron*.

megabyte	megadeaths	megaliths	megaphones	Megaplex

1. Computer engineers created the term _____ to talk about a storage unit equal to 1,048,576 bytes.

2. Cheerleaders with _____ are more picturesque than are cheerleaders with microphones.

3. Stonehenge is only one of many ancient _____ whose purposes are still being figured out.

4. Nuclear war is bound to bring about _____.

5. Our new cinema is named the _____ because it has 24 theaters.

G. *Poly-* comes from Greek and means *many* as seen in such words as *Polynesia* (many islands), *polygamy* (many spouses), and *polygon* (many angles). Most people think of *polygamy* as when one man has more than one wife, but that is actually *polygyny,* while the term for a woman who has more than one husband is *polyandry.*

polyester	polyglot	polygraphs	polyphone	polytheists

1. A _____ is a letter of the alphabet that has many different sounds as with *a*.

2. _____ cloth is made from a chemical substance with repeated units of ester.

3. A _____ is a person who can speak several different languages.

4. Lie detector tests are called _____ because they measure (or *graph*) several different aspects of one's bodily reactions.

5. People who believe in many gods are called _____.

H. *Arch-* from the Greek *archein* means *to rule* or to be the highest and most important, and so in that sense it refers to something that most fully embodies the principle of its kind. *Archetypes* in literature are such characters as The Villain, The Hero, The Caregiver, and The Innocent. An *archconservative* is a prototypical conservative, while an *archvillain* is one of the worst characters anyone can imagine.

archangel	archbishops	Archie	archrival

1. In the Catholic Church, _____ are leaders of large church dioceses.

2. The _____ is the chief angel in a celestial order.

3. Robert Cormier said that in his book *The Chocolate War,* he chose the name of _____ for the head of the Vigils to communicate that he was ultimately evil.

4. During the 1960s and 1970s, Russia was the _____ of the United States.

Workshop 8.1: A. I. 1. prospects, **2.** provoke, **3.** protrudes, **4.** proposes, **5.** propelled. **II. 1.** protest, **2.** promotion, **3.** programs, **4.** prognosis. **B. I. 1.** contravene, **2.** counteroffensive, **3.** contradiction, **4.** counterindicated, **5.** controversy. **II. 1.** contrasting (against), **2.** convocation (together), **3.** contraband (against), **4.** Congress (together), **5.** contractions (together). **III. 1.** contractor's (together), **2.** conspire (together), **3.** Contras (against), **4.** confederates (together), **5.** conjurers (together). **C. 1.** antipathy, **2.** antithetical, **3.** antitoxin, **4.** antioxidant, **5.** antibiotics.

Workshop 8.2: A. 1. eulogy, **2.** Eugene, **3.** euphonious, **4.** euphoric, **5.** euphemisms. **B. 1.** malignant, **2.** malice, **3.** malpractice, **4.** malformed, **5.** malnourished. **C. 1.** benefactors, **2.** benefits, **3.** benediction, **4.** benevolence. **D. 1.** Orthodox, **2.** orthodontics, **3.** orthoscopic. **E. 1.** miscarriages, **2.** misaligned, **3.** misdiagnosed, **4.** misgivings.

Workshop 8.3: A. 1. complete, **2.** compared, **3.** comfort, **4.** combined. **B. I. 1.** disbands, **2.** disagreement, **3.** distrust, **4.** discovered. **C. 1.** defaced, **2.** despise, **3.** decriminalization, **4.** decentralizes, **5.** decried. **D. 1.** transcend, **2.** Transcontinental, **3.** transmission, **4.** transfer, **5.** transact. **E. 1.** infringes, **2.** inoculated, **3.** *in loco parentis,* **4.** indigenous. **F. 1.** interacting, **2.** interchange...international, **3.** to intermarry, **4.** interception. **G. 1.** intrapersonal, **2.** intravenously, **3.** intraspecies, **4.** intraplate.

Workshop 8.4: A. 1. ...an exclusive organization tries to keep people out. **2.** ...an extramural program competes with other schools. **3.** ...an excision cuts something out of a person's body. **4.** ...an external memo goes to people outside of the office. **5.** ...expose someone you put the person or the person's actions in a position to be viewed by others. **B. I. 1.** *The Exorcist,* **2.** extremities, **3.** extradited, **4.** expired, **5.** extraordinary. **II: 1.** expelled, **2.** expedition, **3.** ex cathedra, **4.** expurgate. **C. 1.** Today people *express* their thoughts and feelings or send *express* mail or get in the *express* line at a store. **2.** When we speak about *an exodus*, we are more likely to be thinking not of the road but of many people leaving as when refugees are forced to leave their homeland. **3.** Although employees regularly *execute* the orders given by company *executives*, the most dramatic example of following orders is the killing of someone, which is the meaning that people usually think of when they hear about an *execution*. **4.** The common, contemporary meaning is to get money or information from people probably by twisting more than their arms. **5.** *Exoneration* is now used mostly for emotional burdens as when an accused criminal is *exonerated* and hence freed from the resentment that comes with being falsely accused. **6.** The meaning of *excusing* someone has been softened to such simple actions as smiling at someone who accidentally bumps into you or who comes late to class, etc.

Workshop 8.5: A. Arrows for direction: Insider, incumbents, *in vitro*. Xs for negative: incredible, independent, insubordination, indignities, incognito. **B. 1.** indecency, **2.** indifferent, **3.** inanimate, **4.** infirmaries, **5.** incomparable. **C. 1.** illiterate, **2.** illegible, **3.** illogical, **4.** illegitimate. **D. 1.** imperfection, **2.** impassable, **3.** immaterial, **4.** immortal, **5.** imprudent. **E. 1.** irradicable, **2.** irreconcilable, **3.** irretrievable, **4.** irreproducible, **5.** irrespective. **F. 1.** amoral, **2.** apolitical, **3.** anonymous, **4.** atypical, **5.** atrophy.

Workshop 8.6: A. I. 1. submits . . . subservience, **2.** submerge, **3.** subzero, **4.** subscribe. **II: 1.** subtitles, **2.** subdivide, **3.** subjugating, **4.** subjects, **5.** sublease. **B. 1.** superlatives, **2.** *Superman,* **3.** supersonic, **4.** Super Bowl, **5.** "The Super." **C. 1.** hypercritical, **2.** hyperventilate, **3.** hyperbole, **4.** hyperirritability, **5.** hyperglycemia. **D. 1.** hypoxemia, **2.** hypotension, **3.** hypocenter, **4.** hypogastric.

Workshop 8.7: A. 1. biennial, **2.** Anno Domini, **3.** anniversaries, **4.** annuals, **5.** annuity. **B. 1.** antepasto, **2.** antediluvian, **3.** antecedent, **4.** ante meridian. **C. 1.** postlude, **2.** postpone, **3.** post hoc, **4.** post mortem, **5.** P.S. **D I: 1.** premonition, **2.** prefabricated, **3.** preflight, **4.** preparing, **5.** preface. **II: 1.** prep, **2.** prequel, **3.** prelude, **4.** preposition, **5.** prefixes. **E. 1.** foreword, **2.** forecasting, **3.** foreshadowing, **4.** foreboding, **5.** forecloses. **F. 1.** neologism, **2.** neophyte, **3.** Neosporin®, **4.** neolithic, **5.** neon. **G. 1.** reconcile, **2.** recurrent, **3.** recreation, **4.** renewal, **5.** reflect.

Workshop 8.8: A. 1. donors, **2.** transformers, **3.** dictators, **4.** tractors, **5.** counselors. **B. 1.** trainee, **2.** employees, **3.** absentee, **4.** devotee, **5.** attendees. **C. 1.** illumination, **2.** situation, **3.** extermination, **4.** elongation, **D. 1.** beautification, **2.** beautify, **3.** putrification, **4.** putrify, **5.** clarify, **6.** clarification, **7.** modification, **8.** modify, **9.** crucify, **10.** crucifixion, **11.** mortification, **12.** mortify.

Workshop 8.9: A. 1. circumference, **2.** quintessence, **3.** reticence, **4.** pretense, **5.** preferences. **B. I: 1.** expeditious, **2.** scrumptious, **3.** obsequious, **4.** penurious, **5.** egregious. **II. 1.** salacious, **2.** obnoxious, **3.** lugubrious, **4.** fortuitous, **5.** capricious. **C. 1.** miniscule, **2.** miniseries, **3.** minimalist, **4.** minivans. **D. 1.** microbus, **2.** microfilms, **3.** microcosm, **4.** Micronesia, **5.** micrometer. **E. 1.** maxed, **2.** maxi, **3.** maxim, **4.** Maxwell, **5.** maximum. **F. 1.** megabyte, **2.** megaphones, **3.** megaliths, **4.** megadeaths, **5.** megaplex. **G. 1.** polyphone, **2.** polyester, **3.** polyglot, **4.** polygraphs, **5.** polytheists. **H. 1.** archbishops, **2.** archangel, **3.** Archie, **4.** archrival.

End-of-Chapter Activities

1. Choose a pair of either prefixes or suffixes that somehow "match" each other and make posters illustrating the difference as with something *maxi* versus something *mini*, *super* versus *sub*, *pro* versus *con*, *antagonist* versus *protagonist*, something *accelerating* versus *decelerating*, a person suffering from *hypertension* versus someone suffering from *hypotension*, or an *intramural* tournament versus an *extramural* tournament. If you want to be more subtle, you can illustrate the difference between an *antiwar* protest and the *antebellum* period in U.S. history, or you can make a poster showing several different interpretations of *ex*.

2. As an illustration of the productivity of prefixes and suffixes, look in your medicine cabinet at home and in the kitchen cupboards to see how many new product names you can find that will include one or more of the prefixes or suffixes studied in this chapter. You can look for more examples to cut out from magazine and newspaper advertisements so that you can make a poster. Do not be surprised at the "invented" spellings because companies have to make their product names unique so that they can register them as trademarks.

3. Try to think of a new product that you might invent and then create an original name for it. Experiment with various prefixes and suffixes. Thinking up names for new products is a challenge because to register a trademark, the name must be new enough that it will not already have been chosen by someone else. Also, it needs to be easy to say and easy to remember, and it needs to have positive connotations. When you have settled on a name, sketch out two or three ideas for how it can be used in advertising or how it will look on a product label.

CHAPTER NINE

Numbers

Teacher's Preface

Linguistic principles being illustrated in this chapter include:

1. The names for numbers are some of the most basic words in our language.

2. While their primary use is for counting, they are also used for a myriad of other communication purposes.

3. Because numbers are intimately connected with travel and trade, English speakers have adopted and adapted many "foreign" names for numbers.

4. The same number words are used both as rough approximations and as exact figures.

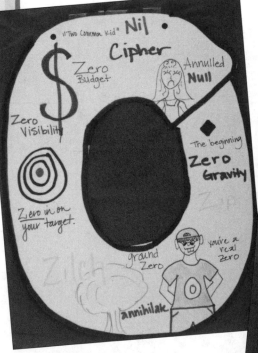

As a concluding activity for this chapter on numbers, students enjoyed working in small groups to illustrate large cut-outs of the numbers 0 through 10.

Fifteen-year old Britton is amused at finding a picture of a Route 66 water tower with his name on it.

5. Number words illustrate linguistic specialization in the way they sometimes lose their actual numerical meanings and take on meanings unique to particular situations.

6. Number words also illustrate the concept of markedness by showing how speakers use number words to mark things that are unusual.

It is more than a coincidence that the English word *nimble* is related to *number* because people who are good with numbers have nimble brains. They can *figure* things out, *sum up* advantages and disadvantages, and *calculate* the effects. Especially with this chapter, keep dictionaries handy so that students can look up further meanings for words that we just mention, for example, *figuratively speaking* and the new slang term, *"Go figure!"*

Over the course of history, people have developed intellectual and emotional attachments to numbers quite apart from their mathematical meanings. For example, there was a big difference between the intensity with which people celebrated the new millennium when the calendar turned to the number 2000 as opposed to when it turned to 2001. As news commentators and others kept pointing out, the 2001 celebrations were more authentic because they marked the actual passage of 2,000 years, but the general public was less interested in accuracy than in the changing of the number.

Public lotteries grew popular in the United States only after people were allowed to choose the numbers that would be on their tickets. When they had to take whatever number a machine handed them, they did not feel the sense of ownership and control that they experienced when they could make up combinations of numbers with which they identified, such as their childhood street number or phone number, a loved one's birthday, the license plate on their first car, or some other number that had proven lucky in another context. Feeling that certain numbers are luckier than others has a long history, as shown through numerology, which is the study of the occult significance of numbers. Numerologists are paid to tell people's fortunes based on the day and hour of their births in combination with other astrological information.

Another way people view the names of numbers as words separate from numerical designations is shown in the way they playfully combine numbers and letters to create such messages as *FARM 2-U PRODUCE* (Farm to you produce), *10SNE1* (Tennis, anyone?), and *O4SURE* (Oh, for sure). Speakers also attach extra meanings to addresses. For example, *Fifth Avenue* in New York has such prestige that people joke

Here are some of the number-related clippings that a community college class enjoyed discussing. They include the U.S. Army's slogan "I Am an Army of One," the V-8 brand name that alludes to Ford's powerful V-8 engine, a photo of Alan Iverson of the Philadelphia 76ers (shortened to *Sixers*), and Microsoft's 99.999 advertising campaign.

about "not every Fifth Avenue being *The Fifth Avenue*." A national chain of clothing stores takes advantage of the joke by calling itself *Off 5ᵗʰ Avenue*. *Heinz 57*, taken from the slogan of the Heinz pickle and food processing company, made its way into the language as a playful way to refer to a mongrel dog and then by extension to anything that is a mixed bag.

The use of number and letter combinations became commonplace during World War II when technological developments came so fast and in such quantities that people were left scrambling for ways to keep track of all the new inventions. Examples include the *B-29* bomber, *WD-40* (now a household product but originally the fortieth formula for a substance that would displace water), and the *AK-47* or *Ak-Ak* gun for the Russian *Avtomat Kalashnikova*.

Based on this practice, World War II soldier Joseph Heller created *Catch-22* as the title of his famous book. *Catch-22* is now defined in dictionaries as "a problematic situation for which the only solution is denied by a circumstance inherent in the problem." In Heller's book, the way to get out of flying bombing missions was to be insane. However, Catch-22 "specified that a concern for one's own safety in the face of dangers that were real and immediate was the process of a rational mind." This meant that people who didn't want to fly were the very ones who had to fly. Heller said he chose *22* because of the alliteration and because it was far enough down a list to fit with other army regulations, but not so far down as to be unimportant.

Code numbers and letters give potential customers the idea that high technology is involved in a product as with the *Infiniti Q45*, where the *45* identifies the displacement of the engine while the *Q* identifies the size and body style. The *BMW 740i* is from the company's seventh series (their largest sedan) and has a 4.0 liter, fuel-injected engine. The effect of such names is usually more emotional than intellectual because few people know what the numbers stand for.

CONVERSATION STARTERS

1. **Numbers used for purposes other than counting:** Encourage students to bring in clippings from newspapers, magazines, and other media in which numbers have been used for some reason other than basic counting. Students will be

more successful at finding examples if you bring in a few as starters. Let students work either individually or in small groups. Depending on how much time is available, students can simply share their clippings and observations or write one-line explanations to mount with their clippings for a bulletin board or a class notebook, or they can prepare more formal reports. See the picture of the high school student who made two posters for his investigation and report on the aura of the name of *Route 66*. In a community college class, students looked at such entertainment names as television's "Sixty Minutes" and "Twenty-Twenty" and the Arnold Schwarzenegger film, *The 6th Day*. They brought in advertisements with such slogans as, "BIG TWO: #1 Dealer in the Nation!" an ad for *accenture. com*, "Chinese to Become #1 Web Language by 2007 (Now it gets interesting)," and "Admit 35,000," printed on an oversized ticket for the Colorado Convention Center. On an ad for Lexus cars, the only large-sized print was *180°*, pointing to the contrasting pictures of a sink full of dirty dishes and a beautiful new car. The small print on a full-page picture of beans read "We are more than bean counters," followed by the name of a symphony orchestra seeking donations. A news story and photograph of the Phoenix Suns honoring basketball player Kevin Johnson by retiring his *No. 7* triggered a conversation about numbers in sports. Students talked about the role played by statistics and how sportscasters devise ways to keep from repeating the same number as when they refer to *double-digit* scores and to *nickel defenses*.

One student brought in some high-end catalogues and showed how Roman numerals on a watch and how model numbers on a shoe, for example, "No. 5580 from the Santoni Handmade Collection" communicate prestige. A Microsoft Windows campaign showed five colorful flags of the number nine over the message, "The mythical five nines. 99.999%. As close as you can get without breaking some law of nature." Students also enjoyed conjecturing about the psychology behind an advertisement for a university fund drive, "The Power of One: One Person. One Fund. One Incredible Difference." They compared this to the U.S. Army's new slogan, "I AM AN ARMY OF ONE," and talked about why readers want to be identified as individuals rather than group members.

2. **Exact versus Approximate:** Another good area for conversation is how sophisticated speakers have the ability to know when a number is exact and when it is approximate. John Allen Paulos in his book *A Mathematician Reads the Newspaper* (Doubleday, 1995) illustrates how fond people are of what he calls "meaningless precision." He tells about a museum guide explaining to visitors that a particular dinosaur is 90,006 years old. When questioned as to how the age was figured, the guide explained that when he started working he was told that the dinosaur was 90,000 years old and that was six years ago. What the guide did not understand is that people often round off large numbers as when someone reports that "*thousands* of complaints have been filed," or says something like, "I wouldn't go there for a *million* dollars."

Lead students to think about whether the number words in the following sentences should be interpreted literally or figuratively and whether they are exact numbers or a kind of metaphorical exaggeration. For example, *half* (and its imported alternates *semi, hemi,* and *demi*) are sometimes used with exact or literal meanings and sometimes with metaphorical and/or approximate meanings.

  a. A *semiannual* newsletter comes out twice a year. (literal and exact)
  b. A *demigod* has more power than a mortal, but less than a god. (metaphorical and approximate)

c. The Northern and the Southern *hemispheres* are each half of the sphere that is the earth and its atmosphere. (literal and exact)

   d. In sports tournaments, the *semifinals* are halfway between the finals and the *quarterfinals*. (literal and exact)

   e. *Semitractor-trailers* (usually shortened to *semis*) are powerful trucks that pull add-on sections. (literal but approximate because the trailer and the truck are not exactly the same size.)

   f. She was *half-crazed* over not hearing from her son. (metaphorical and approximate)

   g. The brownies were gooey because they were only *half-baked*. (literal but approximate)

   h. We were surprised when he presented such a *half-baked* idea. (metaphorical and approximate)

   i. I'm better at playing *half-court* than full-court basketball. (literal and exact)

   j. With a *half-volley* in tennis, players surprise their opponents by hitting the ball before it bounces. (literal but approximate)

   k. He's been released from jail but has to live in a *halfway* house. (metaphorical and approximate)

3. **Numbers Used to Reveal Markedness:** Speakers use number words to point out that something is different from what is expected. For example, the Wright Brothers' first airplane had double wings, so this was just what was expected from airplanes. A few years later when it was discovered that planes could fly with only one set of wings, people were surprised and gave the new invention the special name of *monoplane*. But as more and more monoplanes were built, they became what was expected, and people began referring to them just as *planes*. The special identifying word *biplane* came into use for what is now unusual; that is, planes with two wings. This is similar to how people talk about *monorails* as being different from the majority of trains, but if technology changes so that most trains are monorails, then a new term will probably develop to talk about the unusual trains that run on two rails.

   Here are some other terms in which number-related words serve to mark the item as different from expectations. Lead students to figure out what is different about them:

   - *The Four Corners* area: This is the only place in the United States where the boundaries of four states (Utah, Colorado, New Mexico, and Arizona) meet to form perfect right angles.

   - Intersections in many cities have such names as *Five Points, Five Corners,* or even *Six* or *Seven Corners*: These intersections differ from typical street crossings, which we expect to be four corners.

   - *Four-poster* beds: It is unusual for a bed to have four equally tall corner posts.

   - *Four-wheel drive, 4 x 4s,* and *four-wheelers*: Traditionally, in most cars, only the back wheels had power while the front wheels coasted, so the unusual pattern of giving power to all four wheels, as in SUVs, gets a special name.

   - *Twins, triplets, quadruplets, quintuplets, sextuplets,* and *septuplets*: Most people are born in single births and so multiple births get marked names.

   - *Four-on-the-floor*: In modern cars, the gear shift is usually attached to the steering column, so the unexpected design of sports cars gets a marked name.

The Importance of *Zero*

Name: _____ **Period:** _____ **Date:** _____

The basic names that English speakers use for numbers were taken from Indo European languages, but the numbering system itself was borrowed from Arabic. One of the main advantages of the Arabic system over Roman numerals is that Arabic contains the concept of *zero*, whose design of a circular or oval line (in Arabic script, just a dot) around nothing illustrates its meaning. This meaning of "nothing" is often seen in metaphors, but in mathematics, the importance of zero is its use as a place marker in such numbers as 10, 100, 1,000, 10,000, 100,000, and 1,000,000. In the 2001 movie *Finding Forrester*, the boy who plays an inner-city kid on scholarship at an exclusive prep school refers to his classmates as *two-comma kids*. When his friend and teacher questions him, the boy explains "You know, one comma, zero, zero, zero, two commas, zero, zero, zero," meaning that the kids are millionaires.

While this particular phrase focuses on the commas and the zeroes as place markers, metaphorically *zero* is not so easy to figure out, as shown by these examples:

- Describing someone as *a real zero, a nothing,* or *a cipher* illustrates the way that metaphors tend to exaggerate.
- Dictionaries define *zero gravity* as the "apparent" lack of gravity to hint at the difficulty in knowing what conditions would be with absolute *zero gravity*.
- As shown by local controversies, it is hard to know what is meant by school policies of *zero tolerance* for weapons or drugs.
- At least during daylight hours, it is an exaggeration to describe weather conditions as causing *zero visibility* because even in the worst storms, people can see something.

While the following allusions are to real numbers, people who do not know how to read the terms are likely to get false impressions.

- *Zero population growth* does not mean that no new babies are born. Instead, it means that people are born or immigrate to a country at the same rate that people die or emigrate from a country.
- A *zero-based budget* does not mean a budget with no money; instead, it means that whenever a new budget is made, each category has to be examined and figured out from scratch, or from what some people might call *ground zero*. A similar principle is involved in a *zero sum* arrangement in which there are no new resources so that whatever is gained by one group has to be taken away from the other group.

The following examples are more metaphorical.

- In the 1940s, *ground zero* became the way to talk about the direct point at which a nuclear bomb exploded. Although it was not a nuclear bomb that brought down New York City's Twin Towers on September 11, 2001, the devastation was so awful that people began talking about the site as *ground zero*.

- Based on the countdown before an attack or the launching of a rocket, *zero hour* is the time at which an important decision must be made. After *zero hour*, it is too late to turn back.
- *To zero in* on someone or something developed during World War I from adjusting the sites on a gun so as to concentrate firepower on an exact target. A more metaphorical use is the *targeting* of someone or something without a gun, as when scientists *zero in* on finding a cure for a particular disease.

Joking or slang ways to say *zero* include *zip* as in "The final score was *three-zip*," and *zilch* as in, "He claimed to know *zilch* about it." These are both fairly new (*zip* from the 1920s and *zilch* from the 1960s), and since they both start with *z*, we can guess that they were created as playful one-syllable alternatives to *zero*. *Nothing* and *null* were already in English before speakers borrowed *zero* in the early 1600s from Arabic. *Nil*, also meaning *nothing*, came into English in the early 1800s. Although we all know the basic meaning of *nothing*, we still have to think about what is meant in specific situations. Choose the most appropriate terms and write them in the blank spaces below.

annulled	ground zero	nihilist	null and void
null hypothesis	a real zero	zero population growth	

1. When a contract is declared _____, the idea is that nothing of it is left.

2. The same is true when a marriage is _____, but most people disagree that "nothing happened."

3. A _____ is someone who believes in "nothing," or at least not in traditional values and beliefs.

4. A researcher who sets out to prove the _____ will not be satisfied with learning "nothing."

5. The United States would have _____ were it not for immigrants moving in.

6. When the funding was lost, the group had to start from _____.

7. Do not worry; your opponent is a *nothing*—_____.

Numbers from *One* to *Four*

Name: _____ Period: _____ Date: _____

After the brief discussions of these basic English number words, see if you can figure out the appropriate "foreign" words to write in the blank spaces.

One appears in such basic phrases as *number one, one-on-one conversations, one-way streets, a one-time only sale,* and *a one-man show*. More metaphorically, people talk about playing *one-upmanship*, having a *one-sided* argument, or being a *one-dimensional* person.

A. UNI (LATIN=*ONE*)

> *E pluribus unum*   unified   unique   universal   universities

1. A _____ school district has one superintendent and one governing board for several schools.

2. _____ *product codes* are not really everywhere in the universe.

3. _____ take pride in being united in a search for knowledge while still having diversity.

4. Because _____ is based on *one*, describing something as "most unique" is considered an error.

5. The Latin slogan _____, printed on U.S. money, means "from many, comes one."

B. MON (GREEK=*ONE*)

> mono   monochromatic   monomania   monotheism

1. It looks neat when men wear _____ shirts and ties.

2. _____ is believing in one Supreme Being.

3. _____ (short for *mononucleosis*) is a fairly common illness for teenagers.

4. A person with _____ is overly focused on one idea.

C. PRIMUS (LATIN=*FIRST*)

> premier   primatology   prime the pump   primitive

1. With _____ peoples, *primeval* means "first age," while *primordial* means "first order."

2. To _____ means giving something in order to get something based on the practice of pouring a little water down a pump to get it wet so that the ground water can flow up more easily.

3. _____ is the study of the species considered to be the most important.

4. The World _____ of a film is its first showing.

Two is seen in such basic words as *twosome* (a couple), *two-by-fours* (boards 2" thick and 4" wide), and *two-way streets* (traffic goes both ways). A *two-way mirror* works as a mirror on one side and a window on the other side. Because *between* is based on *two*, careful writers use *among* instead of *between* when they talk about something shared by three or more people. A *two-handed job* is challenging because you have to work at it with both hands, while a *two-fisted approach* means attacking something as if to fight. Restaurants and airlines advertise *twofer* sales when customers can buy two items for the price of one.

D. AMBI, AMPHI (LATIN=*TWO*)

> **ambidextrous**   **ambiguous**   **ambivalent**   **amphibious**   **amphitheaters**

1. _____ are good for rock concerts because they work as both theaters and stadiums.

2. If you have _____ feelings, your thoughts are leaning in two directions.

3. An _____ person is equally skilled with both hands.

4. I want an _____ vehicle to drive to a beach and on into the water.

5. _____ statements can be interpreted in two ways.

E. BI (LATIN=*TWO*)

> **biannual**   **bilabial**   **bipeds**   **bisecting**

1. Such sounds as *m* and *b* are _____ sounds because speakers must use both lips.

2. We used to complain about railroads _____ communities, but today it is freeways.

3. To save money, some banks are sending out _____ statements rather than quarterly reports.

4. Creatures who walk on two feet are known as_____.

F. DUO (LATIN=*TWO*)

> **deuce**   **doubling**   **dozen**   **dualistic**   **dubbed**   **duels**

1. Once a tennis game gets to _____, you have to win by two points.

2. Traditional _____ were fought with guns or swords, but today people mostly use words.

3. If you have a _____ eggs, you have "two plus ten."

4. When the sound track of a film is _____ into a second language, the producer is _____ the number of sound tracks.

5. _____ thinkers divide everything into opposites as in right versus wrong, boys versus girls, Democrats versus Republicans, etc.

Three is seen in such phrases as *three of a kind, three-ring circuses,* and *three-way* stops. It is also seen in the titles of many stories and films, and in practices varying from "Three strikes and you're out!" to families showing a preference for having three children.

G. TRI (LATIN *TRES,* GREEK *TREIS = THREE*)

triage	triceratops	trigonometry	triptych	triumvirate	troika

1. Joseph Stalin came to power as a member of a _____, which in Russian refers to *three* leaders.

2. In English, the group would have been called a _____.

3. In emergencies, medical personnel use a system of _____ to divide people into those who are too seriously injured to benefit from help, those who can wait for help, and those who should be treated immediately.

4. The study of triangles is known as _____.

5. A *tridactyl* is a dinosaur with three toes, while a _____ is a dinosaur with three horns.

Four lends a sense of regularity and dignity to statements as when Abraham Lincoln began his *Gettysburg Address* with "Four score and seven years ago...." While today's scientists list more than 100 elements, ancient peoples decided there were four: Earth, Fire, Air, and Water. They also used *four* as a way to organize thoughts around the four seasons of the year (spring, summer, fall, and winter), the four directions of a coordinate system (up, down, right, and left) and the four directions of the earth (north, south, east, and west), and more metaphorically, "the four corners of the earth." One of the few places where *four* has negative connotations is in the phrase *four-letter words,* which are forbidden words. The first one was the Hebrew word for God, which, out of respect, orthodox Jews do not say. Today most people think of *four-letter words* as swear words or vulgarisms, regardless of whether the words have exactly four letters.

H. QUARTUS (LATIN=*FOUR*)

quadriplegic	quarter	quarter-finals	quarter horse	quarter-pounders

1. In schools, a _____ is one-fourth of the year or one-half of a *semester*.

2. A big seller at McDonald's restaurants are the _____.

3. A _____ can run very fast, but only for about one-fourth of a mile.

4. A _____ is paralyzed in both arms and legs.

5. In NCAA basketball championships, the _____ are called the *Sweet Sixteens.*

The Numbers from *Five* to *Ten*

Name: _____ **Period:** _____ **Date:** _____

In this workshop, continue as you did in Workshop 9.2 by choosing the most appropriate words to write in the blank spaces. Use a dictionary to find out more about these words and to find other words that we did not have space to include.

Five is an easy number to visualize because people have five fingers and five toes. This fact is so closely related to the number *five* that linguists conjecture that the word *fist* came from Old English *fif*, meaning *five*. Today when we give someone a *high-five* as a celebratory greeting, we are showing an open hand—one not formed into a *fist* nor holding a weapon. In some ancient cultures, *five* played the role that *four* seems to play in modern English. Flowers with five petals were considered symbols of good fortune, and the early Chinese considered five a sacred number and hence listed five elements: wood, fire, earth, metal, and water. In Asian cultures, these five elements, along with the sun and the moon, became symbols for the days of the week. Other cultures have valued five forms of earthly happiness (wealth, longevity, peace, virtue, and health), along with such other groupings as five colors, five types of animals, five human relationships, and five degrees of nobility.

A. PENTE (GREEK=*FIVE*)

> pentacle   pentadactyls   Pentagon   pentameter   Pentecost   pentecostal   Pentium

1. William Shakespeare helped to make iambic _____ the most common pattern for English poetry.

2. Humans are _____ because they have five fingers and five toes.

3. Michelangelo made a famous drawing of a man whose body makes a _____ (a five-sided star) in a circle.

4. _____ is the 50th day (the seventh Sunday) after Easter.

5. One reason that Intel chose _____ as the name for its fifth generation of computers is that the word could more easily be protected as a trademark than could the number five.

6. _____ preachers hope to be filled with the Holy Spirit as were the disciples on the original Day of Pentecost.

7. The _____ is the most famous five-sided building in the modern world, but not in the ancient world, where many of the pyramids are pentagonal.

B. Quinque (Latin=*five*); Cinco (Spanish=*five*)

| Cinco de Mayo | quintessence | quintessential | quintet | quintuplets |

1. Five musicians playing together are called a _____.

2. In the American Southwest _____ (May 5th) is becoming an important holiday.

3. In 1934, the Dionne _____ became world famous as the first such multiple births in which all five babies survived.

4. Ancient philosophers defined _____ as the fifth and highest element, the one from which celestial bodies were formed.

5. Today the _____ mother might be described as "co-dependent" because she goes beyond "normal" expectations.

Six, in the title of the 2000 Academy Award winning film *Sixth Sense* refers to something that people aren't even sure exists. Everyone agrees that people have the five senses of sight, hearing, smell, taste, and touch, but the boy in the movie had a *sixth sense* that allowed him to see and talk to people who were dead. In this usage, *sixth* means something like "beyond the real" or "outside of human experience." Images that most people have in their minds about the American Frontier West are tied closely to the *six-shooter,* the gun with a revolving barrel that could hold six bullets before needing to be reloaded. *Six-pack* is slang for a packaged set of beer. From this comes the term *Joe Six-Pack* for a lazy person who sits around drinking beer. Body builders, however, have brought a more positive image to *six-pack* by talking about well-developed abdominal muscles as *a six-pack of abs* or *washboard abs*.

C. Siex (Old English=*six*); Hex (Greek=*six*)

| hexagonal | hexagram | sexagenarians | sextants | sextuplets |

1. When _____ are born, they are not likely to be identical because they have probably developed from different eggs.

2. _____ forms have six sides.

3. For centuries, sailors have used _____, which are navigational tools with six parts.

4. _____ (people between the ages of 60 and 69) are the fastest growing segment of the U.S. states population.

5. The flag of Israel is decorated with a _____.

Seven is considered by many people to be a lucky number, which is why the owners of casinos reward people who get straight sevens. Author Ian Fleming probably did not want to be so obvious as to use *777*, but he still wanted to hint that his famous spy James Bond was lucky, and so he named him Agent 007. It is interesting that around the world weeks are organized into seven days. Astronomical revolutions determine the length of days, months, and years, but people decided on their own to group days by sevens. *September* used to the the seventh month of the year, while October was the eighth, November the ninth, and December the tenth. But then Julius and Augustus Caesar changed the calendar by giving their own names to July and August. They wanted summer months to honor their military victories, and so they moved September, October, November, and December out of their rightful places.

D. SEPT (LATIN=*SEVEN*); HEPT (GREEK=*SEVEN*)

> heptachlor heptameter heptathlon Heptateuch September septuagenarians septuplets

1. The most grueling Olympic event for women is the _____, which consists of seven events.

2. _____ used to be the seventh month of the year.

3. _____ is a chemical containing seven kinds of chloride.

4. When in 1997, Bobbi McCaughey and her husband gave birth to _____, it wasn't only their neighbors in Iowa who were surprised.

5. A _____ is a line of verse containing seven metrical feet.

6. Now that people live longer, it is not unusual for _____ to hold either full-time or part-time jobs.

7. The _____ consists of the first seven books of the Old Testament.

Eight is a word that generally has positive connotations. The *eight-hour day* (from 8:00 A.M. to 5:00 P.M. with an hour off for lunch) is now a typical work period, but this has not always been the case, nor is it typical around the world. Skaters like to twirl through *figure eights* as do pilots of small planes. When electricians or other workers gather up long extension cords, they wind them over their arms in a *figure eight hitch* to keep them from getting tangled.

One of the few negative connotations of *eight* comes from the game of pool, which is played with fifteen numbered balls. The middle ball is number 8, and in the game of *Eight Ball*, once the game starts, players lose if they pocket the 8-ball before they get their other balls into a pocket. From this comes the expression *behind the eight ball*. When used to describe people, it means they are disadvantaged or about to suffer some kind of indignity.

E. OCTO (LATIN=*EIGHT*)

> octagon octave octavo October octogenarians octopus

1. In music an _____ is eight notes that make up a scale.

2. In printing, an _____ is a big sheet of paper that will be cut into eight sheets after it has gone through a printing press.

3. The _____ ride at a carnival has cars connected to eight arms of a motor that makes them revolve.

4. _____ are considered to be the "very old" of senior citizens.

5. An _____ is an eight-sided figure.

6. The month of _____ is misnamed because it is now the tenth, rather than the eighth, month of the year.

Nine is often used to communicate "a bunch" of something. While baseball teams literally have *nine players* and *nine innings,* and the game of *Ninepins* (an old-fashioned bowling game) is played with nine bowling pins, when people say that *a cat has nine lives,* they are not speaking literally. The expression is an exaggeration growing out of people's surprise at how cats fall from high places without getting hurt and how they disappear for days and then come home none the worse. Likewise, if people hear about someone going *the whole nine yards,* they interpret the phrase to mean that the person is enthusiastic and is giving maximum energy and attention to a task. Two stories explain the origin of this phrase. One is that during World War II, the belts of bullets loaded onto fighter planes were nine yards long. When gunners came back from a run, they would be asked if they had shot *the whole nine yards.* The other explanation is that the biggest cement trucks carry nine cubic yards of cement, so getting *the whole nine yards* is getting the whole load.

F. NOVEM (LATIN=*NINE*)

nine	9-11	November	Novena

1. Because _____ is so easy to say, it gets spoken with vigor, which may be why it was chosen for the *911* emergency code telephone number.

2. Even if a new system for calling for help is devised, people will remember _____ because of its coincidental association with the September 11th terrorist attack .

3. *Novem* is seen in _____, which used to be the ninth month of the year.

4. In the Roman Catholic Church, a _____ is a special kind of prayer and devotion repeated for nine days.

Ten is an unusually important number because people have ten fingers and can therefore easily envision what ten is. This is probably why the English numbering system is based on ten and also why people have a fondness for lists of ten. The most famous list of ten is *The Ten Commandments,* which was given to Moses in the Old Testament. A *ten-speed* bike actually has ten gears, but a *ten-gallon* cowboy hat does not hold ten gallons. The name was borrowed from Mexican sombreros decorated with ten strands of braid, which in Spanish is *galón.* English speakers misunderstood the allusion and thought it was an exaggeration communicating that the hat was big.

G. DECEM (LATIN=*TEN*)

> Decalogue   decapods   decathlon   decennial   decibels   decimal   decimate

1. I should think that _____ could lose a couple of feet and still walk.

2. _____ points are an efficient way to mark units of ten.

3. Olympic teams should get more points for winning a _____ than for winning a single event.

4. An ancient custom in war was to _____ a captured army by killing every tenth soldier.

5. Rock music is played at such high _____ that people worry about teenagers going deaf.

6. A _____ is a group of ten teachings or rules, sort of like "The Ten Commandments."

7. In today's economy, a _____ celebration is a big accomplishment for computer-related companies.

H. DIX (FRENCH=*TEN*); DIXIÈME (FRENCH=*TENTH*)

> dime   Dixie   Dixieland   Mason-Dixon

1. The southern United States is called _____ because early in its history when it was closely connected to France the word *Dix* was printed on Confederate $10 bills.

2. The nickname was coincidentally reinforced by the naming of the _____ line, which divided slave and free states.

3. In the 1920s, the *Original* _____ *Jazz Band* gave new popularity to the term *Dixie*.

4. A tenth of a dollar is called a _____ as a result of English speakers dropping the *x* from *dixième* and making the *i* long.

An Analogous Crossword Puzzle

Name: _____ **Period:** _____ **Date:** _____

Use the blanks in these analogous sentences as clues to the words to go in the crossword puzzle.

ACROSS

2. Seven is to *heptathlon* as ten is to _____.

4. Five is to *quintuplets* as two is to _____.

6. Five is to *pentagon* as eight is to _____.

8. Monogamy is to *polygamy* as monotheism is to _____.

10. Half is to *semester* as fourth is to _____.

11. Four is to *quartet* as five is to _____.

DOWN

1. Ten is to a *decade* as one hundred is to a _____.

3. A *sound bite* is to speech as a _____-liner is to print.

5. Three is to *triplets* as seven is to_____.

7. Binoculars are to *monocles* as bicycles are to _____.

9. Single is to *double* as simplex is to _____.

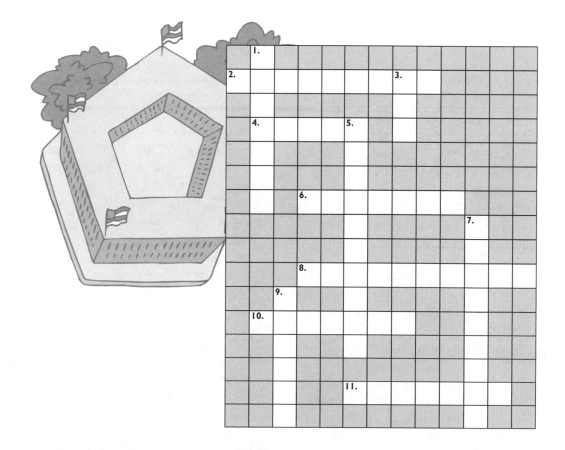

Workshop 9.1: **1.** null and void, **2.** annulled, **3.** nihilist, **4.** null hypothesis, **5.** zero population growth, **6.** ground zero, **7.** a real zero.

Workshop 9.2:A. 1. unified, **2.** universal, **3.** universities, **4.** unique, **5.** E pluribus unum. **B. 1.** monochromatic, **2.** monotheism, **3.** mono, **4.** monomania. **C. 1.** primitive, **2.** prime the pump, **3.** primatology, **4.** premier. **D. 1.** amphitheaters, **2.** ambivalent, **3.** ambidextrous, **4.** amphibious, **5.** ambiguous. **E. 1.** bilabial, **2.** bisecting, **3.** biannual, **4.** bipeds. **F. 1.** deuce, **2.** duels, **3.** dozen, **4.** dubbed…doubling, **5.** dualistic. **G. 1.** troika, **2.** triumvirate, **3.** triage, **4.** trigonometry, **5.** triceratops. **H. 1.** quarter, **2.** quarter-pounders, **3.** quarter horse, **4.** quadriplegic, **5.** quarter-finals, **6.** quarters.

Workshop 9.3:A. 1. pentameter, **2.** pentadactyls, **3.** pentacle, **4.** Pentecost, **5.** Pentium, **6.** Pentecostal, Pentagon. **B. 1.** quintet, **2.** Cinco de Mayo, **3.** quintuplets, **4.** quintessence, **5.** quintessential. **C. 1.** sextuplets, **2.** hexagonal, **3.** sextants, **4.** sexagenarians, **5.** hexagram. **D. 1.** heptathlon, **2.** September, **3.** heptachlor, **4.** septuplets, **5.** heptameter, **6.** septuagenarians, **7.** heptateuch. **E. 1.** octave, **2.** octavo, **3.** octopus, **4.** octogenarians, **5.** octagon, **6.** October. **F. 1.** nine, **2.** 9-11, **3.** November, **5.** Novena. **G. 1.** decapods, **2.** decimal, **3.** decathlon, **4.** decimate, **5.** decibels, **6.** decalogue, **7.** decennial. **H. 1.** Dixie, **2.** Mason-Dixon, **3.** Dixieland, **4.** dime.

Workshop 9.4:Across: **2.** decathlon, **4.** twins, **6.** octagon, **8.** polytheism, **10.** quarter, **11.** quintet. **Down:** **1.** century, **3.** one, **5.** septuplets, **7.** unicycles, **9.** duplex.

End-of-Chapter Activities

Choose a number that is especially interesting and make a presentation to the class about it. Perhaps in your area there is an athletic team with a number name (e.g., *The Philadelphia 76ers*), a restaurant (e.g., *Club 21* in New York), or a place (e.g., *Fifth Avenue* in New York or *10 Downing Street* in London). Or you might look at a famous number from sports or as when race car driver Dale Earnhardt's #3 flag was made famous after he was killed in February 2001. When you share your findings, try to use a visual aid or devise some other way to make your lesson memorable. Here are some ideas to get you started, but you are welcome to devise your own ideas.

1. *Three* has a long history of being a special number as shown in such phrases from Greek mythology as *The Three Graces, The Three Fates, The Three Harpies,* and *The Three Furies.* William Shakespeare starts *Macbeth* with three witches chanting fearsome predictions, and when you were little you probably heard such folktales as "The Three Little Pigs," "Goldilocks and the Three Bears," and "The Three Billy Goats Gruff." When you were older, you might have watched reruns of "The Three Stooges," *The Three Musketeers,* and "My Three Sons." With *three-ring circuses,* there is always something going on, which is why any confusing and noisy event might be described as a *three-ring circus.*

2. *Seven* is generally considered a positive number except when St. Thomas Aquinas in the thirteenth century described *The Seven Deadly Sins* as pride, covetousness, lust, envy, gluttony, anger, and sloth. Since ancient times, people have leaned toward coming up with totals of seven as with *The Seven Wonders of the World, The Seven Cities of Gold, The Seven Seas,* and *The Seven Hills of Rome.* The Seven Hills of Rome are so well known that tour guides in Bergen, Norway, now point out their seven hills, while a suburb of Cleveland is named Seven Hills, Ohio, and an entertainment center in Provo, Utah is called Seven Parks Water Park. In Greek mythology the story of *"The Seven Sisters"* is about the daughters of Atlas and Pleione, who were chased by Orion and saved by being placed in the sky as the seven stars that make up the Pleiades constellation, the one with the sword hanging from Orion's belt. Their memory is honored by what are informally called *The Seven Sisters,* seven prestigious women's colleges in the eastern United States. The Muslim belief system includes various degrees of reward with *Seventh Heaven* being the dwelling place of God. Folklore is also filled with references to seven as in "Snow White and the Seven Dwarves" and "Sinbad and His Seven Voyages." A guide to films lists over fifty that start with seven, including *Seven Brides for Seven Brothers, The Seven-Year Itch, The Seven Samurai,* and *The Seven Faces of Dr. Lao.*

3. *Eleven* is the hour before midnight, and from this we get *the eleventh hour* as an indication of impending doom or the last chance to save something. Armistice Day, now changed to Veteran's Day, is celebrated on the 11th day of the 11th month (November 11) to acknowledge the world's narrow escape from total disaster in World War I. *7-Eleven* stores got their name from a lucky role of the dice in the game of craps. The clever name communicated the convenience marts' business hours and helped them become nationally famous.

4. *Twelve* came into English after the Danes invaded England in 789. Their language was Old Frisian, and *twelf* was the basis of their counting system. Such English customs as *twelve inches to a foot, twelve eggs in a* *dozen,* and *twelve men on a jury* can be traced to this influence. Twelve was already an important number as shown by the *twelve months in a year, twelve signs of the zodiac, twelve gods in Greek mythology,* the *twelve tribes of Israel,* and the *twelve apostles* in Judeo-Christian beliefs. An alternate way to say *twelve* is *duodenum.* In humans, this is the name for the first part of the small intestine, which is literally named *two + ten* because it is twelve inches long. *Duodecimal* (not to be confused with the Dewey decimal system) has a similar meaning of *two + ten,* and is used to talk about mathematical systems based on twelve.

5. Thirteen, except in reference to *a baker's dozen* where a baker puts in an extra cookie or muffin to be sure of filling weight requirements, is considered unlucky. People who number tall buildings often skip thirteen so that the floors go from twelve to fourteen, and as long ago as 800 B.C., the Greek poet Hesiod warned farmers not to plant seeds on the thirteenth day of any month. There are several reasons that *thirteen* is considered unlucky, in addition to the fact that *thirteen* does not have the convenience of twelve, which can be divided into equal parts by two, three, four, or six. Christians view the number negatively because *thirteen people* (the twelve apostles plus Jesus) attended The Last Supper before Christ was crucified. A pagan belief is that *twelve witches* make a coven, but when the devil joins as their leader there will be a fearsome group of thirteen. Hundreds of years ago, Christian missionaries disparaged Scandinavian beliefs in Norse mythology by teaching that Friday, named after Frea the wife of Thor, was an unlucky day, especially if it fell on the thirteenth day of the month.

6. Sixteen, in the phrase *sweet sixteen,* is a compliment to the freshness and beauty of girls in their mid-teens. Because of its alliteration and positive connotations, the phrase was picked up as the name for the games prior to the quarter-finals of the NCAA basketball tournament. Colleges get almost as much publicity for getting into the *sweet-sixteen* bracket as for getting into the next round of eight, which lacks a catchy name.

7. Eighteen-year-olds are considered in many contexts to be adults. An *eighteen-wheeler* truck is made up of both the truck (with ten wheels) and a trailer (with eight wheels) and is big enough and strong enough to move heavy industrial equipment.

8. Twenty-one, in virtually all legal statutes separates children from adults. The U. S. military reserves a 21-gun salute (seven soldiers firing three times each) as its highest honor.

9. Forty is a number with a heritage. In the Old Testament after Noah built the ark and got the animals safely inside, it rained *"for forty days and forty nights."* When Moses led the Jews out of bondage, they wandered in the desert for *forty years,* while in the New Testament, Christ stayed alone for *forty days* as he prepared for the Crucifixion. In nonreligious contexts, a famous middle eastern story is *"Ali Baba and the Forty Thieves."* Naps are called *forty winks.* The word *quarantine* is based on forty days, which since the 1600s has been the time period that ships could be kept in a harbor or people could be isolated so that they would not spread disease. The time period was chosen long before scientists knew the details of how particular diseases were spread, so the choice of forty days was probably based on the popular conception of forty as a general representation of a long time.

10. One hundred has many extra meanings connected to Latin *centum.* Our U.S. dollar contains 100 *cents* or pennies; *Roman centurions* commanded 100 soldiers (ten groups of ten), a *century* is 100 years long, while a *centenarian* is 100 years old. Since the whole system of percentages is based on 100, people are making playful exaggerations when they say someone is giving 110 percent.

Another idea is to choose a number-related proverb, comparison, or cliché to illustrate with a poster, a cartoon, or a piece of creative writing. Here are some suggestions, but there are many other possibilities.

☐ Two's company, three's a crowd
☐ On cloud nine
☐ In Seventh Heaven
☐ Going the whole nine yards
☐ a 180° turnaround
☐ a millionaire versus a good-for-nothing
☐ a triple-decker ship versus a triple-decker sandwich
☐ It's six of one, a half-dozen of the other
☐ Behind the eight-ball
☐ The terrible twos
☐ Too many cooks spoil the broth
☐ A sixth sense
☐ The quintessential beauty queen
☐ The quintessential football player

Bibliography

Agee, Jon. *Who Ordered the Jumbo Shrimp? and Other Oxymorons*. New York: Harper Collins, 1998.

Allen, Janet. *Words, Words, Words: Teaching Vocabulary in Grades 4–12*. York, ME: Stenhouse, 1999.

Amende, Coral. *Famous Name Finder: Concise Biographies of Over 10,000 Legendary People*. New York: Random House, 1999.

Ammer, Christine. *Fruitcakes and Couch Potatoes and Other Delicious Expressions*. New York: Penguin, 1995.

Barnette, Martha. *Ladyfingers and Nun's Tummies: A Lighthearted Look at How Foods Got Their Names*. New York: Random House, 1997.

Braham, Carol, et al. *The Maven's Word of the Day Collection: Word and Phrase Origins from "Akimbo" to "Zydeco."* New York: Random House, 2002.

Carnicelli, Thomas. *Words Work: Activities for Developing Vocabulary, Style, and Critical Thinking*. Portsmouth, NH: Boynton/Cook/Heinemann, 2001.

Chase, Morgan. *Word Smart: A Visual Vocabulary Builder*. New York: Random House, 2001.

Claiborne, Robert. *Loose Cannons, Red Herrings, and Other Lost Metaphors*. New York: W. W. Norton, 1988.

Ehrlich, Eugene. *You've Got Ketchup on Your Muumuu: An A-to-Z Guide to English Words from Around the World*. New York: Henry Holt, 2000.

Evans, Cheryl, and Anne Millard. *Greek Myths and Legends*. London, England: Usborne Books, 1985.

Falletta, Nicholas. *The Paradoxicon*. New York: John Wiley, 1983.

Fromkin, Victoria, and Robert Rodman. *An Introduction to Language*. 3rd ed. New York: Holt, Rinehart and Winston, 1983.

Frye, Northrop. *Anatomy of Criticism: Four Essays*. 10th ed. Princeton, NJ: Princeton University Press, 1990.

Funk, Charles Earle. *"A Hog on Ice" and Other Curious Expressions*. New York: Harper and Row, 1948.

___. *"Heavens to Betsy" and Other Curious Expressions*. New York: Harper and Row, 1955.

Fussell, Paul. *The Great War and Modern Memory*. Oxford, UK: Oxford University Press, 1975.

Gwynne, Fred. *A Chocolate Moose for Dinner*. New York: Aladdin/Simon and Schuster, 1976.

___. *The King Who Rained*. New York: Aladdin/Simon and Schuster, 1970.

___. *A Little Pigeon Toad*. New York: Aladdin/Simon and Schuster, 1988.

Hendrickson, Robert. *The Henry Holt Encyclopedia of Word and Phrase Origins*. New York: Henry Holt/Owl Book, 1990.

Hofstadter, Douglas R. *Gödel, Escher, Bach: An Eternal Golden Braid*. New York: Vintage, 1980.

Holman, C. Hugh, and William Harmon. *A Handbook to Literature*. 6th ed. New York: Macmillan, 1992.

Hook, J. N. *Family Names: How Our Surnames Came to America*. New York: Macmillan, 1982.

Johnson, Dale D. *Vocabulary in the Elementary and Middle School*. Boston: Allyn and Bacon, 2001.

Jones, Charlotte Foltz. *Eat Your Words: A Fascinating Look at the Language of Food*. New York: Delacorte, 1999.

Jung, Carl G. *Four Archetypes: Mother, Rebirth, Spirit, Trickster*. Princeton, NJ: Princeton University Press, 1959.

Kirkpatrick, Betty. *Clichés: Over 1500 Phrases Explored and Explained*. New York: St. Martin's Press, 1996.

Knowles, Elizabeth. *The Oxford Dictionary of Phrase, Saying, and Quotation*. Oxford, England: Oxford University Press, 1998.

Lakoff, George. *Women, Fire, and Dangerous Things: What Categories Reveal about the Mind*. Chicago, IL: University of Chicago Press, 1987.

Lakoff, George, and Mark Johnson. *Metaphors We Live By*. Chicago, IL: University of Chicago Press, 1980.

___. *Philosophy in the Flesh: The Embodied Mind and Its Challenge to Western Thought*. New York: Basic Books/Prometheus, 1999.

Lederer, Richard. *Word Circus*. Springfield, MA: Merriam-Webster, 1998.

Levin, Samuel R. *The Semantics of Metaphor*. Baltimore, MD: Johns Hopkins University Press, 1977.

Lodwig, Richard R., and Eugene F. Barrett. *Words, Words, Words: Vocabularies and Dictionaries*. Rochelle Park, NJ: Hayden Book Co., 1973.

Marckwardt, Albert H. *American English*. New York: Oxford University Press, 1958.

Meltzer, Tom. *Illustrated Word Smart: A Visual Vocabulary Builder*. New York: Random House, 1999.

Nilsen, Alleen Pace. *Living Language: Reading, Thinking and Writing*. Boston: Allyn and Bacon, 1999.

Metcalf, Allan. *Predicting New Words: The Secrets of Their Success*. New York: Houghton Mifflin, 2002.

Nilsen, Alleen Pace, and Don L. F. Nilsen. "Language Play in Y2K: Morphology Brought to You by Pokémon." *Voices from the Middle* 7.4 (May 2000): 32-37.

___. "Lessons in the Teaching of Vocabulary from September 11 and Harry Potter." *Journal of Adolescent and Adult Literacy* 46.3 (November, 2002): 2–8.

___. "Metaphor." *Encyclopedia of 20th Century American Humor*. Phoenix, AZ: Oryx Press, 2000, 199–200.

___. "A New Spin on Teaching Vocabulary: A Source-Based Approach." *The Reading Teacher* (February 2003): 436–439.

___. "Vocabulary Development: Teaching vs. Testing." *English Journal* 92-3 (January 2003): 31–37.

Nilsen, Don L. F. "Creativity, Metaphor, and Poetry." *Humor Scholarship: A Research Bibliography*. Westport, CT: Greenwood, 1993, 84–-92.

___. "The Grounding of Metaphors: An Exercise in Computer-Aided Writing." *Editors' Notes* 4.1 (1985): 16–20.

___. "Live, Dead, and Terminally Ill Metaphors in Computer Terminology." *Educational Technology Magazine* 24.2 (1984): 27–29.

___. "The Nature of Ground in Farfetched Metaphors." *Metaphor and Symbolic Activity* 1.2 (1986): 127–138.

___. "A Note on the Process of Synesthesia." *Humor Scholarship: A Research Bibliography*. Westport, CT: Greenwood, 1993, 257–258.

___. "Some Metaphors in Kabul Dari." *Adab* 16.5-6: 7–14.

Nilsen, Don L. F., and Alleen Pace Nilsen. *Language Play: An Introduction to Linguistics*. Rowley, MA: Newbury House Publishers, 1978.

___. "Out of the Frying Pan and into the Hot Water: How to Mix a Metaphor from Scratch." *Arizona English Bulletin* 23.2 (1981): 1–6.

O'Brien, Conan. "What I'll Miss about Bill Clinton." *Time Magazine* 157.1 (January 9, 2001): 80.

Orgel, Doris. *We Goddesses: Athena, Aphrodite, and Hera*. New York: DK Publishing, 1999.

Osborne, Mary Pope. *Favorite Greek Myths*. New York: Scholastic, 1989.

Panati, Charles. *Extraordinary Origins of Everyday Things*. New York: Harper and Row, 1987.

Parish, Herman. *Amelia Bedelia 4 Mayor*. New York: HarperCollins, 1999.

___. *Bravo, Amelia Bedelia*. New York: HarperCollins, 1997.

___. *Calling Doctor Amelia Bedelia*. New York: Greenwillow/HarperCollins, 2002.

Parish, Peggy. *Amelia Bedelia*. New York: HarperCollins, 1963.

___. *Amelia Bedelia and the Baby*. New York: Avon, 1981.

___. *Amelia Bedelia Goes Camping*. New York: Avon, 1985.

___. *Amelia Bedelia and the Surprise Shower*. New York: HarperCollins, 1966.

___. *Come Back, Amelia Bedelia*. New York: HarperCollins, 1971.

Pearson, Carol S. *Awakening the Heroes Within: Twelve Archetypes to Help Us Find Ourselves and Transform Our World*. San Francisco, CAP/Harper, 1991.

Prelutsky, Jack. *Monday's Troll*. New York: Greenwillow Books, 1996.

Pugh, Sharon L., Jean Wolph Hicks, and Marcia Davis. *Metaphorical Ways of Knowing: The Imaginative Nature of Thought and Expression*. Urbana, IL: National Council of Teachers of English, 1997.

Scarry, Richard. *Best Word Book Ever*. Racine, WI: Western Publishing Company, 1980.

Sommers, Christina Hoff. *The War against Feminism: How Misguided Feminism Is Harming our Young Men*. New York: Simon and Schuster, 2000.

Soukhanov, Anne H. *Word Watch: The Stories Behind the Words of Our Lives*. New York: Henry Holt, 1995.

Stockwell, Robert, and Donka Minkova. *English Words: History and Structure*. New York: Cambridge University Press, 2001.

Terban, Marvin. *Scholastic Dictionary of Idioms, Phrases, Sayings, and Expressions*. New York: Scholastic, 1996.

Vygotsky, Lev. *Thought and Language* (Translated by Alex Kozulin). Cambridge, MA: MIT Press, 1986.

Walker, Barbara G. *The Woman's Dictionary of Symbols and Sacred Objects*. New York: HarperCollins, 1988.

___. *The Woman's Encyclopedia of Myths and Secrets*. New York: HarperCollins, 1983.

Index

www.ablongman.com/nilsen